KV-013-498

Child Protection
and Child Welfare

of related interest

Vulnerable Children and the Law
International Evidence for Improving Child Welfare,
Child Protection and Children's Rights
Edited by Rosemary Sheehan, Helen Rhoades and Nicky Stanley
ISBN 978 1 84905 868 1
eISBN 978 0 85700 456 7

Child Protection Systems in the United Kingdom
A Comparative Analysis
Anne Stafford, Nigel Parton, Sharon Vincent and Connie Smith
ISBN 978 1 84905 067 8
eISBN 978 0 85700 254 9

Improving Outcomes for Children and Families
Finding and Using International Evidence
Edited by Anthony N. Maluccio, Cinzia Canali, Tiziano Vecchiato,
Anita Lightburn, Jane Aldgate and Wendy Rose
Foreword by James K. Whittaker
ISBN 978 1 84905 819 3
eISBN 978 0 85700 248 8
Part of the Child Welfare Outcomes series

Understanding Costs and Outcomes in Child Welfare Services
A Comprehensive Costing Approach to Managing Your Resources
Lisa Holmes and Samantha McDermid
ISBN 978 1 84905 214 6
eISBN 978 0 85700 448 2
Part of the Child Welfare Outcomes series

Improving Child and Family Assessments
Turning Research into Practice
Danielle Turney, Dendy Platt, Julie Selwyn and Elaine Farmer
ISBN 978 1 84905 256 6
eISBN 978 0 85700 553 3

Culture and Child Protection
Reflexive Responses
Marie Connolly, Yvonne Crichton-Hill and Tony Ward
ISBN 978 1 84310 270 0
eISBN 978 1 84642 454 0

Child Protection and Child Welfare

A Global Appraisal of Cultures,
Policy and Practice

Edited by
Penelope Welbourne
and
John Dixon

Jessica Kingsley *Publishers*
London and Philadelphia

First published in 2013
by Jessica Kingsley Publishers
73 Collier Street
London N1 9BE, UK
and
400 Market Street, Suite 400
Philadelphia, PA 19106, USA

www.jkp.com

Library of Congress Cataloging in Publication Data
Child protection and child welfare : a global appraisal of cultures, policy and practice / edited by Penelope Welbourne and John Dixon.
pages cm
Includes bibliographical references and index.
ISBN 978-1-84905-191-0
1. Child welfare. 2. Child welfare--Cross-cultural studies.
3. Children--Social conditions. 4. Children--
Services for. I. Welbourne, Penelope.
HV713.C382626 2013
362.7--dc23
2013023659

British Library Cataloguing in Publication Data
A CIP catalogue record for this book is available from the British Library

ISBN 978 1 84905 191 0
eISBN 978 0 85700 421 5

Printed and bound in Great Britain by Bell & Bain Ltd, Glasgow

For Penelope's parents
and
John's family: Tina, Piers and Aliki

Contents

List of Figures and Tables

Figures

Tables

Preface

This book provides a range of perspectives on child welfare and child protection from a range of countries that vary in terms of their history and politics, type of welfare system, level of affluence, and social and religious composition. It explores the different ways in which childhood wellbeing is promoted through organizations and services such as childcare institutions, schools, health services and social work services, as well as by parents, other family members and communities.

To present information about each country included in this book in a way that allows for some comparison, contributors were asked to respond flexibly to a core set of questions (summarized in Table P.1).

It is noticeable that, even with such a guide, the chapters present a diversity of styles, voices and ideas, while retaining a common focus. This diversity of ways of thinking about children, and the state's obligation to them, is an important part of what the book as a whole has to say. The process of thinking and writing about child welfare in different parts of the world has a different emphasis and each account is distinctive.

One challenge in carrying out this project was the fact that, if contributors are to have scope to develop their ideas in some depth, and if the book is to have a manageable length, then only a limited range of countries could be included. We wanted to reflect the diversity of economic and political systems and social and religious contexts. We aimed to include 11 countries from different parts of the world. This means that there are many regions that we have not been able to cover. Some countries we would have liked to have included were omitted because it proved impossible to find an author who could provide a chapter in English.

Table P.1 Guidance questions for contributors

1. The social, political, religious and cultural context for child welfare services: The demographic and economic context for child welfare services; the size of the population of children; an outline of the political structure and the structure of the welfare state, especially in relation to child welfare and the funding of welfare services; funding available for child welfare; and the ethnic, linguistic and religious composition of the country.
2. The evolution of child welfare services: An overview of the direction of welfare policy for children over the recent past, and current directions in policy and child welfare and child protection practice. This may include also a discussion of the main drivers for the development of policy and practice, including economic issues, political philosophy and governmental approach, child welfare crises or scandals, and research or other findings concerning child welfare.
3. Family policy and family values: The way family is conceptualized and defined by the state and in society more generally. This section may address issues such as the threshold for welfare support for children and families, and the threshold for defining parental behaviour as neglectful or abusive. Policies concerning education may be relevant here too. The main features of the legal framework for intervention in family life will be included here, in particular the threshold for compulsory intervention when parenting is deemed to have fallen below a prescribed standard. It will consider instances where parents have been neglectful or abusive, and children who need parenting by people other than their biological parents because of the death or absence of parents, including 'social orphans'.
4. The state as parent: A discussion of the factors that shape the form taken by welfare services for neglected, abused and other children who are in need of support. Each country may pick out different factors, including, for example: • economic development and its benefits and costs • features of the system of public administration and child welfare provision • religious and traditional values • the developing culture of children's rights • cultural views as to the responsibilities parents have in terms of equipping their children for adult life, and the contribution children should make to their families, either as children or as adults.
5. Conclusion: An overview of the key points about child welfare and child protection that are the subject of the chapter.

All the countries included are made up of diverse groups of people, and it is arguable that no single commentator is likely to be able to reflect the full range and diversity of cultures present, even within a single country. For each country, the views of the authors, all of whom have specialist knowledge about child protection practice in the country they are writing about, represent their own views on how the national context for childcare affects the way children are cared for in their country, and also on what the key themes are in relation to bringing up children, especially those in the most vulnerable situations. Another commentator on the same country might focus more on other issues, or have different views. However, each chapter presents an informed expert view on child welfare and child protection in their country. We are pleased to present a body of scholarship that reflects a common commitment to social justice and a belief in shared social responsibility for the wellbeing of children.

The matter of the order of the chapters is something we would like to comment upon. Once we had collected the chapters, we then had to decide how to place them in sequence. We wish to emphasize that the chapter order does not reflect a preference for Anglo-European countries. The sequencing started with the decision to place Hessle's chapter on Sweden first because it includes a unique conceptual framework for considering different countries' approaches to child welfare policy. We believed that it would be helpful to the reader to put this at the beginning of the book so that it could inform the reader's appreciation of the other country chapters. The contrast between the approach to services for vulnerable children and outcomes for them in the US and Sweden is interesting, given their similarity in terms of economic prosperity and the sharing of theories about the best way to work with children and families. Juxtaposing allows the reader to appreciate this commonality and contrast. The rest of the chapters follow in the order they do either because they reflect certain key themes from the preceding chapter, or for contrast. Since each is independent and freestanding, the reader may choose to read them in sequence, or pick and choose. In whatever order the chapters are read, one feature that is striking about them collectively is the emergence of common themes and ideas that cross both jurisdictions and cultures.

It is reasonable to consider what value comes from a book that addresses the issues of child welfare and child protection from an international perspective. One value is an enhanced appreciation of the range of possible approaches, beyond our own immediate experience, that offer the possibility of finding ideas that might work in our own setting. Thus, better solutions may be found to problems similar to those we are confronting. Knowledge about approaches and issues in other contexts also gives us ideas to help us think more critically and reflexively about what we offer to children in our own national setting, wherever we happen to be. A third reason for assembling the discussions of child welfare and welfare services found in this book is the contribution it makes to emergent knowledge about the plight of children, and the challenges they present to the state, that comes from having a range of perspectives from different countries together in one place. A more broadly based understanding of the ways gender and poverty interact with cultural beliefs about childrearing is an example of this emergent knowledge.

As a whole, this book illustrates powerfully the impact of both long-term influences (such as the legacy of the caste system in India) and more recent global events (such as the development of international trade in Ghana) on the way countries meet the need for a structured national approach to supporting families and children. Our own child support provision and child protection practices, wherever we are, are intrinsically conditioned by their context. We hope that each reader will find ideas in this book that resonate with them in terms of their own experience of child welfare and child protection services, and provide the basis for critical reflection on the role of culture and context in the way societies care for their most vulnerable citizens.

All editors have their debtors. Our debt is to the contributors who took up the challenge of writing to a predetermined framework. Without exception, they did so with good grace and enthusiasm. We must also thank the editorial team at Jessica Kingsley Publishers for their patience and their professionalism, which is evidenced by the quality of the end product.

1

Introduction

Penelope Welbourne and John Dixon

The idea of international social work and the concept of globalization are both rightly important in social work education, research and commentary (Harrison and Melville 2010). The role of the state varies widely from place to place, as well as from time to time. Changes in the political environment can have dramatic effects on the way a society values children.

The broader cultural context is highly significant in determining the extent and type of support available to children and parents. Law is also important, since practice takes place within 'interacting layers of contextual and often contradictory factors'; law is key among these (Braye and Preston-Shoot 2006, p.22). Choices made by societies about the services they provide are influenced by shared cultural ideas about individual and collective responsibility for child wellbeing; the value placed on family privacy and autonomy; child and family rights; and values relating to the best way to bring up children. Some welfare regimes are finding that economic difficulties challenge assumptions about what can be provided and create prioritization dilemmas, so that choices have to be made based on ideas about what matters most.

In Europe and North America, interventions to support children and families tend to fall into one of two broad models: those that emphasize safeguarding children against harm (the child protection model); and those that emphasize the promotion of wellbeing through family support (the family welfare model) (Fargion 2012). The *child protection* approach has a focus on a smaller number of children at high risk. The *family welfare* approach, often identified with the Scandinavian countries, emphasizes service provision for a much larger proportion of children and parents, aimed at enhancing parenting capacity. Generous provision for parental leave, financial support for childcare and the ready availability of advice and support for parents are examples of features of such regimes. Children's rights are important, too, but the emphasis is on provision of an environment in which all children can flourish and achieve their potential as far as possible, through widely accessible support for children within their families. Flexible early intervention and prevention strategies are characteristic of such approaches. This may be seen as a future-oriented approach, following the ideal of society making a social investment in children (Stafford, Parton and Vincent 2011). A more child and family welfare-focused approach has developed in many countries that were once identified with a child protection approach (Gilbert, Parton and Skivenes 2011).

In countries with limited state resources juxtaposed with large numbers of people living in poverty, both models are problematic. There are not the resources for the more generous provision associated with the child and family welfare model, and child protection services have to contend with the moral issues raised by coercive intervention where families may be confronting challenges to physical survival. Parents are often struggling to provide basic care for their children in difficult circumstances. Distinguishing between neglect and the effects of poverty can be difficult. There may be tension between targeting small numbers of children for intensive child protective services when services are desperately needed for the many children living in poverty. This dilemma between targeted and universal services is increasingly affecting some developed countries too, as discussed in the context of Italy, where economic difficulties increase the level of need and demand on services while public budgets are shrinking, limiting service capacity. As a result, policies do not always deliver what they promise. In India, for example, aspirational legislation is described as attenuated in its impact, or subject to delayed implementation, because of national fiscal strictures.

States provide for the needs of their citizens according to the philosophies that underlie their society with respect to personal responsibility and independence; social solidarity; human worth and dignity; and the proper role of the state. Culturally informed constructions of appropriate child and parental behaviour also influence social policies, as well as parenting itself. These cultural constructions inform the way children are cared for by their families: how far they are seen as having inherent worth as persons; the contribution they are seen as making to their families simply by being members of it; expectations about their responsibilities as contributors to family wellbeing or survival as workers and income earners in childhood and after; the value they have linked to their potential as supporters of their parents in old age; their responsibility for the continuation of the family line; and their role in upholding the honour and esteem of the family.

Child welfare and child protection are increasingly international issues, not simply national matters. People increasingly move between countries and cultures, bringing ideas about the upbringing of children from their country of origin, while sometimes absorbing those of their adopted country. Those families that stay in one place are increasingly exposed to ideas from different cultures about childhood and the upbringing of children through direct contact with diverse people, and through the media. This happens at the level of practical parenting, not only at the level of academic debate. The media-based debate about the relative merits of 'Chinese' disciplinarian childrearing ('tiger mothers') versus a 'Western', more permissive approach is a recent example of public debate about the merits of different cultural approaches to childhood, in which the benefits and disadvantages of two contrasting philosophies have been explored as a result of parents' exposure to ideas from other cultures.[1]

In Western countries, the 1940s and 1950s marked the beginning of the influence on parenting of seminal academics such as Benjamin Spock (1946) and John Bowlby (1953). These clinicians' ideas about childhood, child wellbeing and acceptable limits to parenting behaviour raised the profile of debates about good enough childcare and the need for a coherent, theoretically justifiable child policy. Over more recent years, the influence of globalization has added a new dimension to this debate. The Eurocentrism of some subsequently established ideas about families and family intervention has been critiqued (Robinson 2003), and new ways of working with families have evolved that take account of the diversity of family structure. An example is the practice of Family Group Conferences, developed originally in New Zealand (New Zealand, Child, Youth and Family Services 2012) and now used in over 20 countries worldwide. Books such as Harrison and Melville's (2010) discussion of social work and globalization, and Williams' (2011) analysis of the demands and possibilities of working with street children in Africa, are expanding our understanding of the way globalization challenges individuals and professionals. Most social workers practise in environments in which people come from a variety of places and cultures, and many of those with a transnational or supranational cultural heritage still inhabit in part, through their family life, that cultural environment in which their ideas about family, childhood, parenting, wellbeing, responsibility, kindness and care first developed. This increasing globalization of family life is mirrored by increasing interest in sharing knowledge about individual and family wellbeing internationally, in both academic and practice communities. For example, of the 122 articles accepted for publication by the *British Journal of Social Work* in the year from September 2011 to August 2012, 33 (27%) explicitly concerned practice in countries outside Britain.

---

1   See Amy Chua's website about her book entitled *Battle Hymn of the Tiger Mother* at http://amychua.com.

The social and political contexts for childhood are very different in the different countries covered in this book. If the economic circumstances and political histories of the last quarter of a century are taken into account, the challenges that have been overcome, and yet to be overcome, by the states concerned are extremely varied. As discussed, social policies and interventions in family life are located within specific historical and cultural contexts, which are the product of social, economic, religious and political developments. Ideas about adoption, support for single parents, investment in the education of children, especially girl children, marriage and the role of the extended family are just a few examples of issues that fundamentally affect children's experiences, which are often affected by the context in which they arise. Some of the countries included here have undergone dramatic changes as a result of, for example, the break-up of the former Soviet Union (Romania and Kazakhstan). Despite the elements of common history they share, the policy solutions they are currently pursuing to address problems and issues differ widely, shaped by national conditions and re-emerging local cultural identities.

The United Nations Convention on the Rights of the Child

One recurring theme in the chapters of the book is that of the *United Nations Convention on the Rights of the Child* (UNCRC) (UNICEF 2012). This was an attempt to formulate a universal set of principles about what children have a right to expect from the world created for them by adults. To be universal, it has to be applicable across widely divergent contexts. This was a major challenge. It has clearly succeeded to an extraordinary extent, as evidenced by its adoption globally. At the same time, some regions, such as Africa, have felt the need to develop their own *Charter on the Rights and Welfare of the Child*, to complement the UNCRC and reflect specifically African concerns and interests (ACERWC no date).

This book illustrates its value across varied national contexts, and the way different elements of the Convention have particular salience in different countries. Although widely welcomed, as evidenced by being the most widely ratified treaty in the world, it has not been without its critics. For example, in the United States of America (the US), now the only country not to have ratified it, the rationale for not doing so includes a fear that it will undermine parental choice. Some of the premises on which it is based have been contentious because of that same diversity of ideas, often very fundamental ideas, about the role of parents, the status of children and the responsibilities of the state, reflected in this book. We now consider how this diversity of approaches and the convergent aspirations of the UNCRC interact.

The Convention does not, of course, attempt to replace parental choice with state control. However, it does hold national governments to their commitment to protecting and ensuring children's rights, as defined in the Convention, and holds them accountable before the international community (UNICEF 2012). The first country to sign and ratify the treaty was Ghana, just one week after it opened for signature on 29 January 1990. The post-UNCRC international community has shown it has the power to make positive changes in children's lives, as demonstrated by changes in practices concerning child labour in the cocoa farming industry in Ghana. International pressure to meet the standards set out in the UNCRC helped accelerate the process of reform in Romania. The Convention provides a common starting point and language for states to consider how best to support each other, and support children in other countries, to achieve the objectives of the Convention.

Children are seen as active rights holders by the Convention, which firmly challenges historical ideas about children as 'property'. It:

> reflects a new vision of the child. Children are neither the property of their parents nor are they helpless objects of charity. They are human beings and are the subject of their own rights. The Convention offers a vision of the child as an individual and a member of a family and a community, with rights and responsibilities appropriate to his or her age and stage of development… Previously seen as negotiable, the child's needs have become legally binding rights. No longer the passive recipient of benefits, the child has become the subject or holder of rights. (UNICEF 2012)

Achieving universal agreement about children's rights is problematic, even after ratification of the UNCRC. The extent and nature of those problem areas is illustrated by looking at some of the interpretative declarations and reservations recorded on the United Nations CRC treaty web pages.[2] Agreement about exactly what needs to be done to promote children's rights has to some extent been concealed by the apparent consensus achieved by almost universal ratification. The chapters on the Middle East, India and the US illustrate this divergence. Ideas about how children's rights interact with the rights of adults, especially parents, continue to cause difficulty. Ideas about children's participation and choice in matters that affect them are another area where the range of approaches in different jurisdictions belies

---

2   All quoted reservations from the UNCRC are available at http://treaties.un.org/Pages/ViewDetails.aspx?src=TREATY&mtdsg_no=IV-11&chapter=4&lang=en.

apparent agreement based on shared commitment to the UNCRC. One of the first areas to present difficulty, taking the Convention in terms of the sequence of its provisions, is the lack of agreement even over how a 'child' should be defined. Social, religious and cultural factors impact on consensus even at this early stage in the UNCRC document. The three reservations cited below reflect fundamental disagreement over when a child starts to exist as a rights holder (at conception or at birth), and over the outcome of conflict between the right to life of an unborn child (and whether such a right exists), and adult rights to make choices about parenthood and their bodies:

- 'With reference to article 1 of the Convention [which defines a child as a human being under the age of 18], the Government of Guatemala declares that article 3 of its Political Constitution establishes that: "The state guarantees and protects human life from the time of its conception, as well as the integrity and security of the individual."'

- 'The United Kingdom interprets the Convention as applicable only following a live birth.'

- 'The Government of the French Republic declares that this Convention, particularly article 6, cannot be interpreted as constituting any obstacle to the implementation of the provisions of French legislation relating to the voluntary interruption of pregnancy.'

There is also a lack of agreement between countries about such basic issues as when a child ceases to be a child, and when they may take on adult responsibilities, including choosing to participate in risky activities, such as participation in armed conflict:

- 'With reference to article 1 of the Convention, the Government of the Republic of Cuba declares that in Cuba…majority is not attained at 18 years of age for purposes of the full exercise of civic rights.'

- 'Spain…wishes to express its disagreement with the age limit fixed therein and to declare that the said limit appears insufficient, by permitting the recruitment and participation in armed conflict of children having attained the age of fifteen years.'

The rights of children involved in legal processes are also the subjects of some reservations from the Convention. One example is in respect of adopted children's rights, and even the right to an opportunity to be adopted if the biological parents are unable to care for a child:

- Egypt opted out of any commitment relating to adoption on the basis that this is not part of Shari'a law, with the assertion that although

Shari'a provides various ways of providing protection and care for children, this does not include adoption.

- Poland reserved the right to limit adopted children's right to know who their natural parents are, instead preserving the right of adoptive parents to maintain the confidentiality of the child's origins where the law provides for this.

The attempt to develop a universal approach to children's rights has served to highlight differences in the way legal systems approach children, often linked to longstanding cultural values. Children living in countries with legal systems based on Shari'a law may find that UNCRC ideas about child rights are eclipsed by Shari'a principles, as in Afghanistan.[3] Local commitment to local legislation means that signatories to the UNCRC express their commitment to its principles in very different ways, and in some cases derogate from those principles altogether.

Such reservations have the potential to reduce the effectiveness of ratification as a way of strengthening the ideals embodied in the UNCRC. The chapters on the Middle East and India demonstrate how ideas about gender roles and the value of women place some girl children at heightened risk of various forms of abuse, exploitation and even death from birth to adulthood. Laws passed to protect girl children may be ineffective in the context of entrenched social attitudes and limited resources to enforce them. The aims and aspirations of child protective services, and the kinds of resources available to protect children, continue to be highly contingent upon local and national conditions. The challenge for agencies working to protect children is to find a way of meeting the aims of the Convention without contravening local customs and laws – or to find a way of starting a dialogue about the possibility of change, as in India, with the Convention as a focus.

The aspirational nature of Convention rights has to be recognized when applied in places where existence itself can be a struggle. India has reserved the right to *progressively* implement provisions relating to the economic, social and cultural rights of children, in view of the scale of the challenge that full implementation implies. This means that certain kinds of protection, such as protection from engaging in child labour, may not be achievable immediately but its importance as a social goal is recognized. We can see that while the UNCRC is aspirational, it is also a significant force for social and cultural change. And while it reflects the cultural and social values of those who framed it, which may not be compatible with all the values of

---

3   Afghanistan's reservation to the UNCRC reads: 'The Government of the Republic of Afghanistan reserves the right to express…reservations on all provisions of the Convention that are incompatible with the laws of Islamic Shari'a and the local legislation in effect.'

some societies that have signed up to it, it provides a vision of childhood which people in all countries may use to reflect on what is an acceptable and culturally important difference, and what harms children even when it is tolerated culturally. Children's rights are *individual* rights. Societies that place a particularly high value on social cohesion while placing a lower level of emphasis on individual rights, or that value adult rights more strongly over children's rights, are those in which the alternative philosophical starting point of the UNCRC may lead to the sharpest ideological conflict over the application of the Convention, as opposed to countries in which non-implementation is linked to economic circumstances. The contrast between India and the Middle East in the chapters of this book would suggest that this could be the case in some regions.

In the early 1990s, Korbin (1991, p.70) wrote:

> By the year 2007, we should strive to have more satisfactory answers to the following definitional questions: What is the spectrum of caretaker behaviour accepted by different cultures? Under what conditions does an act exceed the cultural continuum of acceptability? ... How much overlap exists between cultures? Is a universal definition possible, or will definitions of necessity be culture specific?

Over 20 years later, there are still no authoritative answers to Korbin's 'definitional questions', although this book represents an approach to developing answers. We may however be able to define more closely what we would look for in a satisfactory answer. Ideas about acceptable caretaker behaviour may vary from place to place and culture to culture, but all should meet the standard set by the Convention. The answers to Korbin's four questions need to incorporate an appreciation of the role of, and degree of freedom of, parental agency in a social context. How do parents make the choices they make, how free are they to choose how they parent, and what is there to support them in making good choices, and succeeding as parents? In seeking to understand the way individual parents respond to the challenge of parenting under both difficult and supportive circumstances, it is essential to understand more about the importance of culture and culture-specific values. The chapters of this book illustrate in particular how potent are ideas about the role of women in society, and the influence of social structures that perpetuate oppression and poverty. In addition, the material and social difficulties faced by many parents mean that it is often difficult to identify neglect and abuse by looking at the condition of a child alone, and sometimes even by looking at parental behaviour taken in isolation from its context.

Appreciation of context is of critical importance. Finkelhor and Korbin (1988, p.4) defined child abuse as 'the portion of harm to children that results from human action that is proscribed, proximate and preventable'. This serves two purposes: it distinguishes child maltreatment from other social, economic and health problems facing children in a diversity of national settings, and it is flexible enough to apply to a range of social and cultural contexts (Korbin 1991, p.68). However, defining 'preventable' is not straightforward, as discussed above. Regarding ascertaining what is proscribed, there will always be a range or continuum of accounts of the limits to acceptable parenting, and each parent must choose between them. The idea that harm must be proximate to be called abuse – that is, caused by someone close to the child rather than by the distal and more abstract social structures that marginalize and exclude some members of society – exonerates social and economic systems from being labelled abusive. Instead the majority of the blame is placed at the level of individual parents. However, a more nuanced appreciation of the social processes and power structures that impact on parents and children might lead one to question how far such a binary separation of responsibility reflects the reality of parents in difficult circumstances. The chapters on the US and Ghana highlight this in particular. The history of forced adoption of children from England, the US and Australia provides another example of the apparent permeability of this boundary between proximate harm and harm rooted in cultural and social practices.

Korbin (1991) defines three categories of harmful practices:

- Harm caused by cultural differences in childrearing behaviour and the practices that may be judged to be harmful by those outside the culture, such as female genital circumcision.

- Harm caused by the idiosyncratic departure from the norms prevalent in a culture.

- Harm caused by society because of poverty, war and the lack of healthcare or nutrition.

We might consider the advantages and disadvantages of adding a fourth category:

- Childrearing behaviour or prevailing social conditions that would be judged harmful to children in any culture or society.

If there exists a core of behaviours that would be accepted as 'good parenting' in all cultures, as Korbin believes, then this category defines that set of parental behaviours and social conditions impinging on parenting that would be considered unacceptable in all societies. The 'country' chapters of this book do not answer all of Korbin's broad-ranging questions, but they do provide rich material for considering parenting in context: the way culture-specific discourses, family policies, welfare services and family circumstances interact to promote or jeopardize the welfare of a child.

Children in state care and adoption

Another recurring theme in this book is that of institutional care of children. Caring for children in institutions has been contentious at least since English Poor Law practices led to the separation of many children from their impoverished parents. Its potential to be a tool for social manipulation was identified half a century ago in a prescient comment by John Bowlby (1953, p.182): 'One must be beware of a vested interest in the institutional care of children!' Sweden, however, has re-evaluated residential care, and examined some of the negative assumptions made about it, identifying its value for some children. However, the way it is designed is all-important. Both modern Romania and Kazakhstan inherited childcare systems based on large-scale institutionalization. Efforts to unpick this are ongoing in both countries, and both are making progress towards remedying the situation, with good results. The potential of institutional care to provide a valuable service or to be an instrument of social engineering is thus highlighted. The chapters relating to Romania and Kazakhstan also reveal the magnitude of investment needed in alternative community-based services if the former practice of institutionalization is to be successfully phased out.

In Australia, state care, particularly compulsory adoption, has resonance with oppressive practices that were an assault on Aboriginal culture, as well as on some other vulnerable groups such as single mothers (Australia, Australian Human Rights Commission no date; Australia, Australian Institute of Family Studies 2012). The social impact of those practices continues to resonate even now, decades later. Any use of compulsion used in an attempt to remedy problems in the present has inevitable echoes of earlier discriminatory practices, although the objectives are different now.

In Japan, by contrast, the state has historically placed strong emphasis on parental rights, and continues to do so. There is a reluctance to interfere with parental choice even when parenting is problematic. The initiative to place children 'for the sake of the child' in Japan is one with a relatively recent history. Adoption is used very differently in different countries, according to ideas about the importance of family ties and the availability of alternatives to permanent removal of children from their families. It is rarely used in Sweden, whereas in the UK policy makers see it as a priority for children in care. In some countries forms of adoption are being developed that are 'open' in the sense that ties with the birth family are not always eliminated and may continue to be valued by the child as well as the birth family. In Kazakhstan, the practice of permitting children to be adopted from orphanages by overseas adopters has been stopped and formal adoption by Kazakh families has begun to develop. In Japan, the practice of adoption of children by non-relatives and strangers is a relatively recent development.

Children as ends in themselves, not as means to an end: Population and child welfare

Children are the future of any country. As well as investing in their children's wellbeing, countries have sometimes considered what the size of the future population should be, because of fears about under- or over-population. In Romania, the objective of increasing population size was one causal factor in the evolution of a situation in which many children were born who were not wanted by their parents, or whose parents could not afford to care for them. Inadequate investment in their care by the same state whose policies had directly contributed to the birth of so many unwanted children led to a humanitarian crisis in Romania in the 1990s, the repercussions of which continue today. The legacy of this, after the fall of Ceausescu in 1989, was the need to find homes for thousands of children living in institutional care under appalling conditions. These children were the result of a social policy that viewed children as a means to an end, rather than as ends in themselves. One of the messages from the overview of adoption and institutional care that comes through the chapters of this book is that both forms of care can can be the means to offer many children and young people safety, security and sometimes love, but they must be provided in the context of a broader policy framework that is firmly child and family-centred in order to prevent their abuse or distortion by 'vested interests'.

Population size has become a public issue in other countries. In both Italy and Japan, low rates of childbirth are giving cause for concern. Negative population growth has acted as a trigger for evaluating support services for parents, in order to promote families choosing to have children. In contrast to falling birth rates in parts of Europe, the expanding child population in India presents the challenge of meeting expanding demand for services, especially for the poorest children. Selectivity about the gender of children is another issue the consequences of which have yet to play out in full, as populations with an unbalanced gender mix come of age. What this strongly suggests is that when children are viewed as a means to an end rather than as ends in themselves by the society they are born into or conceived in, there are likely to be negative consequences for the children, for their parents and for the society as a whole.

Changing family structures and work–life balance

One of the threats to child welfare, as illustrated throughout this book, is the challenge of trying to parent and work to support a family at the same time. Gendered expectations place the burden of caring for young children primarily on mothers, but economic pressures often make working outsde the home an essential survival strategy for mothers as well as fathers, from Japan to Ghana to the US. Some parents are overwhelmed by the challenge, responding by placing children in institutional care, sometimes anonymously as 'cradle babies'; engaging children in work, sometimes as bonded labourers or as trafficked children; arranging early marriages for them; and even committing infanticide. However, the traditional way of coping with the varied demands of raising a family is to draw on the resources of the extended family or clan. In many countries, the extended family is breaking down; new patterns of living and working mean that members often no longer live within easy reach of each other, thus diminishing the potential for mutual support. This has major implications for child welfare.

The urbanization that accompanies globalization and modernization has led to the weakening or breakdown of traditional forms of family life for many families. This process probably started in Britain about 250 years ago, at the beginning of the Industrial Revolution, when changes in industry, agriculture and trade changed social structures in Britain forever. What is perhaps surprising is the length of time it has taken for this change to work its way around the world, and the resilience and persistence of traditional extended family networks into the twenty-first century. However, the pressures of accelerating globalization, linked to increasingly globalized markets, have recently changed family patterns even in places that were able to maintain their extended family structures well into the twentieth century. Pressure on parents to balance work and childcare responsibilities on their own, when once children's other relatives would offer security and care while parents worked, affects children as well as parents. Childcare arrangements may be poor or insecure or non-existent, and the security of having a group of caring relatives for nurture and protection is replaced by reliance on the emotional and material resources of just one or two parents. This is an issue in the US as it is in Ghana; in Japan as in Ghana there are fears about the effect of social isolation on those living in small family units. Children may suffer when new forms of family life are unable to replace that which was lost in the process of urbanization. However, it should also be noted that traditional cultural practices maintained and transmitted within extended families can offer threats to children. This may be seen in the chapters on the Middle East and India, where risks to children can include violation of

Convention rights associated with personal and religious choice. Penalties for non-compliance may be very severe, often imposed by family members drawing on long cultural traditions that regulate both protection from harm and coercion and punishment.

The additional hazards of being a female child

Another notable theme in the chapters of this book is the relationship between a society's attitude to its women members and the welfare of its children. Girl children appear particularly vulnerable in societies that assign a lower value to being female. Poverty is a major and most significant risk factor for many children, but the gender of a child appears to interact with their economic circumstances, to shape the way their life chances are affected by poverty. Poverty is bad for children: it is the most influential factor in children's development and social outcomes, with social capital as the next most influential factor (Ferguson and Lavalette 2006; Putnam 2000).

The description of the combined effects of poverty together with gender discrimination in India in this book is particularly concerning, from their combined impact on survival rates in infancy to their effect on girls' access to education. By contrast, in Japan, where poverty is a relatively rare hazard and children have better life expectancy and educational opportunities, the high expectations of mothers place them under great pressure to ensure their children conform to the stereotype of a well-brought-up child. Stresses on those mothers who struggle to conform to the stereotype of the competent and effective parent with 'perfect' children can even trigger acts of suicide and filicide, including so-called 'altruistic filicide' (Friedman *et al.* 2005; Horwitz and Resnick 2005). If experiencing difficulty in parenting is not a socially acceptable possibility, mothers may feel the need to conceal difficulties, and obtaining help for children will be difficult whether it is the parent or the child that is showing signs of difficulty. Reluctance to interfere with parental rights will play out very differently in terms of its impact on children in need of protection when there is access to universal non-stigmatizing support services, compared with situations in which parental help-seeking is viewed negatively. The issues discussed in the chapter on the Middle East, highlighted above, provide another example of the way a strongly gendered society presents particular risks to female children.

Conclusion

Hessle, in his chapter on Sweden, presents a model for making international comparisons concerning children at risk. The three dimensions of family policy, child welfare and the culture-specific discourse are interacting factors that describe the predisposition and responsiveness of the state to child welfare problems, reflecting different kinds and levels of 'preparedness for action' in the prioritization of protection of children within different national systems. It also offers a framework for the identification of areas of family policy and practice in need of development: where it is under-developed in relation to the level of need experienced by those children and parents most in need, or ineffective in improving the condition of children in need of support. The way national family policy responds to child and family need is a result, at least in part, of predisposing factors in the child and family welfare discourse, as well as the actual needs of the children themselves. Analysis of states' responses to child protection based on states' approaches to policy, specific regional challenges to child welfare and the culture-specific discourse about children may help us to consider not only what has been achieved, and what remains to be addressed, but also which cultural factors are influencing the direction of policy.

The chapters of this book reflect a diversity of approaches to child welfare services, linked to philosophies and political contexts and discourses about family life and the role of welfare. They also reflect the diversity of challenges facing children: many severe, some life threatening and sometimes fatal. They also illustrate the impact social, economic and political change has had on family life in many parts of the world over recent decades. This is perhaps most marked in those regions of the world that have been affected by major political upheaval, but globalization has affected families in many and diverse countries in ways that may be for the good, or add stress to already difficult lives.

This book also illustrates how the search for consensus about children's rights, through implementation of the UNCRC, has opened up global dialogue about children's rights. The ratification of the Convention, in almost every country of the world, has in itself highlighted variation in how children are seen in those different countries, and how children's rights are accommodated, to a greater or lesser extent, by pre-existing structures of adult rights, and existing social and cultural norms and values. It highlights enormous variation in beliefs and expectations about the 'proper' role of the state in supporting family and child wellbeing, and some of the challenges associated with achieving state intervention to support children that is both just and effective.

Policies are developed following a process of inquiry and exploration of issues, during which certain issues gain prominence. The choice of issues is linked to both presenting need and to the discourse that marks certain issues as socially important, or sometimes, as appears to happen occasionally in the case of child protection policy in the UK, as the focus of a 'moral panic' (Cohen 1972), or otherwise significant. Influences such as traditional values and global events impact on the identification of certain issues as pressing, while others are relegated to lower priorities. Ideas about acceptable childcare practices and the reasonable threshold for intervention – or for offering state support – come from the culture-specific discourse about children's welfare, but are shaped by policies and changing expectations about what children should expect. The UNCRC is an example of a document that had its origins in an international attempt to capture key elements of the global discourse about children's rights, and these in turn have influenced thinking about children's rights globally. A virtuous circle is thus created, although in too many regions progress may be overwhelmed by poverty, warfare or other social, political and economic ills.

Children merit special protection because of their vulnerability, and because of this, adults need to use their power over children with discretion, and take their responsibilities to them seriously. Most parents do this, in all countries and cultures, even when they may suffer hardship themselves as a result. In those relatively rare cases in which parents, or others with power over children, fail to respect their need for care and protection, the power of the state should come in to play to act as a fail-safe as they meet their responsibilities to their youngest citizens. The chapters of this book are about the various ways in which that power is exercised, and how the governments of the various countries meet those responsibilities. Giving children rights only helps them if they can exercise them, and children are very dependent upon adults to be able to exercise those rights, including the rights they hold under the UNCRC. This book is about the challenges children face in different regions of the world, but it is also, perhaps more importantly, the way children are protected by those who have ultimate responsibility for shaping the child's world at the level of policy, and influencing the discourse of childhood and child protection towards a robust defence of children's right to grow up free from neglect and abuse.

References

ACERWC (no date) *The African Charter on the Rights and Welfare of the Child.* Available at: http://acerwc.org/the-african-charter-on-the-rights-and-welfare-of-the-child-acrwc.

Australia, Australian Human Rights Commission (no date) *Bringing them Home: The 'Stolen Children' Report.* Available at: www.humanrights.gov.au/social_justice/bth_report/index.html.

Australia, Australian Institute of Family Studies (2012) *Apology in South Australian Parliament over Forced Adoptions.* Available at: http://aifs.govspace.gov.au/2012/07/18/apology-in-south-australian-parliament-over-forced-adoptions.

Bowlby, J. (1953) *Child Care and the Growth of Love.* Harmondsworth, UK: Penguin.

Braye, S. and Preston-Shoot, M. (2006) 'The role of law in welfare reform: Critical perspectives on the relationship between law and social work practice.' *International Journal of Social Welfare 15*, 19–26.

Cohen, S. (1972) *Folk Devils and Moral Panics.* London: Routledge.

Fargion, S. (2012) 'Synergies and tensions in child protection and parent support: Policy lines and practitioners cultures.' *Child and Family Social Work.* Available at: http://onlinelibrary.wiley.com/doi/10.1111/j.1365-2206.2012.00877.x/full.

Ferguson, I. and Lavalette, M. (2006) 'Globalization and Global Justice: Towards a social work of resistance.' *International Social Work 49*, 309–318.

Finkelhor, D. and Korbin, J. (1988) 'Child abuse as an international issue.' *Child Abuse and Neglect 12*, 3–23.

Friedman, S.H., Horwitz, S.M. and Resnick, P.J. (2005) 'Child murder by mothers: A critical analysis of the current state of knowledge and a research agenda.' *American Journal of Psychiatry 162*, 578–587.

Gilbert, N., Parton, N. and Skivenes, M. (eds) (2011) *Child Protection Systems: International Trends and Orientations.* Oxford: Oxford University Press.

Harrison, G. and Melville, R. (2010) *Rethinking Social Work in a Global World.* Basingstoke, UK: Palgrave Macmillan.

Korbin, J.E. (1991) 'Cross-cultural perspectives and research directions for the 21st century.' *Child Abuse and Neglect 15*, 67–77.

New Zealand, Child, Youth and Family Services (2012) *Family Group Conferences.* Available at: www.cyf.govt.nz/youth-justice/family-group-conferences.html

Putnam, R. (2000) *Bowling Alone: The Collapse and Revival of American Community.* New York: Simon and Schuster.

Robinson, L. (2003) 'Social Work through the Life Course.' In R. Adams, L. Dominelli and M. Payne (eds) *Social Work: Themes, Issues and Critical Debates* (2nd ed.). Basingstoke, UK: Palgrave.

Spock, B. (1946) *The Common Sense Book of Baby and Childcare.* New York: Duell, Sloan and Pearce.

Stafford, A., Parton, N. and Vincent, S. (2011) *Child Protection Systems in the United Kingdom: A Comparative Analysis.* London: Jessica Kingsley Publishers.

UNICEF (2012) *United Nations Convention on the Rights of the Child.* Available at: www.unicef.org/crc/index_30229.html.

Williams, A. (2011) *Working with Street Children: An Approach Explored.* Lyme Regis, UK: Russell House.

2

Sweden

Sven Hessle

Introduction

In this chapter there is a discussion of the development of child welfare in Sweden within the context of discourses on the child, family and society. These discourses are mainly the fruit of social and welfare developments in Sweden during the twentieth century. It also presents a framework for international comparison of services for children at risk. In the concluding section, two challenges to the progression of the Swedish welfare state model are outlined: first, the emergence of the context-bound family, without strong bonds to their own traditions; and second, the long-term project of transcultural progression, which is linked to increased immigration from all parts of the world.

Current challenges facing child welfare in Sweden provide the starting point for the chapter. An increasingly multi-ethnic society is becoming established in Swedish secular society, with migrants representing diverse religious beliefs coming from all corners of the world. In contrast, the Swedish model for the welfare state has its conceptual roots in the 1930s, when Swedish society was very different. A historical emphasis on the pedagogical and social dimensions of welfare has left traces in child welfare legislation, which has been built on administrative decision making, rather than court orders, as happens in most Anglo-Saxon countries. The creation of municipality social service centres has created an increasing need for professional social workers occupied with family and child issues, including support for the elderly. During recent decades, there has been a noteworthy increase in the number of schools of social work. Currently, 15 schools and departments of social work are educating graduate and postgraduate students for a market still in need of professional social workers.

The social, political, religious and cultural context

Sweden is an outpost of northern Europe, sharing land borders with Denmark through a bridge, and Norway and Finland on the Scandinavian Peninsula. Topography and vegetation vary widely, from fertile plains in the south to barren mountains in the north. It is an elongated country that is more than 1,600 kilometres long. Half of its nearly ten million inhabitants are concentrated in just 3 per cent of the country's area. Large-scale immigration during recent decades has brought about a rapid change in the formerly homogenous population, and now about one in four children have roots in a foreign country. Most immigrants have settled in the metropolitan areas, which have become multicultural zones. In Malmö, for example, the third largest city in Sweden, 40 per cent of children have an immigrant background.

Demography

Population density is 20.6 people per square kilometre (53.3 per square mile), substantially higher in the south than in the north. About 85 per cent live in urban areas. The capital city, Stockholm, has a population of about one million inhabitants, with about double this in the metropolitan area. It has the third lowest infant mortality rate in the world: 2.74 deaths per 1,000 live births (US, CIA 2012).

Sweden also has the lowest Gini coefficient of all countries (0.23) (UNDP 2012), which makes it the most equal country on earth in terms of income distribution. In national and local politics, some 45 per cent of representatives are women. Women's participation in the labour force is equal with men. A tax reform from the mid-1970s has been helpful in promoting female employment, conferring on married women the status of independent taxpayers, but the Swedish labour market has the same gender-related segregation patterns as in many other countries. Women form the vast majority of employees in all care sectors, such as nursing, childcare and social work. Thirty per cent of working women are in part-time employment, compared to 5 per cent of men.

The population of Sweden is expected to increase from 9.5 million in 2011 to 10 million inhabitants by 2018. The birth rate is 1.92 and is increasing slowly, so the increase in population is mainly explained by increasing immigration, discussed in more detail later. There are 1.9 million children under 17 years of age (19% of the population), and a similar proportion of older people. Life expectancy at birth is 83.5 years.

Immigration

Sweden has been transformed from a nation of emigration, which was ended by the Second World War, to a nation of immigration after the war ended. Sweden was mainly a poor agricultural nation until the First World War (1914–1918). About one million people emigrated, mainly to the United States of America (the US), during the inter-war years. About the same number of people have immigrated to Sweden since 1945. In 2010, there were 1.33 million foreign-born residents in Sweden, corresponding to 14.3 per cent of the total population (EC, Eurostat 2012). In 2009, 102,280 people migrated to Sweden, with immigration reaching its highest level since records began. Included in the migrant stream are asylum seekers, from Afghanistan and Somalia, and other countries where there have been armed conflicts, notably Serbia, Kosovo and Bosnia and Herzegovina; also those suffering discrimination, such as the Roma; and those seeking family reunion. During 2011, nearly 30,000 individuals asked for asylum in Sweden (Sweden, Migration Board 2012). Among them were more than 2,600 unaccompanied children and young people, which puts Sweden top of the list of European countries with this category of children and young people. Migrants tend to settle in large urban areas and have become a challenge both economically and socially, since their unemployment rate is much higher than that of the Swedish-born population (currently around 8%). Depending on country of origin, the unemployment rate among immigrants varies between 20 and 80 per cent. Some implications of this are discussed further below.

Religion

Religion is an important issue when considering migration flows. At the end of 2009, 71.3 per cent of Swedes belonged to the Lutheran Church of Sweden (Church of Sweden 2012). This number has been decreasing by about one percentage point a year for the last two decades. However, only approximately 2 per cent of the church's members regularly attend Sunday services. Some 275,000 Swedes are members of various free churches. In addition, immigration has meant that there are now some 92,000 Roman Catholics and 100,000 Eastern Orthodox Christians living in Sweden. Because of immigration, Sweden also has a significant Muslim population of about 500,000. Some studies have found Sweden to be one of the least religious countries in the world, with one of the highest levels of atheism, but religion in Sweden continues to play a role in cultural identity. This is evidenced by the fact that a majority of adults continue to remain members of the Lutheran Church despite having to pay a church tax where rates remain high; church weddings are popular and increasing in Sweden (Church of Sweden 2012).

The welfare state

Sweden is usually described as a social welfare state, characterized by a universal approach, with tax-financed benefits and services for everyone so as not to stigmatize the few. The combination of the universal approach with earnings-related programmes is known as the *encompassing model* (Korpi 2004; see also Hessle 2012a). Everyone accesses some of these benefits at some time during their lifetime through a national social insurance system created by tax transfers and without means testing. This model has been evolving since the 1930s when the Social Democrats came into political power. Swedish society generally supports it, and at present, with a political right wing alliance steering the country since 2006, there are no indications that any political party will attempt to question the model. Welfare for children at risk has not, however, 'grown out of its poverty-relief shell' (Cocozza and Hort 2011, p.107). The current discourse in Sweden is about the increasing income gap, with an increasing number of children in poverty (Salonen 2011). Residential care in Sweden is still class-based, but 'now with an added ethnic twist' (Cocozza and Hort 2011, p.107).

Overview of social work in Sweden: Development and current features[1]

The history of social work in Sweden is similar to that of many other European countries. Charity and philanthropy provided by religious and voluntary organizations, carried out mostly by women, were the typical ways of fighting poverty before and during the nineteenth century. The industrialization process set in motion mass migration to the cities where working conditions were abominable, especially for women, and criminality was common. It also led in the latter part of the nineteenth century to mass migration to the US, especially by poor farmers who either owned no land at all or had been left with small unprofitable holdings after the great agriculture reform at the beginning of that century.

The first Poor Laws in Sweden were enacted in 1847 and 1871. These gave local communities the responsibility of caring for poor people, especially children and the elderly living under their jurisdiction. Ever since the Middle Ages, caring for the poor had been the province of the church (mainly the Swedish Lutheran Church). However, subsequent reforms in Sweden led to the gradual replacement of the church with secular service providers.

---

1   This overview is partly inspired by the author's chapter in Weiss and Welbourne (2007).

The first signs of a more advanced social policy appeared at the beginning of the twentieth century, largely through the efforts of three Swedish CSOs (charitable organizations): the Central Association for Social Work (CSA), *Svenska Fattigvårdsförbundet* (the Swedish Association for Poverty Care)[2] and the *Fredrika Bremerförbundet* (the Fredrika Bremer Association).[3] These organizations recruited activist middle-class women to take frontline positions in the fight against urban poverty. With the CSA as the main instigator, these CSOs organized the first courses for voluntary social workers and lobbied parliament for new legislation, resulting in the first child welfare legislation in 1903 and the Poor Laws of 1918.

The campaign to organize professional social work education led to the founding in 1921 of the *Institutet för socialpolitisk och kommunal utbildning och forskning* (the Institute for Social, Political and Municipality Education, Training and Research). Located in Stockholm, this was the first recognized school of social work in the country. The study programme was directed toward educating a generalist corps of community administrative workers whose tasks included both practical social work and deciding on issues of social policy. Another aim of the programme was to promote the development of the social sciences.

Basically, social workers provide social assistance to marginalized groups who fall through Sweden's universal social safety net; these populations have varied over time. Social workers also participate in social planning at the policy level, for instance in neighbourhood development and reconstruction. The majority of professional social workers are employed by public authorities, mostly in the municipalities, where they handle complex assignments, such as individual or community psychosocial work and social investigations into child and family welfare.

The exact number of professional social workers in Sweden today is unknown, but close to 40,000 would not be an unreasonable guess.[4] This means that there are approximately four professionally educated social workers per 1,000 inhabitants. The ratio of social workers to the general population is rising as schools and departments of social work are producing more graduate social workers than ever before. Ninety per cent of social workers in Sweden are employed in the public sector (Dellgran and Höjer 2005),

---

2 This Association was established at the beginning of the 1900s to work with administrative and educational issues connected with poverty. It provided a non-confessional alternative to the Swedish Lutheran Church, which had been the major dispenser of charity and had educated deacons since the mid-1800s.

3 This Association promoted the ideas of liberalism and feminism and was headed by Fredrika Bremer, one of the frontline figures in the Swedish feminist movement.

4 Estimate from *Academ SSR*, the Swedish trade union, which represents more than 80 per cent of professional social workers.

and the majority of municipal social workers are employed in social service centres (SSCs), providing social services for children, young people and families, substance misusers and elderly people, as well as dispensing basic financial support.

The field of family and child welfare is by far the most popular social work specialization in Sweden (Bergmark and Lundström 2005). Most social workers in child welfare are familiar with advanced methodologies, such as networking and family therapy, which take a holistic view of family problems. In times of economic recession, however, much of the daily work of the social services, including services for children in need of support, is concerned with deciding on individual applications for financial assistance. Migrants from other cultures constitute a new group of clients. After arriving in Sweden, they are often faced with unemployment and social exclusion. This relatively new situation entailing decision making in transcultural conflicts is one of the contemporary challenges facing Swedish social workers (Hessle 2007a).

Social workers (and other professionals) who leave the SSCs to start their own businesses, or to be in the employment of private companies, have been the focus of much debate in recent years. Private enterprises mainly providing residential care, case investigations and drug misuse care, and care homes and day centres for the elderly, are on the rise in the Swedish social welfare market (Bergmark and Lundström 2005; Szebehely 2011). Critics argue that it is unethical to sell tax-founded public services in the marketplace. However, entering private employment does not seem to be a mass movement, with only 7 per cent of social workers having done so, the majority on a part-time basis (Dellgran and Höjer 2005). The Swedish social welfare service will continue to be mainly publicly provided in the long run, but with some temporary niche projects where private enterprises or voluntary organizations can be quicker at providing solutions in emergency situations (Bergmark and Lundström 2005).

The evolution of child welfare services

The twentieth century has been described as the 'century of the child'.[5] What this means differs of course depending on what part of the world we have in focus. In Sweden, there are reasons to believe that children, generally and incrementally, have become more and more visible in terms of their needs and are increasingly respected for their personal voice. For

---

5   After the Swedish feminist and author Ellen Kay, who published the book entitled *Barnets Århundrade* in 1900, which was translated into English in 1909 as *The Century of the Child*.

example, during the twentieth century, poverty was eradicated as the main reason for placing children in public care in Sweden. Nowadays there are other reasons behind the assessment of a child as being in a high-risk situation (Hessle 2012b). There are at least three qualitative paradigmatic steps forward that child welfare has taken in Sweden in terms of the history of ideas and the development of the discourse of child welfare. During the twentieth century, Swedes learned first to approach the child as a partner and subject in dialogue and not as an object to manipulate; second, to establish a holistic view of the child and family and their context; and third, to activate the child's social network on all levels to benefit the best interests of the child.

The child as a partner

During the first half of the twentieth century, adolescents undergoing coercive treatment in large institutions were released from authoritarian programmes, where they had been objects for behaviour change treatment. In the second half of the twentieth century, large institutions were dismantled, replaced by more family-like group homes. *Milieu therapy* became the key term for a treatment ideology that formed the basis for dealing with children and adolescents at high risk (Hessle 2003a). Seventy-five per cent of such institutions have less than nine adolescents. Most placements of children under 13 years of age accept parents and children together. Children have gradually become seen as agents – subjects in a dialogue with their environment. Isolation from society has always been a characteristic risk associated with residential care treatment, so opening the doors to the surrounding world was an important movement in child welfare development (Hessle 2003b). Institutions not only became small but they also tended to move from the countryside to the cities, close to the homes of the children.[6]

Even the limitations of foster care became obvious through comprehensive research carried out in Sweden, which was inspired by international discourse (for an overview, see Hessle 1998, but see also Fanshel and Shinn 1978; Vinnerljung 1996). Maas and Engler (1959) already pointed out in the 1950s the general problems and risks with foster home placements for children who have been placed permanently, who may be abandoned by the social welfare authorities. Numerous Swedish research

---

6 Three general principles are embedded in the 1989 Social Service Act (SoL): the *Principle of Nearness* – public placements and interventions should be in the client's neighbourhood; the *Principle of Normality* – giving all citizens the right to lead a normal life; and the *Principle of Continuity* – giving children the right to have continued contact with relatives when in public care.

reports identify the same tendencies (Hessle 1988; Sallnäs, Wiklund and Lagerlöf 2010; Vinnerljung and Sallnäs 2008).[7] Under the 1989 *United Nations Convention on the Rights of the Child* (UNCRC) (UNICEF 2012), a child's voice is privileged to have the right to be heard in situations that concern him or her. This declaration came as no surprise to the Swedish authorities. The child's right to be 'a partner' is clearly written into many parts of the legislation that concerns children and young persons.[8]

A holistic view of the child and family in their context

During the twentieth century, Swedish child welfare provision expanded considerably, both in practice and in theory, especially after the Second World War. Since the 1950s there has also been interdisciplinary experience of working together: medical doctors, psychologists, social workers and others working clinical psychosocial cases with families in child psychiatry. One reason for this collaborative success is the development of theory. Psychodynamic theory was initially the common interpretative language for these cases, then systems theory and communications theories, which bound families in theoretically defined relationships. Other kinds of theoretical frameworks were also imported (Båge 1972). All these were explored by experts in these interdisciplinary teams to enable them to get closer to a common understanding of the child or adolescent in vulnerable situations, within their family context. More than 250 frameworks are available to aid interpreting and working with families (Hansson 2001). Another factor is that psychiatry moved out of the hospitals in the 1970s and into the neighbourhoods. Psychiatry needed a framework that connected the psychiatric patient with society (Borgengren and Costa 1997).

Activating the social network

Another factor that made interdisciplinary working a necessity was the increase in immigration during and after the 1970s. Migrant families from all over the world dominated the new suburbs of the big cities. New methods were needed (Grosin and Hedén 1984), and the answer to the new situation was to import the Family Networks Model from the US (Speck and Attneave 1973).

---

7   In a 20-year longitudinal study of children in care, Andersson (2008) found that children who sustained a positive relationship with their relatives had better outcomes than those who did not. Hessle and Wåhlander (2000) showed in a longitudinal study that children who were placed with their family in a treatment setting, especially girls, had a better prognosis than children placed in foster homes or residential care.

8   For instance, the Care of Young Person's Act (LVU) provides: 'The young person's point of view shall be made clear as far as possible. Account shall be taken of the wishes of the young person, with due consideration of his or her age and maturity.'

Working with family networks in their environment was an approach welcomed by professionals working in the new globalized world in the Botkyrka metropolitan area of Stockholm. They had specialist training in working with the wider circles of people around defined 'problem carriers'. The Family Networks Model opened up participation by neighbours, friends and relatives in families' informal networks, their formal representatives and others involved in the family's problem. It was possible to handle difficult childcare cases, youth problems and criminal gangs in situ. Many users of social services are substance misusers in need of treatment in addition to the usual range of social services. Above all, this new way of working became a successful tool with migrant families. *Botkyrka Kriscenter* (Botkyrka Crisis Centre) became the node from which the new method was spread to professional networks all over Sweden and Scandinavia. Theoretically, Bronfenbrenners' bio-psycho-ecological model was very suitable for the social network specialists (Hessle 2003b, 2007b). The original US methodology was exported from the team in Botkyrka and used for the education of various professional teams in Russia. The basic idea is defined as: to be working side by side in the everyday psychosocial reality of vulnerable families, not upside down, not from the bottom up, but side by side!

This method was by no means the only bridge between the different levels of child–family–*Umwelt*.[9] Other child welfare and protection investigation methods have developed their own systematic ways of getting information from the various people involved in a child's problem situation, but mostly from an 'above' position, which can be described as 'upside down'. The New Zealand approach – Family Group Conferencing, which comes closest to the Family Networks Model – is another side-by-side investigation method that is familiar to Swedish child welfare workers.

An important message in this part of the chapter is that Swedish professional social workers in family and child welfare know how to engage vulnerable families side by side, in their habitat. Since the last century it has been recognized that in child welfare and child protection problem solving, everyone can be a partner, including a child. The value of networking is that even an informally linked (non-professional) person who is of importance to the child can be a partner. Formally linked people from different professions can also be partners. The skill lies in getting these partners together to advance the best interests of the child. It is a challenge and takes much skill for a professional in child welfare to act side by side with literally anyone, without losing their professional status. After the turn of the twenty-first century, networking ideas have taken further steps forward. Social media

---

9   *Umwelt* is a German systems theory concept for the bonding relationship between person and environment.

might, for example, be the next forum for mobilization of support in child welfare.[10]

Child welfare laws become the Social Services Act

Child welfare legislation was passed successively throughout the twentieth century. In 1902 Sweden passed a law that clearly established public responsibility for high-risk children and young people. Decisions about young people were to be taken by administrative order issued by local politicians rather than in the courts, unlike the approach that had been the preferred solution in the Anglo-American parts of the world. From 1924, the municipalities were obliged to investigate and make decisions about children who were abused or neglected at home. From 1942, psychological abuse was included in the legislation. From 1960, the municipalities were given preventive responsibilities, and parents were able to appeal against decisions taken at the municipal level. The 1989 Social Services Act (henceforth SoL) was the next step (amended in 1996 and again in 2001). This is a framework law that guides the actions of professional social workers. A framework law is one that sets out basic values and principles rather than detailed regulations. The first of the 76 sections of that Act (Paras 1 and 2) is fundamental in that it gives an idea of how everyday social work should be carried out:

> *Para 1.* Public social services shall, on the basis of democracy and solidarity, promote people's economic and social security, equality of living conditions and active participation in the life of the community. With due consideration for the responsibility of the individual for his own social situation and that of others, social services shall be aimed at liberating and developing the innate resources of individuals and groups. Activities shall be based on respect for people's self-determination and privacy.
>
> *Para 2.* When measures affect children, the requirement of consideration for the best interest of the child shall be specially observed.

The principal goals of the social services are outlined here, as are the principal measures for supplying these services. The client's participation at this point is entirely voluntary, relying on cooperation between social authorities and citizens.

---

10 This suggestion was brought forward in the International Conference on Social Work Social Development – Action and Impact, in Stockholm in July 2012 (see www.swsd-stockholm-2012.org).

The care of children and youth using compulsion is regulated by the 1990 Care of Young Persons Act (henceforth LVU), which has been successively developed into the first decade of the twenty-first century. Embedded is the proposition that the child's view should be considered as much as possible:

Section 1

Measures for children and young persons within the social services are to be undertaken on the basis of agreement with the young person concerned and his or her custodian, as provided in the Social Services Act (2001: 453). All measures should be characterized by respect for the human dignity and integrity of the young person...

Care pursuant to this Act is, however, to be provided for a person under 18 years of age if any of the situations referred to in Section 2...prevails and the necessary care cannot be given to the young person with the consent of the person or persons having custody of him or her and, if the young person is aged 15 or over, with his or her own consent...

The young person's point of view shall be made clear as far as possible. Account shall be taken of the wishes of the young person, with due consideration given to his or her age and maturity.

Section 2

A care order is to be issued if, due to physical or mental abuse, exploitation, neglect or some other circumstance in the home, there is a palpable risk of detriment to the young person's health or development. (2003 Care of Young Persons Act)

Responsibility for providing social services rests with the municipal government, both at the long-term preventive level and at the level of individual assistance. The municipality has responsibility for providing assistance to anyone in need who resides within its jurisdiction. In cases that might require compulsory care, the municipality must refer the matter to the county court for determination.

Since the SoL does not set out the details of when and how social workers should intervene, considerable responsibility is placed on the shoulders of the individual social worker. Final responsibility, however, rests with the elected politicians of the municipal council, who set the framework for what is possible within the budgetary restrictions in their municipality. Nevertheless, the lack of detailed regulations gives social workers considerable freedom in developing their professional identity;

for instance, concerning how to engage with clients, reaching decisions on individual cases, and implementing preventive measures in their districts.

In emergency situations, the municipal councils have mandated social workers to act in the best interest of the child. Social workers employed in the SSCs are responsible for conducting social investigations when children (or other potential clients) are at risk. The law stipulates that everyone working professionally with children (such as teachers, doctors, psychologists, nurses and preschool teachers) is obliged to report to the social authorities if they suspect that a child is in a high-risk situation. Social workers are generally family-oriented in their approach, and the child's perspective has always to be taken into consideration.

Statistics concerning children and young people in receipt of care and preventive services

The official statistics on children and young people who were recipients of social service measures in 2010 contain information about use of '24-hour' measures,[11] and information about needs-tested non-institutional care (preventive measures).[12] Around 10,500 children and young people were subjects of intervention measures initiated in 2010. About 7,600 were debutants (children making their first contact with the service within a five-year period).

Children and young people subject to 24-hour measures. During the whole of 2010, around 24,900 children and young people were subject to one or more 24-hour measures at some time. Of the approximately 17,500 children and young people who were the subjects of 24-hour measures on 1 November 2010, about 12,100 (69%) received care with the support of the SoL; about 5,100 children and young people (29%) were subjects of care under the LVU; and about 300 children and young people (2%) were subject to immediate custody under the LVU. Foster home was the most common form of placement among children and young people in care. Seventy per cent of children in care under the SoL, and 67 per cent of the children in care under the LVU, were in foster homes on that day.

The statistics on children and young people in residential care (group homes) over the period from 1998 to 2010 are presented in Figure 2.1. These reveal a marked increase in the number of boys in care, especially

---

11 This measure comprises: care outside the home under the Social Services Act (SoL); immediate custody under the special provisions for the Care of Young People Act (LVU); and care under the LVU.

12 This measure comprises: structured non-institutional care programmes under the SoL; personal support under the SoL; contact person or family under the SoL; and contact person and treatment under the LVU.

adolescents between 13 and 17 years of age. There has been a small general decrease in the number of girls in residential care, but girls in the 13–17 age group show a small increase over this period. These tendencies can partly be explained by increasing incidence of asylum-seeking unaccompanied minors being placed in group homes while awaiting decisions by migration authorities.

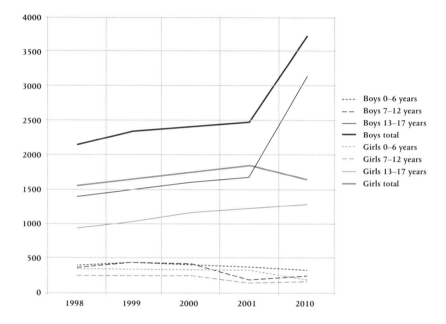

Figure 2.1 Children in residential care in Sweden: 1998–2010
Source: Sweden, NBHW 2012

Children and young people subject to non-institutional measures.
On 1 November 2010, about 28,300 children and young people were subject to one or more non-institutional preventive measures. Needs-tested personal support was the measure that affected most children and young people (87%). About 20,700 children and young people received support from a back-up person or family, and around 9,800 were subjects of structured non-institutional care programmes at some time during 2012.

Concluding remarks

An ongoing economic recession is putting pressure on municipalities to implement child welfare policies that give priority to preventive measures. Current child welfare development should be understood against the backdrop of a progression of ideas which began during the last century, with new preventive strategies developed during the last decade. Another source of pressure on municipalities is increasing migration, particularly an influx of refugees from all over the world. One in four children in Sweden has roots in other countries, and immigrant children are overly represented in childcare statistics. This gives an indication of the problems associated with the adjustments required in increasingly multi-ethnic Swedish society.

All care placements in Sweden are looked upon as parenthetical events[13] in a child's life. The basic work of child welfare involves accessing a range of alternative interventions targeting the child as well as the family within the community setting. However, there has been a tendency in recent years towards longer stays in care, especially in residential care. This could be interpreted as a consequence of the high treatment ambitions of institutional staff: belief in the efficacy of treatment rather than punishment has a long tradition in Sweden. Young people at risk undergo treatment to change their behaviour. For young adolescents in residential care, it is not unusual for their parents and family to be brought regularly into treatment sessions or social network interventions during their stay.

Foster family placements have been the preferred form of care for centuries in Sweden, but an increasing demand for residential placements for children is challenging the dominance of family placement. Close to 50 per cent of new placements in care are in different forms of residential care. Institutions for children under 13 years of age offer, as a rule, placement for the child and parents together. The increase in child placements in Sweden in recent years mostly concerns teenagers (between 13 and 17 years of age). There has been an increase in the number of girls in foster family placements, and boys in residential care. The most stable placements seem to be those in a family consisting of the child's relatives.

Residential institutions are small: 75 per cent have less than nine residents. Increasing privatization of institutions has resulted in the dominance of private provision. Periods of treatment in private institutions are twice as long as in the publicly operated institutions. Institutional placement is nearly five times as expensive as placement in a foster family, and this is a challenge for the municipalities under the present conditions of economic recession. There is a need to extend control over residential institutions, including private ones, and evaluate their programmes. In Sweden, adoption of children is negligible, with fewer than 20 children being adopted annually (Hessle 2003c; Sweden, NBHW 2012).

---

13 Parenthetical events are outside the normal progress of the child's life. This means that a
   child should ideally not stay long in a placement. Child welfare authorities have to work
   actively for a solution to the problem that was the reason the child was placed in care.

Family policy and family values

Family policy: Child protection or family orientation

From international comparisons, it is clear that there are important variations between countries with different family policies concerning the pattern of reporting of child abuse (Gilbert 1997). It seems important to distinguish between *child protection* and *family orientation* when considering the issues of child abuse and neglect. Gilbert, Parton and Skivenes (2011, p.3) found that:

> in a child protection system, abuse was considered as an act that demanded the protection of children from harm by 'degenerate relatives'; whereas in other systems, abuse was conceived as a problem of family conflict or dysfunction that arose from social and psychological difficulties but which responded to help and support.

The Anglo-Saxon countries seem to fall into the child protection category, and the Nordic countries are more likely to treat child abuse and neglect issues from a family orientation position. Sweden belongs to the family orientation category. It follows from this that problems concerning children at risk are dealt with through dialogue and partnership with the family concerning their psychosocial needs, rather than an investigatory approach that places the family in conflict with the authorities.

State support for families and children

Modern Swedish family policy was introduced in the early 1930s, at a time of deep economic recession. Even during periods of high unemployment, few Swedes have questioned the fundamental goals of family policy, which are:

- to establish good conditions for raising children

- to provide social security for families

- to uphold the principle of the equal right of men and women to participate in life and work, while good childcare is provided.

Because birth rates were very low, it was deemed necessary to improve conditions for families as an incentive to encourage family formation and to increase completed family size. In addition to the introduction of monthly child allowances, generous loans were given to newly married couples. The ideal was promoted of modern housing as a civil right rather than a privilege, and government subsidies were used to hasten the restructuring of the housing market. The reforms of the 1930s and 1940s reflected not just ambitions for material improvement, but also a far-reaching social engineering vision: to change the social context for families through reforms.

While around 75 per cent of Swedish children live in traditional nuclear families with birth parents, 50 per cent are actually born out of wedlock, since many couples only get legally married after they have had their first child. The average ages for first marriage in 2009 were 32.5 years for women and 35.1 for men (Sweden, Statistics Sweden 2012). Sweden's high divorce rate means that the probability of finding a child with divorced parents increases with the age of the child. Among 17-year-olds, one in every three has experienced divorce and is most likely to be living with his or her mother. Current developments with new family constellations, for instance increasing gay and lesbian family constellations, create challenges for statisticians (Bäck Wiklund and Johansson 2012).

Social and medical support systems for parents and children expanded radically during the decades after the Second World War. Today they include preventive services with free (or very inexpensive) healthcare during pregnancy; prenatal and postnatal education programmes; and regular health checks for children during the school years. The Swedish parental insurance system, which has gained international recognition, aims to enable both men and women to combine parenthood with employment. In particular, leave covered by parental cash benefits can be taken for up to 480 days, and can be used until the child is 8 years old. A total of 390 days is paid at 80 per cent of previous income, and 90 days at a flat rate of SEK 60 per day. Furthermore, parents have the right to stay home from work to care for a sick child under 12 years of age for up to 60 days a year, qualifying for a cash benefit equal to 80 per cent of their income. Labour laws secure parents' employment unconditionally during absence for the care of children and while in receipt of parental benefits.

New reforms have been added more or less continually over the last decades, even during the recent economic recession, although tax-financed benefits have been reduced. The municipalities are responsible for guaranteeing subsidized childcare for every child between one and six years of age if parents are employed or studying. A maximum fee has been introduced to avoid too much service cost differentiation between municipalities. Since the overwhelming majority of parents work through their children's preschool years, having access to childcare has become a necessity in everyday life. The formerly heavily subsidized high-quality daycare system – often regarded as a striking phenomenon by overseas visitors – has seen relatively large cuts in personnel and in the subsidy rate in recent years, but still, by international comparisons, it remains quite well resourced.[14]

---

14 In 1980 the group size for young children was 10 children to 4 adults. Today, the ratio has increased to 17 children to 3 adults.

Reporting of child abuse as an obligation

Every citizen has a legal duty to report concerns about child harm, but those employed by authorities carrying out activities that concern children are mandated to report immediately to social service authorities if there is reason to believe that a child needs protection.[15] One might expect a stream of referrals to follow this message from the law. Studies in this field show wide variation, with an estimated 11 to 24 cases per 1,000 children under 18 years of age referred to social services, but only 16 per cent of referrals resulting in interventions (Cocozza and Hort 2011). In their analysis of this gatekeeping level of child protection, Cocozza and Hort (2011, p.99) report that 'it is estimated that of the approximately 100,000 children investigated each year, half get support, which should correspond to 3 per cent of all children and young people'. It might be added that, in Sweden, NGOs and CSOs have for many years had an important role as gatekeepers for, and whistle-blowers about, children at risk. In this role they are complementing the child welfare authorities, without taking their public responsibilities away from them. Save the Children and UNICEF, to mention a couple of the organizations with international links, are following up on the implications of the 1989 *UN Convention on the Rights of the Child* (UNCRC) (UNICEF 2012) in Sweden, together with the Public Office of the Children's Ombudsman.[16]

Prevention

When people fall through society's safety nets, welfare legislation states that social services shall compensate for their vulnerability. General social policy has so far been unable to compensate for poverty in the lower-income section of the population. Most high-risk children belong to this group, with single-parent families the most vulnerable type of household. Since the 1980s child welfare policy makers have devised advanced community-based preventive strategies targeting vulnerable children at risk. For example, support groups for children with alcohol misusing parents are offered in many municipalities. Other child welfare-initiated or welfare-supported self-help groups target children with parents who have mental health problems, for example, or who are refugees or single mothers, or who are victims of sexual abuse. Family counselling is offered by law, as well as daycare for preschool children. Contact families or contact persons are another option. These are neighbours or others who have agreed to assist vulnerable families

---

15 14 Kap, 1 §, Government Prop: 2000/01:80.

16 In Sweden, the first Children's Ombudsman was installed by Parliament in 1993. This is the public authority charged with the protection and promotion of the rights of children and young people.

on a voluntary basis, for example by taking a child into their home on weekends. This option is used by 1 per cent of the child population.

A holistic approach to child welfare is generally widespread, and the social network methodology is used in child welfare prevention strategies. Family centres should also be mentioned here as a preventive measure. These have developed as a unique feature in Sweden, based on antenatal clinics and childcare facilities. They offer a service that is universal, voluntary and free of charge. Antenatal healthcare, child healthcare, social counselling and open preschool facilities are all offered under the same roof. This is not only a meeting place for children and parents, but also a place where different professionals meet and collaborate.

The different target groups and preventive interventions are shown in Table 2.1. On the primary prevention level, the target is children at risk on a broad general level, and intervention is through general preventive measures, such as supplying information, counselling, or setting up and supporting self-help groups in the county or municipality. When a report is made to child welfare authorities that a child might be at risk, an investigation is started that can result in different responses, depending on the outcome. When the assessment is that the child is at high risk, the child welfare authorities must suggest a response that makes a real difference for the child. That might be strong support or intervention for the child within the family, or a decision to place the child in public care, or place the child together with their family.

Table 2.1 Children at risk and at high risk: Preventive strategies

Target	Level	Intervention
Children at risk: General	Prevention	General prevention • Information • Counselling • Support groups
Children at risk: Specific	Investigation	Different models used for investigation
Children at high risk	Support for the child at home	• Home support • Contact person • Family therapy • Special pedagogic interventions
Children at high risk	Public care	Placement of child or the child and family

A children-at-risk model

Presented next is a model that may be used for appraising different national child welfare systems and comparing them (see Figure 2.2). It has three interdependent dimensions, *family policy, culture-specific discourse* and *child welfare*. A model such as this may be able to suggest new or different kinds of explanations for patterns of provision when looking at social welfare policies for children in different countries. With a focus on children at risk, the three interdependent dimensions reflect different kinds of preparedness for action within the child welfare and protection arena in different national systems (Hessle, Ioka and Yamano 2004). There follows analysis of the outcome of applying this model to the child protection system in Sweden.

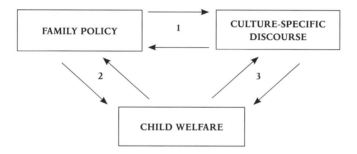

Figure 2.2 A children-at-risk model

Source: Derived from Hessle *et al.* 2004, p.140

NOTES

1. The mutual relationship between family policy and the culture-specific discourse is conjoint in the sense that family policy takes its point of departure from major changes occurring in the culture-specific discourse, with the aim of supporting families that are in a weak position. This aim of the family policy can be more or less well entrenched. The culture-specific discourse is in turn influenced by family policy. How this happens will depend on which model of family policy is applied; on the specific sociocultural tradition in the country; and on how family policy as applied influences families' life course and demographic structure.

2. The mutual relationship between child welfare and family policy is evidenced in the ambition of family policy to provide contextual support for families and children. Child welfare stimulates acknowledgement that there are children at risk who are not covered by family policy, who are growing up under environmental conditions that are considered unacceptable for children.

3. The mutual relationship between child welfare and the culture-specific discourse is evidenced by society's ambition to react (through legislation, or professional action) when children are considered to be at risk. The culture-specific discourse is influenced by the way child welfare is able to deal with the opposition that arises when traditional cultural values pertaining to children's upbringing clash with society's ambition to intervene when children are assessed as being at risk.

In the **family policy dimension**, the wider social policy of the welfare state has gradually established a context for child protection in Sweden. The reasons for state intrusion into family life when children are at risk have changed over time. Swedish standards of living as well as the level of social equality are among the highest in the world. This means that preparedness to intervene when children are at risk tends to be based on psychological assessments, rather than psychosocial assessments or material conditions. We note also that Sweden belongs to a *family orientation* group of states: problems relating to children at risk are dealt with through dialogue and partnership with the family concerning their psychosocial needs, rather than through an investigatory approach in conflict with the authorities.

The **child welfare dimension** in the framework comprises various factors, for example legislative issues, aspects of professionalization (level, availability and discourse) and access to statistics about child welfare. The SoL is concerned with rights rather than with prohibitions. Social workers have, according to the law, a primarily supportive and negotiating function for children and parents. Under the administrative Social Service Council, they have distinctive responsibilities for the welfare of citizens in the community. Compulsory intervention is regulated by separate legislation, the LVU, which stipulates the conditions under which the county court may order the placement of children and young people up to 18 years of age (in some cases up to 20 years) in public care. Moreover, the *right of the child* to have a voice in decisions concerning himself or herself is strongly emphasized in law. With larger numbers of social workers being trained and employed, the preventive sector has advanced greatly, with various innovative community-based preventive strategies targeting vulnerable children and families at risk. Thanks to the inflow to Sweden of many theoretical and methodological models, it has been possible to find a language that binds different professions together in interdisciplinary teams when the focus is on children at risk. In addition, daycare for preschool children is an obligation for all municipalities and, by law, the community offers family counselling when needed. A holistic approach to child welfare is generally widespread, and the *social network approach* is commonly used in child welfare prevention strategies.

The **sociocultural context** comprises both traditional norms (including religious and other faith-related factors) as well as demographic conditions. Providing for the care of children at risk is in this sense based on a learned set of actions and beliefs, shared by those who have internalized a specific informal pattern of culture as an essential guide for making judgements in everyday life. Demographic changes, like changes in the fertility rate, family structure and migration, contribute to the development of the sociocultural context in an ongoing discourse. Any society has to accommodate readiness to intervene when children are at risk. This has to be achieved within its sociocultural context, within the family, and within the norms of the society. From what has been discovered in this chapter so far, there are two challenges shaking up the Swedish sociocultural context: first, the strong development of a powerful public sector, and second, a fast escalating stream of migrants from different parts of the world.

With the progress of the Swedish welfare state, family policy has gradually established a safety net for families, parents and children, according to parents a right to work, and children a right of access to both parents. If families, parents and children fall through the safety net, they are buffered by an impressive capacity of authority representatives (e.g. social workers) through the public dimension of child welfare, which, among other things, protects the rights of citizens according to the SoL.

There are indications that the progress of the welfare state may be challenging elements of the sociocultural dimension in Swedish welfare provision. Our hypothesis is that the family policy of the Swedish welfare state, together with the fast-growing and rapidly developing professionalization of child welfare, has gained ascendancy over the traditional culture-specific discourse, the result being a highly context-dependent (as opposed to culture-dependent) family institution (cf. Hessle *et al.* 2004). We are witnessing strong state support for democratic development at the level of individual families. Is this a bad or good thing? On the one hand, this might mean that the modern Swedish family (and individual) might be easier to manipulate by the state than traditional culture-bound families. On the other hand, a context-bound family, without strong bonds to its own traditions, might be more flexible, finding it easier to adjust to new situations. Future studies might shed light on these questions.

The second sociocultural challenge to consider is increasing immigration, which has established a multi-ethnic society in Sweden, mainly in metropolitan areas. Secularized Swedish society is challenged by a prism of religions carried by migrants from all corners of the world. The strong generous Swedish welfare state, with its basis on trust-based peaceful agreement between the individual and the state, is a challenge for migrants who have been pushed out of their country of origin, where the only people to trust are those belonging to the same clan, church or family. Even if 'pull' factors for immigrants include the Swedish welfare state model and progress in equity, it is understandable through this exploration that developing a 'melting pot', achieving the established inclusion of immigrants into our society, which entails *transcultural progression* in Swedish society, might be a more long-term project than previously envisaged (Hessle 2007a).

Conclusion

It is clear that Swedish family policy has developed along the lines of the institutional and universal model, the so-called *encompassing model*. The welfare state guarantees all its citizens, in principle, a reasonable level of living regardless of what phase in the life cycle in which they find themselves. Swedish family policy also reflects thinking about, and concern for, social justice. It is relevant to conclude by asking: What effect has the massive reform through investment in family policy and child welfare development over the last 50 years had on children at risk? A worrying trend has been increasing numbers of young people in care, mainly boys in residential care and girls in foster care placements. There is also an overrepresentation of young people with origins in other countries in the care system. This leads to the conclusion that child protection has not yet grown out of its poverty-relief origins. What is the reason? There is no simple answer.

Some might blame the ongoing European economic recession, which also impacts on Sweden. Reforms are expensive to implement, and are built upon an assumption of increasing public prosperity through taxes on working inhabitants. Increased unemployment and cuts in welfare provision strike against the most vulnerable groups, and researchers are currently expressing alarm about increasing child poverty (Salonen 2011). Others might blame an observed increase in child welfare cases on 'diagnostic inflation' and the increasing numbers of professionals in the field (see for instance Parton 2006). A third reason might be ongoing neoliberal tendencies in the social care field, such as the ongoing privatization of the residential care system for young people, resulting in longer and more expensive care for the users.

But, when looking at the triad of *child–family–society* in Swedish child welfare, it is clear that remarkable progress has been achieved in each of these dimensions, in practice as well as conceptually, over each dimension. This has been achieved through a paradigmatic change to a family-network approach. No child is isolated in a big asylum or abandoned in foster care. In Sweden, children at risk must be counselled as partners, together with the people closest to them, side by side, through interdisciplinary working, done in the best interest of the child. Whether that is enough investment to support transcultural progress into the future is yet to be seen.

References

Andersson, G. (2008) *Utsatt barndom – olika vuxenliv: ett longitudinel forskningsprojekt om barn i samhällsvård* [*Vulnerable childhood – diverse childhoods: a longitudinal research project about children in child welfare*]. Stockholm: Allmänna Barnhuset.

Bäck Wiklund, M. and Johansson, Th. (eds) (2012) *Nätverksfamiljen* [*The Family Network*] (2nd ed.). Stockholm, SE: Natur & Kultur.

Båge, C. (1972) *Ustötning–Familjebehandling* [*Exclusion and Family Treatment*] (*Del I och II*). Stockholm, SE: Aldus.

Bergmark, Å, Lundström, T, Minas, R. and Wiklund, S. (2008) *Socialtjänsten i blickfånget, organisation, resurser och insatser* [*Focus on Social Service – organisation, resources and performance*]. Stockholm: Natur och Kultur.

Borgengren, M. and Costa, F. (1997) 'Familje-och nätverksperspektiv i en psykiatrisk organization' ['Family and network perspectives in a psychiatric organization']. *Focus 1*, 25–39.

Church of Sweden (2012) *Welcome to the Church of Sweden.* Available at: www.svens kakyrkan.se.

Cocozza, M. and Hort, S. (2011) 'The Dark Side of the Universal Welfare State? Child Abuse and Protection in Sweden.' In N. Gilbert, N. Parton and M. Skivens (eds) *Child Protection Systems: International Trends and Orientations.* New York: Oxford University Press.

Dellgran, P. and Höjer, S. (2005) 'Rörelser i tiden. Professionalisering och privatisering i socialt arbete' ['Movements in time – professionalisation and privatisation in social work']. *Socialvetenskaplig Tidskrift 12*, 2–3, 246–266.

European Commission (EC), Eurostat (2012) *Statistics by Themes.* Available at: http://epp. eurostat.ec.europa.eu/portal/page/portal/statistics/themes.

Fanshel, D. and Shinn, E. (1978) *Children in Foster Care.* New York: Columbia University Press.

Gilbert, N. (ed.) (1997) *Combating Child Abuse: International Perspectives and Trends.* New York: Oxford University Press.

Gilbert, N., Parton, N. and Skivenes, M. (eds) (2011) *Child Protection Systems: International Trends and Orientations.* New York: Oxford University Press.

Grosin, L. and Hedén, A. (1984) *Behandling och omhändertagande. En rapport om arbetet med problemfamiljer* [*Treatment and Care: A Report on Social Work with Problem Families*]. Stockholm, SE: Akademilitteratur.

Hansson, K. (2001) *Familjebehandling på goda grunder* [*Family Treatment on Good Grounds*]. Stockholm, SE: Gothia.

Hessle, S. (1988) *Familjer i sönderfall* [*Families Falling Apart*]. Stockholm, SE: Norstedts.

Hessle, S. (1998) *Child Welfare and Child Protection on the Eve of the 21st Century – What the Twentieth Century has Taught Us* (Stockholm Studies in Social Work 12). Stockholm, SE: Stockholm University Department of Social Work.

Hessle, S. (ed.) (2003a) *Fokus på barn-familj-nätverk metodutveckling i den sociala barnavården* [*Focus on the Child–Family–Network: Development of Methodology in Child Welfare*]. Stockholm, SE: Gothia.

Hessle, S. (2003b) 'Network Collaboration within Swedish Child Welfare.' In L. Dominelli (ed.) *Broadening Horizons.* Aldershot, UK: Ashgate.

Hessle, S. (2003c) *Sweden Country Report 2003.* Stockholm, SE: Stockholm University Department of Social Work.

Hessle, S. (2007a) 'Globalization: Implications for International Development Work, Social Work and the Integration of Immigrants in Sweden.' In L. Dominelli (ed.) *Revitalising Communities in a Globalising World.* Aldershot, UK: Ashgate.

Hessle, S. (2007b) 'The Network Approach – Turning Point in Working with Families and Children with Psychosocial Problems.' In B. Holmberg and A. Trygged (eds) *Social Networking with Russian Families in Crisis* (International Projects). Stockholm, SE: Stockholm University Department of Social Work.

Hessle, S. (2012a) 'Variations and Issues of Survival of European Welfare State Models in the 21st Century.' In L. Healy and R. Link (eds) *Handbook of International Social Work.* New York: Oxford University Press.

Hessle, S. (2012b) 'Högriskbarn i psykosocialt utsatta familjer' ['High-Risk Children in Psychosocial Vulnerable Families']. In M. Bäck-Wiklund and T. Johansson (eds) *Nätverksfamiljen* [*The Network Family*] (2nd ed.). Stockholm, SE: Natur o Kultur.

Hessle, S. and Wåhlander, E. (2000) *Högriskbarn – livskarriär och livskvalitet som vuxna* [*High-Risk Children – Life Course and Quality of Life as Grown Ups*] (*Rapport i socialt arbete*, 97). Stockholm, SE: Stockholms Universitet, Institutionen för Socialt Arbete.

Hessle, S., Ioka, B. and Yamano, N. (2004) 'Key Factors to Consider in International Comparisons of Family Policy and Child Welfare.' In N. Mauro, A. Björklund and C. le Grand (eds) *Welfare Policy and Labour Markets*. Stockholm, SE: Almqvist och Wiksell International.

Korpi, W. (2004) 'The Japanese welfare system in an international perspective.' In N. Mauro, A. Björklund and C. le Grand (eds) *Welfare Policy and Labour Markets*. Stockholm: Almqvist och Wiksell International.

Maas, H. and Engler, R. (1959) *Children in Need of Parents*. New York: Columbia University Press.

Parton, N. (2006) 'Every child matters: The shift to prevention whilst strengthening the protection in children's services in England.' *Children and Youth Services Review 28*, 976–992.

Sallnäs, M., Wiklund, S. and Lagerlöf, H. (2010) 'Social barnavård ur ett välfärdsperspektiv. Ekonomiska och materiella resurser, psykisk hälsa och tillgång till socialt stöd för ungdomar i familjehem och vid institutioner.' *Socialvetenskaplig Tidskrift 17*, 1, 5–27.

Salonen, T. (2011) *Barns ekonomiska utsatthet* [*Children's Economic Vulnerability*] (*Årsrapport 2010*). Stockholm, SE: Rädda Barnen.

Speck, R.V. and Attneave, C.L. (1973) *Family Networks*. New York: Pantheon Books.

Sweden, Migration Board (2012) *News*, July. Available at: www.migrationsverket.se.

Sweden, National Board of Health and Welfare (NBHW) (2012) *Statistics*. Available at: www.socialstyrelsen.se.

Sweden, Statistics Sweden (2012) *Statistics Sweden*. Available at: www.scb.se/Pages/Product____25799.aspx.

Szebehely, M. (2011) 'Insatser för äldre och funktionshindrade i privat regi' ['Caring for elderly and disabled people in private enterprises']. In L. Hartman (ed.) *Konkurrensens konsekvenser. Vad händer med svensk välfärd?* [*The consequences of competition: What is happening with Swedish welfare?*] Stockholm, SE: SNS Förlag.

UNICEF (2012) *United Nations Convention on the Rights of the Child*. Available at: www.unicef.org/crc/index_30229.html.

United Nations Development Programme (UNDP) (2012) *UNDP Report July 2012*. Available at: http://hdr.undp.org/en/reports/global/hdr2010/chapters.

US, Central Intelligence Agency (CIA) (2012) *CIA World Factbook*. Available at: https://www.cia.gov/library/publications/the-world-factbook.

Vinnerljung, B. (1996) *Fosterbarn som vuxna* [*Foster children as grown ups*]. Diss, Lund: Arkiv Förlag.

Vinnerljung, B. and Sallnäs, M. (2008) 'Into adulthood: a follow-up study of 718 youths who were placed in out-of-home care during their teens.' *Journal of Child and Family Social Work 13*, 144–155.

Weiss, I. and Welbourne, P. (eds) (2007) *Social Work as a Profession: A Comparative Cross-national Perspective*. Birmingham, UK: Venture Press.

3

The United States of America

Otrude Nontobeko Moyo

Introduction

The United States of America (the US) is still the richest nation in the world
with a Gross Domestic Product (GDP) at US$15.04 trillion in 2011, and a
GDP per capita of US$47,200. In terms of GDP per capita, the US ranks
eleventh in the world. One would expect that with such an endowment
of material wealth and with grand ideas of democracy that the quality of
life of children would be meaningfully assured across all spectrums of US
society. However, material riches do not necessarily translate to equality and
a better quality of life for all children. According to the United Nation's
Human Development Report (UNDP 2010), the US ranks ninth among the top
ten countries with highest quality of life. This is corroborated by UNICEF
Report Card 7 (UNICEF 2007), which reports on six dimensions of child
wellbeing in 21 rich countries: material; health and safety; educational;
family and peer relationships; behaviours and risks; and subjective
wellbeing. It assigned the US an average ranking position of 18.2 for all
six dimensions.

With the global economic downturn, the US economy contracted,
and many states made substantial cuts to government funding, which have
negatively impacted on the quality-of-life indicators for children (see Kids
Count 2011). White, Chau and Aratani (2010) judge that substantial cuts
in government funding have negative effects that disproportionately impact
on children in low-income households and children of African Americans,
Latino Americans and Native Americans. Further, children in the southern
and southwestern states, and children of colour, are most likely to live with
quality-of-life disadvantages (Kids Count 2011). The US Census Bureau's
American Community Survey shows that about 7.9 million (11% of US
children) are growing up in areas where at least 30 per cent of residents live
below the federal poverty level – about US$22,000 per year for a family of

four; this compares with 6.3 million children (9%) who were living in such communities in 2000 (Kids Count 2011). These children often lack access to resources that are critical to healthy growth and development, including quality education, medical care and safe outdoor spaces.

Currently, the material wellbeing of most children is troubling. Discussing racial disparities and disproportionality in the quality of life of children, Patrick McCarthy, President and CEO of the Annie E. Casey Foundation, states (McCarthy 2011, p.1) that the:

> current body of research shows racial disparities exist in the system level, child-level outcomes and disproportional representation in the child welfare system, starting with reports, to investigations, to interventions, to placement. Relative to white children, kids of color are more likely to drift in care, less likely to be reunited with families, more likely experience group care, less likely to find a permanent family and more likely to have poor educational, social, behavioral and other outcomes…it's fair to say that these disparities in outcomes line up all too well with the disparities in outcomes seen in other areas such as poverty, housing, employment and the criminal justice system.

Thus, the general status of children's wellbeing in the US is troubling.

Demographic breakdown of children

The 2010 Census quotes that there were 74.2 million children in the US, 1.9 million more than in 2000. There were approximately equal numbers of children in the relevant three age groups: 0–5 years (25.5 million), 6–11 years (24.3 million) and 12–17 years (24.8 million) (Children's Defense Fund 2011). Since the mid-1960s, however, children have been decreasing as a proportion of the total population. In 2010, children made up 24 per cent of the population, down from a peak of 36 per cent at the end of the 'baby boom' in 1964. Children's share of the population is projected to remain fairly stable through to 2050, when they are projected to make up 23 per cent of the population (US, Census Bureau 2011); however, racial and ethnic diversity has changed dramatically in the last three decades. This increased racial diversity appeared first among children, and later amongst the older population. The population is projected to become even more racially diverse in the decades to come. In the 2010 Census, 54 per cent were White non-Hispanic; 23 per cent were Hispanic; 14 per cent were Black; 4 per cent were Asian; and 5 per cent were other races. According to the US Census Bureau (2012), the percentage of children who are Hispanic has increased faster than that of any other racial or ethnic group, growing from 9 per cent of the child population in 1980 to 23 per cent in 2010. In 2023, fewer than half of all children are projected to be White, non-Hispanic (Federal Interagency Forum on Child and Family Statistics 2011). The demographic background is summarized in Table 3.1.

Table 3.1 America's children (aged 0–17) at a glance

DEMOGRAPHIC BACKGROUND	2009	2010
Child population	74.5 million	74.2 million
Children as a percentage of the population	24.3%	24.0%
Racial and ethnic composition		
White	75.6%	Data not available
Not White, non-Hispanic	55.3%	53.5%
Black	15.1%	14.0%
Asian	4.4%	4.3%
All other races	4.9%	5.2%
Hispanic (of any race)	22.5%	23.1%

Source: www.childstats.gov/pdf/ac2011/ac_11.pdf

Quality-of-life indicators for children

In terms of material wellbeing, more children in the US live in poverty in comparison with other industrialized countries. According to the 2010 US Census (US, Census Bureau 2012), out of a population of 308.7 million, 72 million (24%) are children and young people up to 18 years of age. In 2010, 31.9 million children (44%) lived in low-income families, and 15.5 million children (21%) lived in poor families (White, Chau and Aratani 2010). Indeed, the number of children living in low-income and poor families has increased since 2005 (White *et al.* 2010). According to Kids Count (2011), a data centre within the Annie E. Casey Foundation, in 2006 there were 13 million children living in poverty and by 2010 this had risen to 15.7 million children. In 2012, 16.5 million children are living in poverty (Children's Defense Fund 2011).

In terms of socioeconomic status, in 2007 at least 3.6 million children (5%) were living with one unemployed parent, which doubled by 2010 to 7.7 million children (11%). Children living in families where neither parent has full-time, year-round employment increased from 23.7 million children in 2003 to 24.3 million children in 2007.

What does this growth in child poverty mean? On average, children who grow up in poverty are more vulnerable. Specifically, they are more likely to be in poor health; to have learning and behavioural difficulties; to underachieve at school; to have early pregnancies; to have lower skills and aspirations; to be in low-paid employment; to be unemployed; and to rely on public assistance for subsistence for long periods of time. These factors tend to be compounded by structural factors and embedded discrimination, which decide the futures of poor children and their families. For example, when looking at housing, between 2007 and 2009 5.3 million children were living in families affected by mortgage foreclosure, and the number of children living in crowded housing rose to 9.9 million children by 2009. Increasing numbers of families are homeless. Moreover, African Americans, Native Americans and Latino Americans comprise a disproportionate share of the low-income population under 18 (Green, Belanger and McRoy 2011).

The health and safety of children dimension is another indicator used by UNICEF to understand child wellbeing. Three components are used: health in their first year of life (measured by the infant mortality rate); the percentage of infants born with a birth weight of less than 2,500 grams; and the number of child deaths from accidents (including murder, suicide and violence). In terms of the infant mortality rate, the US still has over 6 deaths per 1,000 births. Compared to other industrialized countries this is relatively high, reflecting the lack of access to basic preventative health services, particularly for the marginalized populations. The percentage of infants born with a low birth weight (less than 2,500 grams) is relatively high in the US at 8 per cent. The prevalence of low birth weight by racial and ethnic groups is highest among African American children. Many factors are associated with low birth weight, including the experience of living in racialized spaces.

According to the *America's Children* report (Federal Interagency Forum on Child and Family Statistics 2011), 'healthcare' comprises the prevention, treatment and management of illness and preservation of mental and physical wellbeing through services offered by health professionals. Effective healthcare is an important aspect of promoting good health. Given that the health of children depends on preventative services, access to healthcare services is an important indicator of children's wellbeing. Access to health insurance can be used as a measure of access to health services.

In this regard, the number of children without health insurance continues to be high. According to the Children's Defense Fund (2011), 8.1 million children are uninsured. Further, more than 500,000 women are uninsured and lack timely access to essential health services, even given the changes ushered in by President Barack Obama's Affordable Health Care initiative, which mandated health insurance for all.

Another measure of children's health is safety (UNICEF 2007), which is the rate of deaths among children and young people caused by accidents, murder, suicide and violence. In the US this is the critical measure because the safety of children has been the driver of the US child protective services, and hence child welfare. According to UNICEF (2007), the US, like other industrialized countries, has reduced the incidence of death from accidents and injuries to fewer than 10 per 100,000. Further, recently released national child maltreatment data for 2008 shows a generally encouraging situation during the first year of the serious recession that began in late 2007. Overall, substantiated child maltreatment declined 3 per cent from the previous year, including a 6 per cent decline in sexual abuse. Child maltreatment fatalities stayed stable (Finkelhor, Jones and Shattuck 2008, p.1). When the situation is disaggregated by racial and ethnic groups, African American children are disproportionately represented in the child welfare system, starting with reports, moving to investigations, to interventions and, finally, to placement (McCarthy 2011).

The third dimension of child wellbeing is educational wellbeing and childcare. According to UNICEF (2007, p.19), 'the overall wellbeing of children must include a consideration of how well children are served by the education systems in which so large a proportion of their childhood is spent and from which so much of their future wellbeing is likely to depend'. The measures used included the educational achievement of 15-year-olds; dropout rates; percentage of 15–19-year-olds remaining in education; and percentage of 15–19-year-olds transitioning to employment or training. Although there are debates about the comparative use of this data (see Beaton 1999), on the basis of the UNICEF data, the US is not performing well on any of those educational performance indicators.

Childcare is an essential service to most parents who must work to provide for the wellbeing of their children. Increasingly, as most parents must enter the labour force out of necessity, their children need safe and quality places for their care. It is astonishing that a country that values the work ethic so much still has not been able to provide universal childcare to enable parents to work. The US policy frames rest on an antiquated paradigm of a male breadwinner in a two-parent home, where a single salary was sufficient to keep a family out of poverty. Today, there are more lone-parent families who have to work to provide adequately for their children. Living on public assistance means living in poverty! If parents, whether in lone- or two-parent families, have to work out of necessity, there are currently very limited support systems to help them balance work and family responsibilities. How, then, can these families assure the wellbeing of their children? Lindsey (1994) argues that the lack of a comprehensive family policy is a problem of reliance on a predominantly male-oriented legislation that is strongly patriarchal and with little interest in the assurance of childcare for all children. The US continues to be the only country among industrialized nations without paid maternity and parental leaves. Currently, the most vulnerable people in the US are children, and they have a right to safe and quality childcare to grow into healthy individuals.

A token support programme relating to childcare has been Head Start, a federally funded and states-supported programme of educational services for young children in poverty (Barnett and Hustedt 2005). Since Head Start's inception in 1965, more than 21 million children have participated in it (Barnett and Hustedt 2005). Over the years, Head Start has moved towards a comprehensive approach to children's services. It now provides a social, health and nutritional service to children, and thereby seeking to enhance their health, material and educational wellbeing. Its scope was widened in 1994, to serve children below school age (under three years of age) and their families. Barnett and Hustedt (2005, p.16) have argued: 'Head Start remains a promise unfulfilled. Nearly 10 years after Congress authorized full funding, Head Start's budget is still insufficient to serve all eligible children or deliver uniformly high quality services to all enrolled.' Further, the current funding levels for Head Start provide for support to less than 5 per cent of children who are poor, forcing other poor families to rely on the private market and informal care. Although opinions on the long-term benefits of Head Start are mixed, a recent Early Head Start Research and Evaluation Project, involving 3,001 children and families in 17 sites, reported that three-year-old Early Head Start children performed significantly better on a range of measures of cognitive, language and social emotional development than a randomly assigned control group who did not receive Early Head Start support (US, DHHS 2006). Of course, the public school system provides care for children as soon as they turn six years of age. In this regard, schools afford parents with an opportunity to work and earn an income. But children need care before and after school. Moreover the problem of childcare falls heaviest on mothers during the earliest years of a child's life. It is before reaching school age that childcare assistance is most needed. Depending on geographic location, childcare is often one of the highest costs facing families with working parents

(Gornich and Meyers 2003). This is a major expense for poor, low-income and middle-income families. It affects the accessibility of good-quality childcare because poorer families are forced to use cheap and often poorer-quality alternatives or remain in poverty on public assistance, which in turn impacts their children's quality of life.

The fourth dimension used by UNICEF to assess children's wellbeing is young people's relationships. Its components include family structure (measured by percentage of children living in single-parent families and step-families); family relationships (measured in percentage of children who report eating the main meal of the day with parents more than once a week, and the percentage of children who report that parents spend time 'just talking' to them); and peer relationships (measured by the percentage of 11-, 13- and 15-year-olds who report finding their peers 'kind and helpful'). In terms of family structure, about 22 per cent of all children live in single-parent households, which is a similar rate to that in Sweden, the difference being the level of economic hardship experienced by US single parents, particularly single mothers, because of the parsimonious welfare support available to them. The amount of 'parental time' families devote to conversation and interaction with children is critical. Again, US adults tend to work more hours, resulting in difficulties in juggling time for childcare and socialization. About 54 per cent of the young people report peers as 'kind and helpful'.

According to UNICEF (2007), any overview of children's wellbeing must attempt to incorporate aspects of behaviour that are of concern to both young people themselves and to the community in which they live. This dimension is concerned with health-related behaviour, risk-related behaviour and the experience of violence. There are many reasons why children and young people live unhealthy lifestyles. These reflect circumstances, pressures and self-perceptions that undermine wellbeing. Using the UNICEF (2007) Report Card 7, healthy behaviour is measured by eating habits in childhood and adolescence. Those children who eat unhealthily during their early years are more likely to continue that eating pattern into adulthood and risk increased health problems, including diabetes, heart disease and cancer. Among industrialized countries, the prevalence of childhood obesity is highest in the US. Also, the US leads in young people reporting their engagement in risky behaviours, such as teenage births and substance abuse. The troubling experience of young people in the US is the experience of violence. According to UNICEF (2007, p.27), 'aggression and violence in all its forms – bullying, fighting, and abuse – shadow the lives of many children making the time of life that adults like to think as happy and carefree into a time of anxiety and misery'.

In particular, exposure to violence in the home, neighbourhoods (both directly through child abuse and, indirectly through witnessing aggression) and police surveillance can cause enduring distress and damage to children of all ages.

These five indicators drawn from the UNICEF (2007) Report Card 7 highlight the status of children's wellbeing in the US. While the data constitute only snapshots, they provide an alarming picture of the wellbeing of children. They give support to Hutchinson and Sudia's (2002, p.ix) observation that, in the US, children are precious only in the abstract, because, in reality, they appear to be disposable, particularly when the indicators of wellbeing compare the US with other industrialized countries; the US continues to perform relatively poorly. What are the causes of this poor performance? The answer is the intractable child welfare paradigm that guides the US child welfare system, one that has, historically, been framed by the principles of individualism, family responsibility and the residual approach.

The historical context of the child welfare system in the US

Historically, in the US the child welfare system arose as a response to the needs of children whose parents had died, or who had abandoned them because they were unable to care for them (Lindsey 1994). This need is closely linked to the labour force participation. For example, the child welfare system in the US rests on the paradigm that parents are solely responsible for making decisions about their children's wellbeing (Jenson 2004; Lindsey 1994; Pecora *et al.* 2007). The role of child welfare policy is to facilitate parental decisions by opening a range of options allowing parents to make choices. However, finding the necessary resources, especially financial, to support certain options is the sole responsibility of families (Jenson 2004, p.174). Thus, the US child welfare system addresses the needs of children only indirectly.

Further, income support responds and reacts to the needs of adults in the context of their relationship to the labour force, and in particular their capacity to earn enough income for themselves and their families. In the US, the Temporary Assistance to Needy Families (TANF) is a time-limited public assistance programme targeting families with young children who are needy because of unemployment. Only limited adult and family support exists for those adults who are working and who have families. Presently, archaic and racialized assumptions underlie family policy in the US. For instance, through the 'family ethic' it is presumed that a single income is sufficient to support a family; thus mothers are able to 'choose' their relationship to the labour force by deciding whether to seek a job or provide full-time parental care. The rise of lone-parent families in the latter part of the twentieth century has cast a negative light on these punitive public policy measures, which have targeted poorer women and women of colour, who, by their use of public assistance, are labelled lazy and unmotivated to work. The effect of this on poor parents has been to push them into low-wage and insecure jobs, which means that the government can dissociate itself from the family problems associated with low earnings and with women raising children (Abramovitz 1989).

In terms of labour market policies that impact children, they have been very punitive to poor women. In the absence of a job or partner, women with children must turn to the state for assistance. To receive assistance they must be poor with very limited assets. The family ethic inscribed a woman's role as mother and wife in the home, but punitive laws impose mandatory work on women viewed as departing from the prescribed wife and mother roles (Abramovitz 1989). In this regard, the US is an example of a country with high gender inequality. Current labour market policies that support labour participation offer very limited assistance to parents with young children who must work out of necessity. Thus, such policies in the US support work but they do not promote family and/or child wellbeing.

Shireman (2003) argues that children's wellbeing is inextricably linked to the status of their own families. Historically, the ups and downs in the economy, changes in the structure of the economy and changes in the structure of the family are all factors that have shaped the wellbeing of families, and therefore the wellbeing of children. Operating from that residual frame, child welfare agencies have historically expanded to address impoverishment, child abuse and child neglect.

The child welfare system in the US is residual in form and only reactive to social problems facing children. In earlier times, orphanages provided food and shelter, with limited instruction. With public outcries about the state of orphanages – for the institutionalization of children – they began to wane. Their successor, the out-placement of children, marked the beginning of the foster care system, which arose again in public awareness in response to the high costs and limited public satisfaction with large state-operated orphanages (Lindsey 1994). Further, Lindsey (1994) argues that foster care provided a more family-like setting, which was less restrictive and less expensive, therefore shifting the care of children from large custodial institutions into foster family care. This was viewed as progressive reform of the child welfare system. Services have been shaped by the prevailing theoretical approaches to the causation of social problems, for instance that of rescuing and saving children from 'abusive parents'. Indeed, the emphasis on family preservation and then on supporting 'permanency' and kinship care has meant that more children, specifically those of African Americans, are languishing within the foster care system. Today, Alternative Response, also known as Differential Response or Multiple Response, is presumed to be a family-centred approach to children at risk. Alternative Response is a new approach that enables child welfare agencies to respond to allegations of child abuse and neglect by investigating the report, determining whether maltreatment has occurred or if the child is at risk, and putting an appropriate intervention in place (National Quality Improvement Center on Differential Response in Child Protective Service 2012).

Historically, social problems facing children have been viewed as rooted in the individual children and individual parents who are perceived to be 'abandoning' their parental roles. For the most part, individual causation of child problems, which has been legitimized by ecological and psychological theories, has been used to explain and understand child abuse and maltreatment (Turnell and Edwards 1999). Because of this individualistic perspective, engrained child abuse, neglect and maltreatment has been recognized as the result of 'troubled parents' and/or 'troubled children'. Child welfare services arose to care for children whose parents were believed to be incapable of caring for them, and/or children needing substitute care, and questions about the impact of economic factors on children's wellbeing have been neglected.

Throughout the twentieth century the 'child savers' mentality continued to frame the child welfare system. Various theories were harnessed to shape the way the child welfare system developed and functioned, mostly within a residual frame, to provide services to children experiencing abuse and neglect and those perceived to be at risk. These residual services evolved into safety nets to protect those individual children who were at greatest risk of harm through abuse, maltreatment and neglect. Historically, this mentality has been adversarial to parents – casting them as 'dangerous' and advocating the permanent removal and separation of their children from them. As Lindsey (1994) points out, child welfare agencies sought to aid distressed families by removing the children until the families could demonstrate an ability to adequately provide for their children. Further, the intent was to provide families with case-management services aimed at changing the parenting behaviour, before permitting reunification with their children. But few biological families were able to show enough parenting behaviour change to warrant the return of their children. This reflects a deep failure of a child welfare system that is reluctant to consider the impact of environmental and socioeconomic factors on parenting behaviour, and that fails to invest in families in terms of comprehensive family policies.

The more children were brought into the child welfare system, the longer they remained, as the bureaucratic process rigidly reserved to itself the role of assessing the burden of proof (Lindsey 1994), as no one wanted to release children back into possible harm. As a consequence, children began to languish in the foster care system, and the burden of proof shifted from child welfare agencies to parents, where parents have to prove definitively that they could take care of their children. An adversarial role was born between child welfare workers and parents in the child welfare system.

Given the multitude of problems that families experience in a system that is residual in nature, few families could prove definitively that they could take care of their children. In return, the child welfare bureaucracy responded by procedures to terminate parental rights. Children in the foster care system grew exponentially in response, and questions of the cost to the federal government supporting these children came into play. Moreover, literature was emerging that was arguing that foster care was not a harmless intervention for the benefit of children, and can cause severe psychological harm (Lindsey 1994). With the growth in numbers of children in the foster care system, and with the consequences that had for the expense of the foster care system, family preservation became the new frame of child welfare services. But, with only limited resources available, intensive family services and wrap-around services have focused only on 'at risk' families, leaving the wider social and economic problems that underpin many individual instances of neglect and abuse unresolved.

Intractable child welfare paradigms: Family responsibility and residualism

An individualistic framing of family responsibility

In the US, responsibility for the care and nurture of children is entrusted to families, who are expected to provide their children with all necessities (Lindsey 1994, p.3). Collective responsibility for children has been restricted to reclaiming children from situations where the family has been unable to meet its obligation (Lindsey 1994). However, as poverty grows, families continue to struggle to make ends meet, particularly lone parents, who constitute the most common family structure. This means that many children's needs continue to go unmet. For example, in 2010, out of 72 million children under 18 years of age, 31.9 million (44%) live in low-income families and 15.5 million (21%) live in poor families (White et al. 2010).

Children's economic insecurity is directly linked to the employment status of their parents, who are increasingly unable to meet all their children's needs. For poor parents in particular, the contradictory environment they live in violates their right to dignity in parenting the children they have borne. The societal value of autonomy and the presumed equality of opportunity contradict the realities of the situation for poorer families, who have little control over their lives, and many of whom work long hours but cannot lift themselves out of poverty. For others, opportunities are limited by the reality of struggling to exist on incomes below poverty levels, which impacts on food security, health, housing, safe and secure neighbourhoods, healthy development, availability of quality childcare for working parents, and education, all of which are indicators of children's wellbeing.

The US child welfare system is residual in form. It lacks an underpinning coherent family policy that comprehensively supports parents to raise healthy children. According to both Gornich and Meyers (2003) and Poelmans (2005), the US continues to lag behind other industrialized countries in terms of the provision of paid work leave for new parents. It is only recently that the US enacted laws to guarantee breast-feeding breaks for mothers. As economic security stressors mount, and given the residual nature of the child welfare system, there is little support for parents whose parenting capabilities are compromised by the reality of the material hardships they face. Substance abuse and victimization through violence may take over, compromising further the parenting abilities of parents and their capacity to provide adequately for their children. It is under these circumstances that child welfare services have developed, with child protection services, rather than child wellbeing services, being the driver. As Lindsey (1994) pointed out, impoverished families who are unable to meet their children's needs have relied on the child welfare system, but the child welfare system has historically not been shaped to assure children's wellbeing, only to pick up the pieces that result from the laissez-faire social policies of a liberal democratic capitalist system. From its inception the child welfare system has focused on children who are 'left out' (Lindsey 1994).

Hutchinson and Sudia (2002) argue that the US child welfare system is designed to remove children from their 'dysfunctional' families, hence its adversarial attitude to parents. This is arguably an outdated mode of providing children's services in a complex post-industrial world, where service jobs are the order for most low-income family members, and where earnings from these service jobs cannot lift most families out of poverty. Such parents are without support to help them raise healthy children. In work environments characterized by casual, part-time and minimum-wage employment, there is only limited protection for workers' employment rights, including rights relating to parental status, such as maternity leave. Thus, the wellbeing of families is compromised. Moreover, child welfare services are ineffective, with miracles expected from social workers who have high caseloads. There is a paucity of the right kinds of community resources, and there is the reality of underfunded provision, all of which are, among others, reasons for the failure of the US child welfare system (Lindsey 1994).

Residualism as an anchor to the child welfare system

The US has been termed a reluctant welfare state (Jansson 2003). Historically, it is characterized by political control that ebbs and flows between the conservative (neoliberal Republican) and the liberal (Democratic) political parties, with the policies and procedures that are established mirroring the prevailing ideology of the controlling political party. But, despite their political differences, both political parties share ideals of liberalism, which uphold the principle that the market is the instrument best suited to protect the common good. The differences lie in the extent to which they believe that government should support those who are the social and economic losers under the capitalist system. The belief in the supremacy of the marketplace goes hand in hand with individualistic beliefs and values, such as the belief that to work hard begets a better life. So, those who are experiencing hardships are constructed socially and politically as responsible for their difficulties because they are not working hard enough.

The belief in individualism supports and justifies laissez-faire economics, which call for less federal and/or state governmental support to social programmes. The rolling back of government social programmes has intensified with the growth of the neoliberal agenda, yet the public still expects adequate welfare services to be provided. As a result, services, which continued to be funded on a residual basis, are only available to selected population categories, which receive assistance after the application of strict eligibility rules and means testing have established the need for benefits and services. The benefits and services available are designed, and thus considered to be, only short-term solutions to the problems that are the result of what are often intractable long-term and structural difficulties.

The residual approach retains its most enduring appeal in the US because it is hinged to individualistic values, which place a positive value on inequality and mistrust of whole sectors of society, particularly the non-White population and people who are poor. According to Lindsey (1994, p.23), 'the residual perspective has always assumed that the troubles of those families served by the child welfare system derive either from unknown causes or from shortcomings in the parents (that is, a moral, psychological, physiological, or otherwise personal failing) that must be addressed through casework'.[1] As Martin (1985, p.53) observes:

---

1   Casework interventions are based on psychological therapies, often carried out with individuals, but sometimes with small groups, as in couple and family therapy (editors' note).

The residual perspective incorporates the psychological rationale. Underpinning this ideology and mindset is the belief that the US society offers opportunities for all families to provide for the physical, emotional, and social needs of their children, and consequently, that failure in these tasks is a failure of the parent(s) or possibly the family as a whole. Service intervention is thus focused on seeking change at the individual or family level.

The child is seen as needing protection from these parental failings.

Thus, the foster care system emerged as the major tool the child welfare system uses to deal with parental and family problems. This approach has been adversarial and authoritative. The child welfare agencies remove children and then watch, and hope, that the family will sufficiently mend itself to be able to take the child home again. Only occasionally are services provided to parents. The current Alternative Response programme is a contemporary approach to providing intensive and differential support to families. However, the mainstream of child welfare services has given itself over to treating symptoms and avoiding the causes (Lindsey 1994).

The residual perspective does not recognize the importance of structural factors like the feminization of poverty or child poverty. Nor have the social programmes been developed that take proper consideration of the circumstances of lone parenting. Family-leave provisions are often unpaid; mothers are economically penalized for giving birth whilst fathers are precluded from full-time caring for their children. This residual approach has in no way adequately responded to the dramatic effects of labour force participation by women who are sole 'breadwinners', which has today come to be the norm. Moreover, the residual approach does not provide for developing and implementing policies and programmes that would prevent harmful problems facing children from occurring in the first place. Lindsey (1994) argues that the residual approach focuses on the deficits of parents in meeting their parental role responsibilities, and in its concern with psychological shortcomings, it is unable to recognize and/ or embrace new structural realities that impact on children negatively and bring children to the attention of the child welfare system. Overall, whilst the residual approach to the welfare of children may have been appropriate for earlier times, it no longer represents an effective approach to address the social problems that children and families face in the twenty-first century. As Lindsey (1994, pp.85–86) concludes:

> For decades it [the residual approach] allowed society to provide services 'on the cheap,' targeting only those 'most in need.' The residual approach retains its enduring appeal because it promises to do the least and, thus, cost the least. However, it has, over time,

proven itself ineffective in dealing with long-term problems brought about by irrevocable social changes. Somehow a new understanding of the limits and possibilities of child welfare must be developed, one that reflects the enriched knowledge base in the field and an understanding of the social conditions within which public child welfare services operate.

In this regard, the needs of children are similar to the needs of business. Business and industry, for example, routinely look to the government for assistance in developing the capacity to compete in the global economy. Indeed, the business community requires an economic infrastructure that provides assistance in a variety of forms to all businesses, not just those businesses in difficulty. The business community would certainly not accept anything resembling a residual perspective in developing policies and programs that regulate commerce and industry. Likewise, families and children, who represent the country's future, require a broad based infrastructure to support their development and economic opportunity.

Discussion: Reasserting the welfare of children

In the US, child welfare continues to be narrowly conceptualized so as to refer only to the array of services, policies and programmes that have arisen as part of the child protection services (see Pecora *et al.* 2007, p.1). Child protection has become the mainstay of the child welfare system in the US. Since the late nineteenth century, the US has championed policies and programmes to prevent child abuse and neglect. The US spends more money fighting child abuse than any other industrialized country and yet it has long experienced the highest rates of child abuse (Lindsey 1994, p.3). The child welfare system thus conceptualized has been reactive rather than proactive to social problems facing children.

The heavy investment in responsive services, whilst being crucial to abate child abuse and neglect, is associated with a widening of the net of children and families becoming involved with the child welfare system. This has, however, little or no impact on the causes of abuse and neglect. It therefore is only effective in relation to individual children's experiences. The current conceptualization of the child welfare system looks effective only if seen in terms of the individual responsibility-based child-rescue model. It is less effective if viewed through a public wellbeing lens.

The child welfare system in the US has focused on child protection as a way of supporting the wellbeing of children. The residual approach to the welfare of children is detrimental to children and families who have historically experienced social and economic vulnerability – African Americans, Native Americans, Latino Americans, and poor Whites. In a country that has high inequality with a significant rich–poor divide, the individualistic and residual programmatic approaches to child wellbeing are likely to continue the fragmentation of services and the selective and ineffective care of children. Looking at comparative data for industrialized countries, those countries that have comprehensive family policies tend to be more supportive of families by providing paid family leave, childcare, healthcare access and income support, all of which help lower the divide between the rich and poor and, in turn, lower the problematic stigmatization and targeting of poor families. Moreover, the residual approach to child welfare has been adversarial to parents, even with the recent shift of ideology to a differential response in child protection services; as illustrated by the Alternative Response programme in states like Wisconsin, which attempts to fund services for children where there are lower levels of risk. However, what is ironic is that whilst there are presumed to be changes in outlook about children within the Alternative Response paradigm, the structures for providing children's welfare remain the same – residual. The US government has clearly failed to provide more than token support to children and families in the areas of childcare, healthcare, education, safe neighbourhoods, income security and housing.

Conclusion

What should be done to assert concern for the wellbeing of children in the US? Clearly, a multi-dimensional and comprehensive approach to wellbeing is necessary to improve policies, programming and services to support children and their families. Looking at children's wellbeing in a multi-dimensional and comprehensive way requires a broad range of family, labour market and income-support policies. There is no single policy that could positively impact children's wellbeing; a multiple dimensional approach to policies and programming is needed to support children's wellbeing. This should especially involve the adoption of a set of comprehensive family policies that are child oriented; that take into account the variety of family types and structure, and structural changes in the labour market; and that address poverty, the educational and childcare needs of children, and the health and income security needs of families. It is time for a shift in the family ethic, which, over the years, has provided the basis for justifying and promoting the punitive and stigmatized treatment of women who are poor and single. Such a paradigmatic shift with respect to the wellbeing of children should involve a shift away from a paradigm that holds that parents have full responsibility for their children's wellbeing to one that embraces Jenson's (2004) investing-in-children proposition, which holds that the responsibility for children's wellbeing should be shared by the family and the broader community.

References

Abramovitz, M. (1989) 'Women and children-at-risk and in poverty.' Paper presented at the Scholar and Feminist Conference on 'Women and Public Policy: Making the Difference', Barnard College, New York, 1 April.

Barnett, S. and Hustedt, J.T. (2005) 'Head Start's lasting benefits.' *Infants and Young Children* 18, 1, 16–24.

Beaton, A. (1999) *The Benefits and Limitations of International Educational Achievement Studies.* UNESCO–International Institute for Educational Planning. Available at: http://unesdoc.unesco.org/images/0011/001176/117629e.pdf.

Children's Defense Fund (2011) *The State of America's Children 2011 Report.* Available at: www.childrensdefense.org/child-research-data-publications/state-of-americas-children-2011.

Federal Interagency Forum on Child and Family Statistics (2011) *America's Children Key National Indicators of Wellbeing.* Washington, DC: US Government Printing Office. Available at: www.childstats.gov/pdf/ac2011/ac_11.pdf.

Finkelhor, D., Jones, L. and Shattuck, A. (2008) *Updated Trends in Child Maltreatment* (Crimes Against Children Research Center, University of New Hampshire). Available at: www.unh.edu/ccrc/Trends/papers.html.

Gornich, J.C. and Meyers, M.K. (2003) *Families that Work: Policies for Reconciling Parenthood and Employment.* New York: The Russell Sage Foundation.

Green, D.K., Belanger, K. and McRoy, R.G. (2011) *Challenging Racial Disproportionality in Child Welfare: Research, Policy and Practice.* New York: Child Welfare League of America Press.

Hutchinson, J.R. and Sudia, C.E. (2002) *Failed Child Welfare Policy, Family Preservation and the Orphaning of Child Welfare.* Washington, DC: University Press of America.

Jansson, B.S. (2003) *The Reluctant Welfare States.* Boston, MA: Brooks/Cole Publishers.

Jenson, J. (2004) 'Changing the paradigm: Family responsibility or investing in children.' *The Canadian Journal of Sociology 29*, 2, 169–192.

Kids Count (2011) *America's Children, America's Challenge: Promoting Opportunity for the Next Generation.* Baltimore, MD: The Annie E. Casey Foundation. Available at: http://datacenter.kidscount.org.

Lindsey, D. (1994) *The Welfare of Children.* New York: Oxford University Press.

Martin, M. (1985) 'Poverty and Child Welfare.' In K. Levitt and B. Wharf (eds) *The Challenge of Child Welfare.* Vancouver, BC, CA: British Columbia Press.

McCarthy, P. (2011) 'The Alliance for Racial Equity in Child Welfare – Yesterday, Today and Tomorrow.' In *Disparities and Disproportionality in Child Welfare: Analysis of Research.* New York: Center for the Study of Social Policy.

National Quality Improvement Center on Differential Response in Child Protective Service (2012) *Project Abstact.* Available at: www.differentialresponseqic.org.

Pecora, P.J., Whittaker, J., Maluccio, A.N., Barth, R.P., DePanfili, D. with Plotnick, R.D. (2007) *The Child Welfare Challenge: Policy, Practice and Research.* Edison, NJ: Transaction Publishers.

Poelmans, S. (2005) *Work and Family: An International Research Perspective.* Hillsdale, NJ: Lawrence Erlbaum Associates.

Shireman, J.F. (2003) *Critical Issues in Child Welfare.* New York: Columbia University Press.

Turnell, A. and Edwards, S. (1999) *Signs of Safety: A Solution and Safety Oriented Approach to Child Protection.* New York: Norton Professional Books.

UNICEF (2007) *Child Poverty in Perspective: An Overview of Child Wellbeing in Rich Countries. A Comprehensive Assessment of the Lives and Wellbeing of Children and Adolescents in the Economically Advanced Nations* (Report Card 7). Available at: www.unicef-irc.org/publications/pdf/rc7_eng.pdf.

United Nations Development Programme (UNDP) (2010) *The Human Development Report 2010: 20th Anniversary.* Basingstoke, UK: Palgrave MacMillan.

US, Census Bureau (2012) *State and County Quick Facts.* Available at: http://quickfacts.census.gov/qfd/index.html.

US, Census Bureau (2011) *Decennial Censuses: Population Estimates and Projections 2011.* Available at: www.census.gov/prod/2011pubs/11statab/pop.pdf.

US, Department of Health and Human Services (DHHS) (2006) *Early Head Start Benefits Children and Families.* Washington, DC: Administration for Children and Families. Available at: www.acf.hhs.gov/programs/opre/ehs/ehs_resrch/reports/dissemination/research_briefs/research_brief_overall.pdf.

White, V., Chau, M. and Aratani, Y. (2010) *Who Are America's Poor Children?* (National Center for Children in Poverty). Available at: www.nccp.org/publications/pub_912.html.

4

The United Kingdom

Clare Colton and Penelope Welbourne

Introduction

There were estimated to be 61.8 million people resident in the United Kingdom (the UK) in 2009, an increase of 2.7 million since 2001, and an increase of 23.6 million since the start of the twentieth century. Average age has increased from 36 years in 1992 to 40 years in 2009 (UK, Directgov 2012). Some 17.9 million families live in the UK, with 13.2 million dependent children (UK, ONS 2011a). The UK is made up of four countries: England, the largest and most populous country, and Scotland, Northern Ireland and Wales, each of which have their own national political systems. There are variations in terms of population, law and child welfare practices between the four countries. The main focus in this chapter is on England, partly because it would be impractical to cover each country in equal depth in one chapter, and partly because some of the most dramatic events that are shaping child protection practice across the UK have happened recently in London, as discussed later in the chapter. However, we would draw the reader's attention to the fact that there are distinctive elements to the child protection systems in each of the four countries.

For a small country, there are wide differences in terms of ethnic background, cultural practices and religion across and within regions. There are also marked differences between rural and town living. Over the period from 2004 to 2011, the five most common countries of birth for people born outside the UK were India, Poland, Pakistan, Republic of Ireland and Germany (UK, ONS 2011b). The UK's rich cultural mix of nationalities, religions, languages and cultures is especially notable in many cities that have significant numbers of Irish, Indian, Pakistani, American, Polish, German, Bangladeshi, Caribbean, African and Chinese people (UK, ONS 2004a, 2011a). The breakdown of religious practices and beliefs shows considerable diversity: about 78 per cent of the population self-describe as Christian, with Muslims (3.2%), Hindus (1.2%), Sikhs (0.7%) and Jews (0.5%) as the other main religious groups. Sixteen per cent of people describe themselves as having no religion (UK, ONS 2004b).

In 2011, there were 3.5 million children under five years of age in England and Wales, 406,000 more than in 2001 (UK, ONS 2011a). The UK is a highly developed nation, having industrialized early. It is sometimes described as 'post-industrial', and much of Britain's current Gross Domestic Product (GDP) comes from the banking and service industries. It still ranks globally in the top ten nations economically, despite recent economic setbacks linked to wider global financial problems. Although Britain is not a poor country, a substantial minority of the population lives in relative poverty: about one-fifth of children live in families with an income less than 60 per cent of the median UK income (Child Poverty Action Group 2012; UK, DfE 2009). Poverty affects as many as half the children who live in the most deprived areas of Britain, but only 5 per cent of children in the most affluent areas. Poverty is the common background factor that links many of those children whose welfare brings them into contact with services for children in need in the UK, as in so many other countries.

Background to the evolution of child welfare services

> In the little world in which children have their existence whosoever brings them up, there is nothing so finely perceived and so finely felt, as injustice. (Dickens 1860, p.53)

The history of interventions to support children at risk and in need is a relatively long history that has resonance in current services for children, partly because in some sense the UK has been a test bed for social interventions with children and families. This has had a wide-ranging effect outside the UK, sometimes for the good, and other times perhaps to the detriment of the development of locally appropriate services.

As a social commentator, the Victorian author Charles Dickens highlighted the oppression and many abuses experienced by children living in poverty in the nineteenth century. From the sixteenth century onwards, early systems for providing relief from poverty for those unable to work, and their dependants, were collectively known as the Poor Laws. Each of the four countries of the UK had their own versions of the Poor Laws. The Welsh Poor Law closely followed the English law, the Scottish law had some distinctive features, and the Poor Law system in Ireland only came to resemble closely the English system in the mid-nineteenth century. These laws were purposely harsh and punitive to discourage 'idleness' and dependency, offering minimal assistance. Changes to the Poor Laws in 1834 contributed to this deterrent effect by introducing the notorious workhouses for those who could not support themselves financially. 'Houses of Correction' had already been in existence in some areas for two centuries prior to this, fulfilling similar functions of social control combined with a minimal 'safety net', but after the mid-nineteenth century these evolved as a much feared, widely used national institution. As a satirist, Dickens challenged notions of benevolence and charity based on the Poor Law, and critiqued the failings of existing systems of care. Ironically, the year 1834 also saw the banning of slavery in the British colonies, whilst in Britain itself the practice of forcing young children of poor parents to live in inhumane conditions and contribute to their upkeep through harsh work continued.

Church parishes administered the Elizabethan Poor Law of 1601, funded from local levies or taxes. Over the centuries this system evolved into a more centralized system of poor relief based on larger rural areas and cities, especially as Britain industrialized and people moved to cities and towns to find work. The first established workhouse was recorded in Exeter in 1652. Whilst families were admitted, children were separated from their parents, who were only permitted a daily 'interview' with their children. Nearly two centuries later the system was still in place, still with the same philosophy of minimal care for disregarded social 'outcasts': in 1838, Assistant Commissioner Dr James Phillips Kay noted that children who ended up in the workhouse included 'orphans, or deserted children, or bastards, or children of idiots, or of cripples, or of felons' (Roberts 1963, p.714).

Before state organizations – primarily the local authorities – were set up to provide services for children in need of protection, charitable organizations lobbied for reform. These organizations were at that time the only providers of services to poor children and parents, apart from the workhouses. The inhumanity of the Victorian era is summed up in a letter from Reverend George Staite in the *Liverpool Mercury* in 1881: '…whilst we have a Society for the Prevention of Cruelty to Animals, can we not do something to prevent cruelty to children?' (cited in NSPCC 2012a). Following this inflammatory statement, the London Society for the Prevention of Cruelty to Children (SPCC) was established, changing its name in 1889 to the National Society for the Prevention of Cruelty to Children (NSPCC). NSPCC inspectors would visit homes where children were poor, neglected or ill-treated to offer advice, practical assistance and, after the passing of the first child cruelty legislation in England in 1889, instigate legal interventions to protect children. The NSPCC remains one of the largest and longest established of the numerous charitable organizations that sprang up in response to the problem of child abuse and neglect, and recognized its causal association with poverty.

From 1929 onwards the state, as opposed to the parishes, took responsibility for protecting children from ill-treatment and inadequate parental care through the role of the devolved local government agencies known in the UK as local authorities. The 1929 Local Government Act abolished the workhouses, although the buildings remained and many people, including children, continued to live in them until new buildings and facilities were developed. In the immediate post-war period, in 1948, the Labour Government finally abolished the long-lived but much feared Poor Law. The 1948 National Assistance Act marked the beginning of a move towards making local authorities responsible for the provision of services to adult 'persons in need' in the community, although services specifically aimed at children living in the community, as opposed to services for children already in care, had yet to develop. In the same year, the Children Act 1948 established new departments of social work within local authorities to provide services for children in need of care, whose duties were further extended in the 1960s and 1970s:

> While the [UK Government] Cabinet considered the [1948] Act to be reasonably effective, it did not address the problem of children mistreated within the family at home. The Children and Young Persons Act of 1963 extended the power of local authorities to intervene in cases of parental neglect. The Children Act of 1975 extended the rights of children, foster and adoptive parents and local authorities, and reduced those of the natural parent. (UK National Archives no date)

The 1968 Seebohm Report (Seebohm 1969) led to welfare services being integrated into local authority social services departments, with specific central roles for social workers in the new unified departments (Dickens 2011). The factor that spurred the Seebohm Report's compilation was concern about a perception that there were increasing levels of juvenile delinquency and a need for 'an effective family service for children from deprived and troubled backgrounds' (Dickens 2011, p.24). The future of children's welfare services was to include an ongoing flux between more and less integration between those services for children and young people with welfare needs due to a lack of parental care or familial abuse, and those for young people with conduct problems and offending behaviour, and services for those who fitted into both categories.

The start of the modern era in child welfare and child protection: The 1989 Children Act

In the period from the 1940s to the 1960s child abuse was 're-discovered', having been thought to be solved by progress made in the post-war period in advancing social welfare provision and living conditions. This re-awakening awareness of the fact that children were still being abused and neglected was initially framed within a medical framework, in contrast to the moral and social lens applied by the reformers and Poor Law guardians of earlier times. Child abuse was viewed as analogous to a social 'disease', for which a cure must be found (Parton 1985, pp.48–68). Consequently, social casework (developed largely in mental health social work settings) was used widely as a means of intervening and 'treating' families (mainly mothers) that ill-treated or neglected their children. In the 1970s, further extension of the role of the local authorities led to social work expanding to become a public service. It evolved as a profession, with increasing emphasis on education and training. Much of this effort, especially the legislative and procedural changes in the role of social work, was focused upon developing a systematic social work response to child abuse (Corby 2000).

It should be noted that there are significant regional differences between the systems for providing support services and protective services to children in the four countries of the UK. These differences have become more marked since the beginning of devolved regional governments in the latter part of the twentieth century. The system for protecting children in Wales closely resembles that of its English neighbour, with which it shares much relevant legislation, with its own distinctive approach to implementation and some specific legislaion. The devolved Northern Ireland Assembly has had the power to make laws for Northern Ireland since 1998, and is developing its own legislation and regulations to govern interventions in child welfare support and abuse cases. Scotland's child welfare system has some established distinctive features, notably the Children's Hearings System, set up in the 1960s, which employs volunteer lay members from the community to make decisions on what is best for a child or young person, and a more informal 'round table' approach to ascertain what would be in the best interests of the child. This applies to neglect and abuse cases, and cases of crimes committed by children. (For more information about Children's Hearings, see for example Hallett and Murray 1998.) Most of this section concentrates on the English law, given the unwieldiness of trying to cover all four countries in one chapter. However, it should be noted that there are regional differences.

By the latter half of the twentieth century, the laws relating to children had grown and become complex and unwieldy. They were in need of revision: both private law, which largely related to the management of issues in families when parents divorced and were in dispute, and public law, which regulated the actions of public authorities and judicial decision making in cases where the state intervened in a child's life, were in need of overhauling.

The 1989 Children Act was the legislative response to this complicated legal situation. Although the 1989 Act has been much amended, its core principles remain. Its ethos is still consistent with child and family social work as understood in the twenty-first century: using language such as 'participation' and 'partnership' to describe the relationship between state welfare agencies and parents (Section 1.3). Another central tenet of the Act promotes the concept that, whenever possible, children are best cared for in their own homes and by their own families. This Act became the seminal legislation upon which current child protection practices built their foundations. The term 'significant harm' (Section 31), describing the threshold at which the state may use compulsion in its dealings with parents, became increasingly important as child protection became seen as a defining characteristic of the role of the state in child welfare interventions.

Under the Children Act, compulsory state intervention is warranted when a child is suffering harm or is likely to suffer significant harm. Investigation of expressions of concern about significant harm is a duty of local authorities, and families cannot opt out of assessment or service provision for the child. Defensive practice stimulated by trenchant criticism of social workers and other agencies following high-profile child deaths, especially in the 1980s, led to an increase in proceduralism which continued, gathering pace, into the 2000s. Eventually, this proliferating tendency of guidance documents, recording systems and other systems intended as 'fail safes' led to strong criticism, and a process of rationalization has started in response (Broadhurst et al. 2010; Munro 2011). Parton (2007, p.17) argues that the nature of child protection work in England by the 1990s can be characterized as aiming to 'identify "high risk" in a context in which notions of working together were set out in increasingly complex yet specific procedural guidelines'.

The Children Act sought to provide proactive intervention and support for children, to support families before child protective action became necessary. This was through the introduction of a new threshold for the provision of services to 'children in need'. Children in need are defined in Section 17 of that Act as children entitled to assistance because they are failing to meet their developmental potential, where the provision of services could ameliorate this situation and promote the achievement of developmental potential. This contrasts with the earlier focus on resources for children who were known to be suffering harm already, which is still covered in the newer legislation under the rubric of 'significant harm'. In addition, under Section 17 all children who are disabled are considered children in need and entitled to assessment for services. Both 'need' and 'disability' are broadly defined to include children with social, emotional and behavioural developmental needs, as well as physical developmental needs. One of the key aspects of the Children Act was its integration of already existing provision for the protection of children from wilful or neglectful harm by parents, with new provisions for the support of children 'in need', where the cause is neither necessarily child abuse nor a medical problem. Social need is identified and defined as warranting a response to improve the situation and the prospects for the child. In summary, the Children Act defined a minimum acceptable standard of child welfare (welfare that supports a level of development that is as good as might be expected for that particular child); introduced a right to proactive state support before problems become severe; and brought about intervention based on the full range of resources available through a local authority and its partners in healthcare as well as education provision.

The concept of being a 'child in need' was a radical departure that permitted the relatively new integrated local authorities (the system of local government through which many public services are delivered under the 1970 Local Authority Social Services Act)[1] to provide services specially for children who were, or were at risk of, falling behind their peers in their health or development for reasons that were avoidable, including when this was linked to poor levels of care by parents. This could be done without any form of court order. The legislation notably excludes any reference to parental fault or parental conduct when setting out the criteria for provision for children in need. It might, therefore, be expected that such services would not be seen as stigmatizing, and parents would actively seek them for their children when needed. To some extent this is the case, but the negative representation of social workers in the media, which has been overwhelmingly focused on instances of service failure, means that the public have been given a very negative view of state children's services. Nevertheless, the legislative step forward of making free services available to children who need them has led to the existence of preventive services, with a large number of children receiving help and support through social work services and other free services, such as family counselling and parent support. Many of these children are living at home with their parents or

---

1   The 1970 Local Authority and Social Services Act required all local authorities to set up a social services committee and discharge a number of care and protection functions in relation to children and other vulnerable persons under other existing legislation.

other carers in their home communities; some are children being looked after by the state in foster care, or residential care, or looked after by relatives with state support.

This new approach meant that, for the first time, children could be assessed – and had a right to be assessed – and to have something done to help them develop to the best of their potential even when they were not in direst need or suffering abuse or neglect. Seeking to *encourage* use of services for children rather than deter help-seeking was a radical step away from tradition. Proactive preventive provisions might have been expected to reduce the need to intervene on a compulsory basis, but studies of early-intervention projects suggest that such intervention can lead to the identification of more, rather than less, severe need (Pithouse *et al.* 2009).

The balance between promoting welfare and addressing child abuse became a matter of concern in the 1990s. During the early 1990s the government commissioned a set of 20 research studies into child protection practice and the functioning of the 1989 Children Act – into the effectiveness of the state machinery in protecting children from abuse and neglect and promoting their welfare. These studies were published in 1995 as *Child Protection: Messages from Research* (UK, DH 1995). The studies appeared to show that instead of maintaining a balance between supportive non-compulsory early intervention and intervening on a compulsory basis, there were too few children and families receiving early support in partnership with service providers, and too many cases of intervening in family life as 'child protection', including cases in which no services were subsequently offered to the child and family. The inference drawn was that this was due to over-preparedness by local authorities to use their statutory powers of intervention when children had been abused, and slowness in offering early, preventative services.

In *Child Protection: Messages from Research* (UK, DH 1995) it was argued that local authorities and the professionals who worked in them should focus more on identifying and meeting the needs of children who are in need; moving towards what became known as needs-led services (as opposed to offering services on the basis of what is available), although this placed significant strain on resources (Horwath 2007). It concluded that the pendulum had swung too far towards a risk orientation: social work was now focused almost exclusively upon risk and investigation to the exclusion of assessing and providing services to children who are in need. The problematic aspect of this, as the research highlighted, is that 'long-term difficulties seldom follow from a single abusive event' (UK, DH 1995, p.53). Incident-driven and risk-focused assessment therefore fails to identify and serve the many children who need a service before the critical incident that leads to an investigation. Further, it suggested that many vulnerable children were 'falling through the net' because they were not being considered with reference to their position within their wider social and family environment. *Child Protection: Messages from Research* challenged the dominant sociomedical model of child abuse, and reframed the 'dangerous family' in child protection work by redefining it as the result of social stress and unmet need, potentially susceptible to the positive influences of early intervention by the state. This is another theme that has recurred throughout the last nearly 20 years, with the recent Allen Review of early intervention (Allen 2011) representing an attempt to use systematic and scientific methods of inquiry to find out what kinds of early intervention really help children to escape the negative effects of 'untreated' dysfunctional families and poor parenting practices.

After the Children Act was passed in 1989, *Working Together to Safeguard Children: A Guide to Inter-Agency Working to Safeguard and Promote the Welfare of Children* (UK, DH 1991) was published in an attempt to achieve more standardized and accountable practice in child protection. It gave guidance for professionals in all agencies working with children to promote better investigation, and better collaboration between agencies and professionals. It has been revised and updated over the years. The latest edition was brought out in 2013 (UK, HM Government 2013). The aims of this practice guidance were to bring about an improvement in child protection practice, and later, it has been argued, to move local authorities beyond narrow responding to concerns about abuse towards a much wider agenda for children's services associated with social exclusion, as promulgated by the (then) New Labour government (Frost and Parton 2009), based on investment in children as the citizens of the future. *Every Child Matters* was the high-profile policy initiative that set the keynote for government family policy during much of the first decade of the twenty-first century, with family and child policy taking a higher-profile position in government than at any time in the past.

As the parameters for entitlement to services have been drawn with a broader brush, the result has been greatly increased cost to the public purse of funding child welfare services:

> Spending on children's social care rose steadily throughout the last decade, peaking in 2009–10 at £8.54 billion across England and Wales. This equates to just over £650 for each 0–19 year-old, compared with £357 in 2001–02. Projected spend on children's social care for 2010–11 totalled £8.14bn (£620 per young person), but it was set to fall sharply to £6.28bn in 2011–12. This means that 2011–12 expenditure will equate to £478 for every 0–19-year-old,

> slightly below the level in 2005–06… While cuts in spending
> are currently commonplace in all public services, the sheer pace of
> change in spending on children's social care in some local authorities
> is of concern. It is hard to imagine that mistakes won't be made in
> the face of cuts of 40 per cent to some children's social care budgets.
> (NSPCC 2012b, pp.5–6)

High levels of professional as well as public concern about vulnerable
children is evidenced by an increase in the use of statutory powers to protect
children, ironically tending to increase public alienation from state child
welfare services, as well as costs. There has been a marked and sustained
rise in the number of applications by local authorities to the courts for
applications to remove children from neglectful or abusive parents, with
record numbers of applications year on year since 2008, and over 10,000
new applications for care orders in 2011–2012 (CAFCASS 2012).

It is not currently clear how tension between public and government
expectations and local government capacity may be resolved, since neither
lower expectations of services in the sensitive area of child protection, nor
substantial increases in local authority funding, appear to be imminently
available. As a consequence, the local authorities who administer child
welfare and child protection services have to make fine, professional
judgements about making provision for the greatest number of children,
or targeting resources on those most likely to suffer the most severe harm.

The following section will focus particularly on events in England,
because they have been particularly high profile and influential in steering
the course of child welfare service development over recent decades.

Child death inquiries and the development
of child protection practice

It is arguable that in addition to received cultural ideas about acceptable
and unacceptable childcare practices, a strong cultural influence on child
protection practice in the UK has been the very public debate in the media
about child protection services. This debate has seemingly gripped much
of the British public many times since the 1940s. These national debates
in the press have taken place on numerous occasions when a child has died
or been abused in unusual circumstances (by, for example, care workers), or
when interventions to protect children have been seen as over-authoritarian
or unwarranted. The phrase 'damned if you do, damned if you don't' is
often used as a colloquial way of describing the double jeopardy that
child protection and child welfare professionals feel themselves to be in
because of the high professional risks associated with both under- and

over-responsiveness to risk. This creates a feeling by many professionals that an acceptable level of risk is hard to define when complaints about errors of judgement swing between the two extremes.

Such tragic scandals have related to a wide range of failures of care and have been noted in each of the four countries of the UK, encompassing children who have died of cruelty while in care (e.g. Dennis O'Neill, in Wales), sexual abuse of children in care (e.g. children abused by Brendan Smyth, a Catholic priest, in Northern Ireland) or the zealous removal of children from their parents' care (in South Ronaldsay in Scotland and Cleveland in England). Dominant cultural influences on child protection practice include a legal culture that defines and manages child welfare interventions; a political culture that has a varying orientation towards service provision and self-reliance; and a popular culture that is shaped by, as well as reported by, the media. Indeed, newspapers, more than any other medium, have been the epicentre of this process, with particular newspapers identified with particular campaigns or positions in relation to child protection practice.

One early and influential child tragedy that caused a strong public reaction was the untimely and brutal death of Maria Colwell who, at seven years of age, was killed in 1974 by her stepfather. The subsequent inquiry led to more accountable child protection systems by introducing protocols for multi-agency child-protection case conferences, child-protection registers, and better representation for children in childcare court cases.

During the 1980s a series of child deaths led to social work agencies being strongly criticized for failing in their exercise of their duty to protect children. One of the last of these was the Cleveland Inquiry in 1987 (Butler-Sloss 1988), which concerned police, paediatricians and social workers in a hospital in the North East of England. Concern about sexual abuse of a large number of children led to many children being subject to protective action, but questions about the lack of well coordinated inter-agency working or adequate concern for legal safeguards to protect parental rights led to a public inquiry. The subsequent inquiry saw a 'distinct shift in the dominant discourse concerning child abuse away from the "socio-medical" to the "socio-legal"' (Parton 2007, p.16). In other words, a shift within the professional culture followed an instance of media and public outrage followed by a public inquiry headed by a senior judge.

In 2000, the introduction of the *Framework for the Assessment of Children in Need and their Families* (UK, DH, DfES and Home Office 2000) gave structure to what had been locally variable assessment processes. The aim of this new approach was to ensure that assessments were holistic or 'ecological', taking account of all the main dimensions of a child's experience: the child's needs;

the characteristics of the child him or herself; parenting capacity; the family environment in which the child was living; and the wider environment in which the family lived, including factors such as housing, neighbourhood, extended family, and other social and economic factors that impact on the quality of childhood. The needs of the child are thus located and analysed in the context of their family, community and culture. One criticism that was levelled at this generally well-received approach was that it did not provide a specific focus on risk – risk having become a preoccupation of local authority social work and perhaps the public, albeit sporadically (Corby 2000; Horwath 2007).

This approach was extended to include children for whom the level of concern is lower, and for whom services may be provided by professionals employed in universal services such as in healthcare, education and early-years care settings. In this incarnation, this *Assessment Framework* was adapted to become the *Common Assessment Framework* (CAF) (UK, DfES 2004). The CAF domains are similar to the earlier *Assessment Framework* and are designed for early identification of a child's needs (Horwath 2007, p.251).

The threshold for carrying out structured, standardized assessments of children had dropped dramatically from the pre-1989 situation, in which children who were not in severe need would barely be expected to receive any special service, to a situation in which large numbers of children whose welfare could be promoted became eligible for assessment for services.

A particularly shocking child death in London resulted in a landmark inquiry – the Climbié Inquiry – which had repercussions throughout all agencies with child protection responsibilities (Laming 2003). One aspect of this case which set it apart from many other child deaths was the fact that Victoria was a Black child from the Ivory Coast who did not speak English, and the failure of agencies to assess her with due consideration for her cultural background and her circumstances. The resultant misconceptions about the significance of her cultural context were partly responsible for the tragedy. Victoria had been entrusted by her parents to the care of her father's aunt, Marie-Therese Kouao, in whose care she sustained prolonged and sustained abuse. Although seen by many professionals and the subject of a number of referrals, she was never identified as a child in need of protection, and no one ever tried to speak to her in her own language, instead relying on the accounts of her abusive great-aunt. Victoria died in hospital on 25 February 2000. Post-mortem examination found her death was attributable to hypothermia, to severe malnutrition and to being kept in appalling circumstances, with 128 separate injuries on her body (Laming 2003).

This case highlighted the need for all professionals involved in caring for children, including doctors and police as well as social workers, to have regard for children's language and culture. No one spoke directly with Victoria, whose first language was French. Signs that with hindsight were probably of fear were misconstrued as 'respect'. The cultural diversity of Britain has challenged, and continues to challenge, services to find positive ways of responding to the needs of children who have equal rights to protection under the law as any other child, but whose families apply the cultural standards and practices of their country of origin. So-called female circumcision or female genital mutilation, and child marriage, are examples of areas in which there has needed to be recognition of cultural diversity, and an increase in awareness and understanding of the cultural expectations of people in different minority groups. At the same time, however, a strategy is needed to protect children in those communities from actions that would be considered harmful and abusive if they were done to a child in most other communities. The balance between respect for culture and promotion of children's rights is problematic because parents are naturally seen as the people who are most likely to be the most vigorous proponents of their children's rights. Cases of, for example, genital mutilation are different from other kinds of child abuse cases in that the parents' primary motivation is not to harm their child – indeed, it may be done in fulfilment of what they see as their parental duties to the child. The cultural sensitivity of the child protection response is enormously important, but areas like this highlight the need to be clear about the allowance that may be made for culture, whether it is associated with membership of a religious or ethnic group, or a cultural approach to childcare within the White majority culture of the UK, such as more severe methods of discipline that are accepted by some sectors of society (Welbourne 2002).

One area of state involvement in family life that has taken a much higher profile after the death of Victoria Climbié is the monitoring of children who live in the UK under 'private fostering' arrangements. These are children cared for by someone who is not a close relative, sometimes for money, sometimes not. Even though these are private arrangements, made for a variety of reasons including parental commitments, illness or sometimes a choice made by an older child, there is a duty on both carers and parents to inform the local authority so the arrangement can be assessed. The fact that Victoria Climbié was vulnerable in part because she had no one to monitor the quality of care provided for her by her great aunt led to increased awareness of the state's responsibilities towards children, even when private arrangements have been made for them by their parents.

The death of Victoria Climbié, and subsequent reflection on how to improve the child protection system, led to a radical review of policy and practice. At the policy level, in September 2003, a Government Green Paper,[2] *Every Child Matters* (UK, DfES 2003), was launched in response to the Laming Report (Laming 2003), and also in response to a commitment to improving early intervention and social inclusion for all children (Parton 2006). The Green Paper was concerned with addressing child abuse, but it clearly had a much wider interest than this. One of its key features was the introduction of five key indicators or outcomes of children's wellbeing, which were to become well known and widely used in developing policies and evaluating services. They were defined following consultation with a range of stakeholders in British society, including children. This consultation reflects a move under the then New Labour government to widen participation in the political process for all citizens, children included. The five outcomes were:

- being healthy
- staying safe
- enjoying and achieving
- making a positive contribution
- achieving economic wellbeing.

Another aspect of the development of services for vulnerable children in the wake of the Climbié Inquiry was an emphasis on information sharing and inter-agency cooperation. It was in part a failure to recognise and accurately communicate concerns about Victoria that prevented effective action being taken to save her life.

Section 12 of the 2004 Children Act, passed in the wake of the Climbié affair, required local authority children's services to establish Information Sharing and Assessment databases covering all children in the area served by the authority (Parton 2007, p.26). Children's Trusts had to be in place by 2006, combining planning for children's services across a range of departments, including health, education and children's social care. A single senior officer – a Director of Children's Services – appointed to be responsible for the quality of local children's services. Multi-agency local safeguarding children boards would replace the less effective – because of their lack of a clear legal mandate – area child protection committees in England and Wales. Children's Commissioners, positions created in England and Wales

---

2   Green Papers are government consultation documents. Their aim is to allow people both inside and outside Parliament to debate the subject and give the government feedback on its suggestions. For further information, see www.parliament.uk.

by the 2004 Children Act, have been appointed for all four countries of the UK. Their role is to promote the views and interests of all children in their respective regions, in particular those whose voices are least likely to be heard, to the people who make decisions about their lives.

The shake-up of structures for keeping children safe after the Climbié Inquiry went far beyond bolstering child protection systems, although it did also aim to do this. It reflected a different vision of the importance of children in society – giving them a right not only to be cared for in the present, but also to be provided with a context for growing up in which they could become economically and socially integrated individuals. Their ability to participate and contribute to society was taken to begin in childhood, not on becoming an adult. They were to be provided with a positive environment by society, but this was to be the beginning of a two-way process, with children being given opportunities from an early age to make a contribution too, at a proportionate level. It could be argued that these five outcomes were somewhat idealistic, nebulous and open to interpretation, but they appear to have been underpinned by a positive view of what childhood should and could be like – a view that reflected children as active participants in their own cultural context. They were also associated with a move towards using the research base concerning child development and a more evidence-based approach in child care and child protection social work.

In August 2007 news was announced of the death of another child in the same area of London in which Victoria Climbié died. This led to a similar public furore. Seventeen-month-old 'Baby P' (later to be identified as Peter Connelly) died of horrific injuries at the hands of his mother and her boyfriend. His post-mortem revealed that he had died with a swallowed tooth in his intestine after being punched; he had a broken back, broken ribs, damage to his fingers and missing finger nails. The abuse he suffered had been sustained and brutal. Unlike Victoria, who had mostly been kept hidden away, he had been in plain sight of many professionals. The Secretary of State for Children, Schools and Families appointed Lord Laming, who led the Climbié Inquiry, to urgently review child protection procedures in England. Once again, intense media and public interest in a child's death had far-reaching consequences for child protection in Britain. Concern about the vulnerability of children cared for away from home by people who are distantly related to the child, or unrelated, was one of those areas that changed in response to the death of Victoria Climbié. A marked and sustained increase in children entering public care was one of the outcomes of the Peter Connelly case.

Family policy and family values

This section looks first at the way values around parental discipline influence the way child welfare policy is pursued in the UK, and then at two perspectives used to manage dilemmas in the borderline cases. These arise in any system that relies on interpretation of partial evidence, using rules that follow cultural values that are difficult to express with precision. The extent to which children may be punished using physical chastisement, for example smacking or hitting, is an issue that goes to the heart of the tension between individual parental choice over 'lifestyle' and state intervention in family life. There are obvious issues with using physical punishment as a way of teaching children: children are generally expected to learn that they should not rely on physical violence or physical intimidation to achieve their aims. Changing the culture of parenting so as to reduce the use of physical punishment, or even stopping it altogether, by making it unlawful to hit children – as has already happened in a number of European countries, including Sweden, Finland, Denmark, Norway, Austria, Cyprus, Croatia and Latvia – has been the subject of debate and public consultation in the UK, but change does not look likely to happen soon.

The consultation established that the dominant view in the UK is that parents want to retain the right to smack their children. The government concluded that criminalizing such acts would not be in the interests of society: it would be 'intrusive' and incompatible with their aim of helping and encouraging parents. A survey carried out on behalf of the government in 2000, the last such survey, found 88 per cent of respondents were of the view that it was sometimes necessary to smack a naughty child, and only 8 per cent disagreed (UK, DH 2000).

A problem with the use of physical chastisement is that it becomes difficult for child protection and child welfare workers to explain to parents exactly what the position of the state is in relation to the boundary between reasonable punishment and physical ill-treatment. The lack of clarity between permissible and non-permissible acts by parents is problematic (Welbourne 2002): the acceptability of punishment with a hand or an implement, or hitting the face or other parts of the body, the significance of whether a mark is left on the child's body or not, and other issues have become the subject of debate. It is arguable that this is the case with other types of abuse and neglect too. Each case has to be assessed on its own merits. But physical punishment remains problematic because of its widespread use and incompatibility with adult rights to protection from assault. The four UK Children's Commissioners point out that children do not support the use of physical punishment. Their position (2008, p.15) is as follows:

Since 2002, physical punishment within the family has been the subject of regular debate resulting in a change in the law in each nation in the UK. Nevertheless, all legislative changes have fallen short of the standard required by the [UNICEF] Committee [on the Rights of the Child]. Throughout the UK, the physical punishment of children is still permissible within the family. Where a parent hits a child, they are able to claim a justifying defence where such a defence would not be available were the victim over the age of 16. Children are thus denied the equal protection of the law.

The lack of a clear boundary between acceptable and unacceptable punishment of children leaves scope for professional judgement, allowing practitioners who work with parents to take into account the parents' motivations, their commitment to good parenting and their willingness to work with social workers. Practitioners in the UK are expected to consider all these things, and the practice guidance for social workers requires it (UK, HM Government 2013; UK, DH *et al.* 2000). The current social context for child protection work in the UK offers practitioners two main themes, which become important whenever a decision has to be made in borderline cases (Hannon, Wood and Bazalgette 2010):

- The interventionist, 'child protection first' position: children are being left in dangerous situations for too long and are harmed by their parents as a result of social workers' failure to recognize the threat the parents represent to the children. Social workers should be more vigilant and more ready to remove children at risk of harm, especially young children at risk of harm.

- The non-interventionist, 'family rights' position: children do not thrive in state care and are generally better off with their families. This means that the threshold for taking children into care is too high; fewer children should come into care and, if they do come into care, they should stay there for shorter periods. This means speeding up the process of adoption, which currently takes far too long to place children – but adoption is a fundamental severance of family rights, and therefore should only be used in cases in which there really is no other option.

The balance between these two imperatives is influenced by current events. After the high-profile death of the baby Peter Connelly, the number of applications for care orders to remove children from the care of their parents rose to record levels and, five years later, the level of applications remains high.

The state as parent

Hannon *et al.* (2010, p.10) argue that:

> broadly speaking, there has been a 'pendulum' movement in the history of the care system between two approaches, which mirror those relating to the role of the child protection system, outlined above. The first approach sees the purpose of care as supporting families and enabling children to remain with or return to their birth parents (a 'preventative' approach). According to the second approach, the purpose of care should be to safeguard children and provide them with permanency beyond the birth family (a 'permanency' approach).

Both of these philosophies contain the idea that children's exposure to public care should be minimized. They argue that instead of oscillating between these positions of 'prevention' and 'permanency', public care should be used more proactively in the UK:

- to provide support to families as soon as they need it rather than waiting until they reach crisis point

- to achieve early permanency for those children who cannot return to their families

- to provide stability for those children and young people for whom a permanent solution is not desirable or feasible.

Children may be removed from their families for their own safety against their parents' wishes in specific circumstances defined in the 1989 Children Act. This is sometimes as a result of information gathered during a child protection inquiry (under Section 47), which may trigger an application to a court for an interim care order or, in an emergency, an emergency protection order on a short-term basis, for an absolute maximum of 15 days if extended. In cases of the highest gravity, a police officer may place a child under police protection for a shorter period: a maximum of 72 hours, during which they may be looked after in a foster home or other accommodation provided for them by the local authority. If a care order is made (under Section 31), they may remain in care until their eighteenth birthday, and receive support after this, although most stay for a shorter period. Parents sometimes ask for children to be voluntarily accommodated by a local authority (under Section 20). In this situation children may enter state care without any court order, for an indefinite period, by agreement of parents and local authority.

Three-quarters of children in care are in foster care. Foster carers are often very experienced in looking after troubled children, and have something like semi-professional status by virtue of that experience and the training they have to undergo as part of their role as foster carers. They receive remuneration for the work they do, but this is seen as recompense for the cost and difficulty of looking after the child rather than payment in the usual sense of an hourly rate, for example. Of the other 25 per cent, relatives, often grandparents, who are given financial support and oversight by the local authority, care for many. For some young people, foster care is not appropriate; these young people are placed in residential homes, about three-quarters of them privately run. This is very expensive; in 2012 the annual cost of looking after the 5,000 children in residential care homes in England was estimated at around £1 billion (BBC 2012).

In March 2011 there was a record 65,520 children looked after in state care: an increase of 2 per cent from 2010 and an increase of 9 per cent from 2007 when baby Peter Connelly died. In 2011, 54 per cent of children were brought into care due to abuse or neglect. This percentage has increased each year since 2008, when 48 per cent of children were in care for this reason (UK, DfE 2011a). Wales has also seen an increase in the number of children in care: a rise of 44 per cent over the last decade (BBC 2011), possibly attributable to increasing financial stresses. Scotland also has seen a rise in children coming into care (Fostering Network 2012), as has Northern Ireland (BAAF 2012). It is possible that the 'Baby P' effect – an alleged increased readiness to seek to remove a child when there are fears for the child's welfare – may be only one component, albeit a very important one, in a more complex causal picture in relation to the rising numbers of children becoming looked after by the state.

Historically, when the state as parent looks to find a foster carer or adoptive parents for a child, finding a good match between the ethnicity of the child and the carer was seen as central to the process, and this continues to be the case, but with a caveat. Black and other ethnic minority children were frequently left waiting in short-term placements until a cultural and ethnic match to a carer was achieved. Recently, the Children's Minister has recommended that guidance on adoption in England be updated to stress that consideration of a child's race should not be a barrier to finding them a family. Children from ethnic minorities are over-represented in the care system and, typically, it takes three times as long to place them with a permanent family. In March 2012, Prime Minister David Cameron stated that 'this government is going to tear down the barriers that stop good, caring potential adoptive parents from giving a home to children who so desperately need one' (UK, DfE 2012).

The reality is that there are insufficient numbers of potential adopters from all ethnicities to place all children in a 'perfect match'. Social workers looking for adoptive or long-term foster parents for children are required to find a value balance between ethnocentrism and cultural relativism. Ethnocentrism is the belief that:

> one's own cultural beliefs and practice are not only preferable, but also superior, to all others…cultural relativism is the belief that each and every culture must be viewed in its own right as equal to all others, and that culturally sanctioned behaviours cannot be judged by the standards of another culture. An exclusive reliance on either position has serious implications for practice. (Korbin 2007, p.135)

To achieve equilibrium requires 'cultural competence', a term coined by anthropologist James W. Green (1995). Cultural competence features heavily in some serious case reviews, as does cultural relativism, notably in Lord Laming's report into the death of Victoria Climbié. Medical professionals believed marks on her body occurred in her country of origin, and may have been to do with cultural customs. Her social worker heard that Victoria 'stood to attention' in the presence of her great-aunt, and concluded that 'this type of relationship was one that can be seen in many Afro-Caribbean families because respect and obedience are very important features of the Afro-Caribbean family script' (Laming 2003, p.345). This is echoed by Ratna Dutt, Director of the Race Equality Unit, in her evidence to the Climbié Inquiry:

> There is some evidence to suggest that one of the consequences of an exclusive focus on 'culture' in work with black children and families, is [that] it leaves black and ethnic minority children in potentially dangerous situations, because the assessment has failed to address a child's fundamental care and protection needs. (Laming 2003, part 5, para.16)

Black children took on average over 50 per cent longer to be placed for adoption than children from other ethnic groups, and children over five were four times less likely to be adopted compared to children under five years of age (UK, DfE 2011b).

Although a care order can last until a young person is 18 years of age, relatively few children who enter care stay for extended periods.

> Many children entering care are over 10 years of age, and many will only have a short stay in care. Consequently, a child's pre-care experience is one of the most important influences on their care journey. Evidence suggests that many of the children and young people who eventually become looked after already have a high level of mental and physical health problems at their point of entry to care. (Hannon *et al.* 2010, p.11)

This pre-care experience may have a profound and lasting effect on their developmental trajectory. While many children return home to their parents after a short time, others, especially very young children, may be adopted; almost 60 per cent of children adopted in 2010 were between one and four years of age (UK, ONS 2010).

Adoption is seen as the preferred outcome for children in care, and much political pressure has been placed behind initiatives to increase the number of children adopted from care, as noted above, but the number of adoptions in England and Wales in 2010 was 4,472 – a decrease of 4 per cent from 2009. Adoption is currently at a record low in the UK, despite the considerable political will to convert the many children in the care of the state into children permanently adopted into families.

The 2002 Adoption and Children Act made it a requirement that all adopters have an assessment of their need for support, as well as the child's need for support, and resources should be available to support the adopters and the adopted person in terms of services such as counselling and advice to the parents. Unlike foster carers, adoptive parents can choose whether they want to maintain contact with services, and can choose on behalf of their children, too, until the child is old enough to choose for themselves.

The ideal of a happy family life is a very powerful one. Awareness of the power of this ideal of family life with birth parents, together with a professional bias towards working in partnership, means that there has been a tendency to only remove children whose family life has been so difficult that they are often significantly damaged by their experiences. Indeed, the threshold for the compulsory removal of a child is that they have suffered, or be at risk of suffering, significant harm. The same ideal means that, once in care, there is a focus on finding a permanent home where children can put down roots, so building new attachments and a sense of security. The ideal of state parenting is, therefore, to find permanent alternative parents for children – if the birth parents cannot resume care of the child – possibly a person from within the child's kinship network, and, if this is not possible, to find a long-term foster placement that is as close as possible to the ideal of 'ordinary' family life.

Conclusion

The evolution of child welfare and child protection practices in the UK has its roots firmly entrenched in the varied economic and social history of the country; the vastly differing government ethos and policies; and the rich cultural diversity of the population. Child welfare practices have vacillated between risk-averse child protection practices and attempts to construct a welfare environment where families feel able to utilize support and parenting advice, without fear of stigma. Services for children have been affected in their evolution over recent decades by public criticism levelled at social workers as 'failing' in their duty to protect, set against the criticism by family (or parents') rights proponents of being too vigorous and precipitate in removing children in danger of harm. It can only be hoped that a level of stability will be achieved, and a socially accepted equilibrium develop, so that children in the UK can always count on receiving timely, reliable and well-judged services from professionals with a public and political mandate to offer the best protective and preventive services for all children.

References

Allen, G. (2011) *Early Intervention: The Next Steps*. London: The Stationery Office. Available at: www.dwp.gov.uk/docs/early-intervention-next-steps.pdf.

BAAF (British Agencies for Adoption and Fostering) (2012) *Statistics: Northern Ireland*. Available at: www.baaf.org.uk/res/statni.

British Broadcasting Corporation (BBC) (2011) *Children 'Wellbeing' Data Rise in Wales Care Figures*. Available at: www.bbc.co.uk/news/uk-wales-politics-12901950.

British Broadcasting Corporation (BBC) (2012) *Are Some Children's Homes Putting Profit before Child Protection?* Available at: www.bbc.co.uk/news/education-18649389.

Broadhurst, K., Wastell, D., White, S., Hall, C., Pithouse, A. and Davey, D. (2010) 'Performing "initial assessment": Identifying the latent conditions for error at the front-door of local authority children's services.' *British Journal of Social Work 40*, 2, 352–370.

Butler-Sloss, E. (1988) *Report of the Inquiry into Child Abuse in Cleveland* (Cmnd. 412). London: Her Majesty's Stationery Office.

Child Poverty Action Group (2012) *Child Poverty Facts and Figures*. Available at: www.cpag.org.uk/child-poverty-facts-and-figures.

Children and Family Court Advisory and Support Service (CAFCASS) (2012) *CAFCASS Care Demand: Latest Figures for April 2012*. Available at: www.cafcass.gov.uk/pdf/April%202012%20care%20demand%20update.pdf.

Corby, B. (2000) *Child Abuse: Towards a Knowledge Base*. Maidenhead: Open University Press.

Dickens, C. (1860) *Great Expectations*. London: Penguin Classics.

Dickens, J. (2011) 'Social work in England at a watershed – as always: From the Seebohm Report to the Social Work Task Force.' *British Journal of Social Work 41*, 22–39.

Fostering Network (2012) *Rising Numbers of Children in Care in Scotland*. Available at: www.fostering.net/news/2012/rising-numbers-children-in-care-in-scotland.

Frost, N. and Parton, N. (2009) *Understanding Children's Social Care: Politics, Policy and Practice*. London: Sage.

Green, J. (1995) *Cultural Awareness in the Human Services: A Multi-Ethnic Approach*. Boston, MA: Allyn and Bacon.

Hallett, C. and Murray, C. (1998) *Deciding in Children's Interests*. Edinburgh: The Scottish Office Central Research Unit.

Hannon, C., Wood, C. and Bazalgette, L. (2010) *In Loco Parentis*. London: Demos.

Horwath, J. (2007) 'Safeguarding children: the assessment challenges.' In K. Wilson and A. James (eds) *The Child Protection Handbook*. London. Baillière Tindall.

Korbin, J. (2007) 'Issues of Culture.' In K. Wilson and A. James (eds) *The Child Protection Handbook*. London: Elsevier.

Laming, Lord H. (2003) *The Victoria Climbié Inquiry: Report of an Inquiry by Lord Laming* (Cmnd 5730). London: The Stationery Office.

Munro, E. (2011) *The Munro Review of Child Protection: Final Report – A Child-Centred System* (Cmnd 8062). London: The Stationery Office. Available at: www.education.gov.uk/publications/standard/publicationDetail/Page1/CM%208062.

National Society for the Prevention of Cruelty to Children (NSPCC) (2012a) *History of the NSPCC*. Available at: www.nspcc.org.uk/what-we-do/about-the-nspcc/history-of-nspcc/history-of-the-nspcc_wda72240.html.

National Society for the Prevention of Cruelty to Children (NSPCC) (2012b) *Smart Cuts? Public Spending on Children's Social Care*. Available at: www.nspcc.org.uk/Inform/research/findings/smart_cuts_pdf_wdf85752.pdf.

Parton, N. (1985) *The Politics of Child Abuse*. Basingstoke, UK: Macmillan.

Parton, N. (2006) '"Every child matters": The shift to prevention whilst strengthening protection in children's services in England.' *Children and Youth Services Review 28*, 2, 976–992.

Parton, N. (2007) 'Safeguarding Children: A Socio-Historical Analysis.' In K. Wilson and A. James (eds) *The Child Protection Handbook*. London: Elsevier.

Pithouse, A., Broadhurst, K., Hall, C., Peckover, S. and White, S. (2009) 'Engaging early in children's needs through the Common Assessment Framework (CAF): New challenges for practice in England and Wales.' *International Journal of Child Health and Human Development 2*, 4, 395–402.

Roberts, D. (1963) 'How cruel was the Victorian Poor Law?' *Historical Journal 6*, 97–107.

Seebohm, F. (1969) *Report of the Committee on Local Authority and Allied Personal Social Services* [The Seebohm Report] (Cmnd. 3703). London: Her Majesty's Stationery Office.

UK, Children's Commissioners (2008) *UK Children's Commissioners Report to the UN Committee on the Rights of the Child*. Available at: www.childcom.org.uk/uploads/publications/61.pdf.

UK, Department for Education (DfE) (2009) *Ending Child Poverty: Making it Happen*. London: Child Poverty Unit. Available at: www.education.gov.uk/consultations/downloadableDocs/8061-CPU-Ending%20Child%20Poverty.pdf.

UK, Department for Education (DfE) (2011a) *Statistics: Children in Care*. Available at: www.education.gov.uk/rsgateway/DB/SFR/s001026/sfr21-2011.pdf.

UK, Department for Education (DfE) (2011b) *Government to Look at Strengthening Inspection of LA Adoption Services* (press release, 22 February). Available at: www.education.gov.uk/childrenandyoungpeople/families/childrenincare/a0074754/breaking-down-barriers-to-adoption.

UK, Department for Education (DfE) (2012) *Government Sets Out Measures to Speed Up Adoptions and Give Vulnerable Children Loving Homes* (press release, 9 March). Available at: www.education.gov.uk/inthenews/inthenews/a00204964/governmentmeasurestospeedupadoptions.

UK, Department for Education and Skills (DfES) (2003) *Every Child Matters*. London: The Stationery Office.

UK, Department for Education and Skills (DfES) (2004) *Common Assessment Framework: Introduction and Practitioners' Guide*. London: DfES.

UK, Department of Health (DH) (1995) *Child Protection: Messages from Research*. London: Her Majesty's Stationery Office.

UK, Department of Health (DH) (1999) *Working Together to Safeguard Children: A Guide to Inter-Agency Working to Safeguard and Promote the Welfare of Children*. London: Her Majesty's Stationery Office.

UK, Department of Health (DH) (2000) *Supporting Parents, Protecting Children*. Available at: http://dera.ioe.ac.uk/1780/1/dh_4054848.pdf.

UK, Department of Health (DH), Department for Education and Skills (DfES) and Home Office (2000) *Framework for the Assessment of Children in Need and their Families*. London: The Stationery Office.

UK, Department of Health (DH), Home Office, Department for Education and Employment (1991) *Working Together to Safeguard Children: A Guide to Inter-Agency Working to Safeguard and Promote the Welfare of Children*. London: The Stationery Office.

UK, Directgov (2012) *Key Facts about the United Kingdom*. Available at: webarchive.nationalarchives.gov.uk/20121015000000/http:/www.direct.gov.uk/en/government citizensandrights/livingintheuk/dg_10012517.

UK, HM Government (2013) *Working Together to Safeguard Children: A guide to inter-agency working to safeguard and promote the welfare of children*. London: HM Government.

UK, National Archives (no date) *The Cabinet Papers 1915–1981: Protection of Children*. Available at: www.nationalarchives.gov.uk/cabinetpapers/themes/protection-children.htm.

UK, Office for National Statistics (ONS) (2004a) *Focus on Ethnicity and Identity*. London: The Stationery Office.

UK, Office for National Statistics (ONS) (2004b) *Focus on Religion*. London: The Stationery Office.

UK, Office for National Statistics (ONS) (2010) *Adoption Statistics*. Available at: www.ons.gov.uk/ons/taxonomy/index.html?nscl=Adoptions.

UK, Office for National Statistics (ONS) (2011a) *Statistical Bulletin: Families and Households, 2001 to 2011*. Available at: www.ons.gov.uk/ons/rel/family-demography/families-and-households/2011/stb-families-households.html#tab-Dependent-children.

UK, Office for National Statistics (ONS) (2011b) *Taxonomy*. Available at: www.ons.gov.uk/ons/taxonomy/index.html?nscl=International+Migration.

Welbourne, P. (2002) 'Culture, children's rights and child protection.' *Child Abuse Review* 11, 6, 345–358.

5

Italy

Teresa Bertotti and Annamaria Campanini

Introduction: The social, political, religious and cultural context

Italy is a relatively young nation that celebrated 150 years of unity in 2011. On 1 January 2011, the Italian population was 60.63 million, of which 9.65 million (15.9%) were children below 16 years of age (Italy, ISTAT 2011). It is important to note, however, that in Italy the legal age for becoming an adult is 18, so the total number of minors is 10.80 million (17.8%). The annual rate of population growth is 0.6 per cent, with an average number of children per woman of 1.42. Italy was a country of emigration from the early nineteenth century until well into the second half of the twentieth century. It was only towards the end of the twentieth century that this was reversed, and Italy became a country of immigration. Seven per cent of all residents are foreign nationals (4.23 million on 1 January 2010), of whom 22 per cent (0.93 million) are minors; of these, 61 per cent (0.57 million) were born in Italy, with the balance immigrating to Italy for family reunification.

About half of all foreign residents, over two million individuals, come from Eastern European countries, both within and outside the EU. The other half comes largely from Africa (especially Morocco and Tunisia), China, India, Pakistan, the Philippines and Latin America. New arrivals are not spread evenly through the country: over 60 per cent reside in the North, 25 per cent in the central area and the remaining 13 per cent in the South, although the foreign population has grown fastest in the South (Italy, ISTAT 2011).

Although Italy continues to portray itself as a relatively homogeneous, Catholic society, there is also a significant following for Islam – the second largest religion – serving a little over a third of the immigrant population; there are also Orthodox and Pentecostal Churches, as well as the African,

Asian and Latin American Christian faiths. This is changing the social and religious map of Italy (Pace 2010). Nevertheless, the influence of the Catholic Church is still strong, because of the presence of the Pope and the Holy See. It emerges as a very significant voice in all debates that touch on morality and representation of the family. It is no coincidence that in Italy there is no formal recognition given to unmarried couples, or to homosexual unions, and that there is an ongoing public discussion on artificial insemination and even on abortion.

Italy's economy is also changing. The structure of its workforce, as with almost all industrialized countries, has shifted from agriculture to industry and now, progressively, towards the service sector. The employment structure in 2010 was: agriculture (3.9%), industry (28.5%) and services (67.6%). Employed people accounted for 56.9 per cent of the population in December 2011. For men, the employment rate was 67.1 per cent, and the unemployment rate was 8.4 per cent. For women the respective rates were 46.8 per cent and 9.6 per cent. It is important to note that the unemployment rate has increased over recent years, with a significant deterioration in the labour market and a significant differentiation between North and South. At a regional level, unemployment is relatively low in the North, while increasing significantly in the South, where in many areas it exceeds 14 per cent (Italy, ISTAT 2011).

Poverty is also becoming more prevalent. The Caritas report (2011) on poverty in Italy is both noteworthy and of considerable interest, as it documents the seriousness of the economic situation in Italy. In 2010, 13.8 per cent of the population was considered poor, and relative poverty increased over the year, especially among:

- families of five or more members (from 24.9% to 29.9%)

- single-parent families (from 11.8% to 14.1%)

- families in the South with three or more children (from 36.7% to 47.3%)

- families of retirees in which at least one member has never worked and is not seeking employment (from 13.7% to 17.1%)

- families with:
  ○ a self-employed earner (from 6.2% to 7.8%)
  ○ a university or college qualification (from 4.8% to 5.6%).

Research by EURISPES (2012) emphasizes that for people in poverty there are not only basic needs to be met, but also needs associated with the maintenance of social status and meeting social expectations about increasing levels of cultural consumption in a knowledge-based society. This is central to understanding the complexity of the contemporary needs of families. In this sense, marginality is defined by the impossibility of meeting those human needs caused by factors linked to sociocultural influences and consumerism. This strongly emphasizes the multiple and complex character of contemporary poverty in Italy, which urgently needs a revised definition. Indeed, poverty is not always linked in a straightforward way just to the experience of economic deprivation. Material deprivation leads to social exclusion and marginalization with respect to critical opportunities such as access to educational, health and social services.

The structure of the welfare system

The structure of the Italian welfare state was once defined, in terms of the Titmussian model, as *particularistic-clientelistic*, which has since changed to a Mediterranean or southern European welfare system (Esping Andersen 1990; Ferrera 1998). An important feature of the Italian welfare system is the strong dualism in social protection, with the assumption that the networks of solidarity and kinship in families, based mainly on the role of women, remain accessible throughout the life cycle to augment public provision. This dualism is exacerbated regionally by the presence of a universal healthcare and welfare system in the North of Italy. This goes together with client manipulation of the systems, low levels of state agency, a high rate of tax evasion and poor performance on the part of the publicly administered services. These are poorly insulated from outside interests, and are often manipulated and organized by powerful interest groups in other regions of Italy. The profound differentiation of the Italian system at the regional level, specifically between North and South, was highlighted in the late 1990s as the emergence of a model that was particularistic and infused by patronage and dualism (Ascoli 2010).

In comparison with other European countries, the impact of the economic crisis on the Italian welfare system has been distinctive. It has not resulted in the market assuming a more important role, but rather in the greater involvement of non-profit organizations, such as charity groups, social cooperatives, non-profit organizations of social utility (*Onlus*), self-help groups, and social associations and foundations, all of which fall within the Third Sector (Ascoli and Ranci 2003). The model resulting from this situation has been described as the negotiation model (Pavolini 2003) or the marketization model of social care services. This is, according to Paci (2005, p.140):

> based on reduced financial effort by the state and [instead there is reliance on] its ability to identify families' needs for services, in

order to direct [service users] towards a private offer coming from accredited organizations, increasingly structured and formalized, and in competition with each other.

In practice this implies a move from the traditional top-down logic of government to the bottom-up one of governance (Mayntz 2003), where several independent actors from the public, private and non-profit sectors contribute with their own resources to solving problems in a collaborative and horizontal process. In this model, the social partners working at the local or community level can take up the challenge of co-designing social policies and evaluating the results achieved by the chosen mode of delivering social services.

The specific nature of the Italian welfare mix is related to an array of social, economic and political factors. First, there is Italian culture, which is deeply oriented towards social solidarity, along with the key role played by the family. In Italy, families represent the main caregivers (Saraceno 2002), thus defining a family-kinship solidarity model (Naldini 2003). Second, there is the specific nature of the labour-intensive public social services, characterized as having low productivity. This means that they are not profitable enough for private entrepreneurs to be privatized. Third, as Ferrera (2005) argued, the spread of *particularism* has also played a central role in the transformation process, further contributing to the emphasis on the distinctiveness of the case of Italy when compared to other European countries. Finally, there is Italy's recent move towards a multi-tier provision structure. In 2001, the reform of the Constitution delegated the power to legislate on health, education and social services to the regions and local authorities. This was preceded by a national law that reformed the social sector (Law 328 of 2000). Although this law designed a framework, based on Italian territoriality, for the development of an integrated system of social services and social interventions that was expected to be in place for over 20 years, its implementation has been thwarted almost everywhere. The factors contributing to this problematic situation can be identified as: an emphasis on the need to define minimum levels of assistance and homogeneous levels of social performance throughout the country; the change of political climate with the transition from centre-left government to Berlusconi's centre-right era; and the amendment to Title V of the Constitution, which granted additional autonomy to the regions, and has resulted in a 'spotted leopard' pattern of welfare provision.

It is evident that the universality logic, which inspired the reform of compulsory education, the 1969 pension reform and the 1978 healthcare reform, is becoming increasingly irrelevant. A new logic based on corporate provision is clearly overtaking the old logic based on citizenship. The welfare mix, in particular, has seen the growing importance of the private-for-profit sector. Italy devotes just 0.9 per cent of Gross Domestic Product to family policies, which is well below the EU average (2.3%). The difficulties facing Italian families wishing to have children[1] are due, on the one hand, to economic difficulties and, on the other hand, to the failure of government policies to support the family. Child and family policies are financed mainly through fiscal measures involving employment-related taxation (payroll and income tax) related to income and to the number of children. The monetary allowances currently available to support families are wholly inadequate to the maintenance of children. The birth of a first child in Italy leads on average to a decrease in disposable income of between 18 per cent and 45 per cent, with additional expenditure of between 500 and 800 Euros per month, varying according to age and geographical location.

It is likely that where negative conditions related to geographic location, employment status and family size are added together, the probability of being in a situation of economic hardship is dramatically affected. It suffices to say that while in the North poverty affects 11.6 per cent of households with five or more family members, in the South, for the same family size, the percentage rises steeply, reaching 32.4 per cent. Added to this is a significant lack of services for young children. Private services make up, nationally, over 30 per cent of the overall supply of services for young children. The failure of nursery services supported by public funds may only be partially compensated for by the presence of private nurseries, which are available at a higher cost. Moreover, the percentage of applications for entry to nursery schools, both public and private, remains very high, even in areas characterized by a greater presence of private services.

The evolution of child welfare services

Compared to other European countries, Italy moved late, and in fragmented and contradictory ways, towards the adoption of a child welfare policy that conceived a child as a subject with rights, and that is coherently planned and implemented. During the 1980s, the government established national committees specifically aimed at promoting special policies for children, but the main result of their work has been listing the areas of need, rather than improving child welfare services. Even now, policies targeting children are hardly separable from those targeting families. Moreover, Italian child policy follows the residual approach, which addresses only children in need, instead of considering the range of support required by families in

---

1   The average fertility rate for Italian women is only 1.4 children, which would be lower were it not for the presence of immigrant groups in Italy.

their daily life. This is consistent with *child-centredness as appearance* – child-centredness that is present in style but not in substance. Such an approach emphasizes the centrality of the child, but does not deliver the resources needed to support the required services. Saraceno (2002) argues that Italian policies are characterized by ambivalence, where the attention given only to malfunctioning families, together with the lack of public resources and the call for private solidarity within and between families, is the hallmark of the country's Catholic culture. This hides an attempt to control families. The Italian system is, moreover, fragmented, with regional variation of policies giving rise to unequal treatment and opportunities across the country. This regional inequality is related to the dualism of the Italian welfare system. It has worsened with the process of decentralization.

The evolution of child welfare services should be considered within this general framework. In the 1980s, Italy consolidated its welfare system in accordance with the universality model. Since 1978 the national health system has guaranteed medical assistance to all children, with a network of paediatricians and health visitors belonging to the public sector. For children at risk of psychological problems or disabilities there is a network of child psychiatric services. Family counselling centres (*consultori familiari*) were set up in 1975 as a result of the law on abortion and the 'promotion of conscious motherhood'. They are spread across the country in accordance with the population distribution. They are public services offering both medical and psychosocial support, dedicated to family planning; to the protection of motherhood and family; to counselling and mediation in family separation; to abortion for women and minors; to sexual education; to women's health; and to foster care and adoption. Over time, they have gradually changed, adopting a more social approach and less medical care, but they remain an important service for both families and women.

In the 1990s, the national health system was profoundly modified by the creation of a network of public companies – *Azienda Sanitaria Locales* [literally Local Health Agencies] (ASLs) – to deliver healthcare. These sought, as part of a managerialist agenda, to reduce the social component of provision in favour of strengthening the health component of services. The previous emphasis on the integration between social and health services was strongly reduced: healthcare services are now provided by the ASLs, while social and educational services are now delegated to local authorities.

The 1990s were also the decade in which important laws for child welfare were enacted. The 1989 *UN Convention on the Rights of the Child* (UNCRC) (UNICEF 2012) was ratified by Italy in 1991. In 1997 it established the National Observatory on Children, together with a National Study and Documentation Centre, which collects data and monitors the development of conditions for children and the implementation of the laws affecting them (Law 451 of 1997). In 1997 the law on the rights and opportunities of children and adolescents (Law 285) was also enacted. This was the first, path-breaking Italian law to address childhood in a global way. It targeted interventions not just at children in need but also children who live under 'normal conditions'; and it promoted the development and adoption of preventive strategies. This marked a cultural change; no longer is it just the family that is responsible for the care of children, for it is now the responsibility of Italian society to meet the demand for the education and socialization of children. This also marked a shift from the concept of the child as someone who will grow up to be an autonomous adult, to the idea of the child as an active subject who should be directly involved in actions that concern him or her (Bosisio 2006).

In the 2000s, child welfare services were caught in the separation between the partitioned social services and healthcare provision. At the same time, the implementation of neoliberal policies and the spread of managerialism were especially marked in some parts of the country. As ASLs are responsible for planning and purchasing services that are provided by other agencies, their direct engagement in the provision of health services provided by profit and non-profit hospitals and private agencies has reduced. Local authorities are increasingly building closer links with local housing, education and labour market services in relation to the provision of social care for children and families. In the second half of the 2000s, however, children's welfare services were also split into healthcare services and social services. With a centre-right government in power, the focus tends to move from the child to the family, which it valued for its 'private subjectivity' and its right to make decisions autonomously and freely. Resources have been shifted away from service provision to families by local authorities to the provision of private services purchased by tax-funded cash vouchers. Nevertheless, today the main issue under discussion is developments linked to the financial crisis and spending cuts in services for children and families. At issue is: What should be the minimum level of care that can be guaranteed throughout the country?

Welfare for children in need

Children in need of general assistance receive help through the health and the social service systems. All provision is free, or requires only a very small contribution, and services are activated on the basis of a parental request. The specific thresholds for support are determined nationally and locally, according to the multi-tier structure that Italy adopted in 2000. The national government has the duty to establish what minimum levels of assistance should be guaranteed in all parts of the country. The regional and local authorities have the responsibility of providing these services; the regional authorities provide mainly healthcare, while local authorities provide social services.

The threshold for administrative intervention is set locally, and local authorities, according to the national social services reform (Law 328 of 2000), have the duty to act in order to 'promote and support family responsibilities' (Articles 16 and 22). In particular, they have to facilitate the harmonization of working time and family care; to support single mothers; and to intervene in cases of children in distress, at risk or in danger. This is achieved through local support provided to the family, home care or placement with a foster family or in residential care. It is also the local authority's duty to promote the rights of children and adolescents. According to this law, a range of different providers can provide services, and the local authority has the task of the accreditation and evaluation of the interventions they provide.

Children in need of protection receive help in two different administrative settings. Local administrative protection is provided through the framework of the social services provided by local authorities and is based on self-referrals by the family, as well as by schools and other agencies. Judicial protection is granted in the form of a court order, which follows an inquiry, initiated by an alleged breach of the law, which assesses the risk to the child who may be in need of protection. After this, the court establishes what kind of intervention is required, the level of protection needed and the limitation of parental powers. In both contexts, local authorities are responsible for the delivery of services to the children. The social services system provides different kinds of help: social support and counselling, pedagogical support, linking with housing and education resources, home parental support (home visitors), foster care or residential care. Professionals involved in the provision of services are usually social workers, educators and psychologists.

Awareness surrounding the problem of children in need of protection, especially protection for children being abused or maltreated in the family, developed in Italy from the 1980s. The evolution of services for child protection can be summarized as taking place in different phases over three decades, which makes it possible to trace changes in the social and professional culture of child protection in Italy (Bertotti 2010).

In the 1980s, awareness was raised mainly due to the action of the AIPAI (*Associazione Italiana Prevenzione Abusi* [Italian Association for the Prevention of Child Abuse]) journal – *Il bambino incompiuto*. This led to the lively activity of the CBM (*Centro per il Bambino Maltrattato e la cura della crisi familiare* [Centre for Maltreated Children and Treatment of Family Crises]), a non-profit organization created in 1984 and strongly supported by Milan's city council. What soon followed was the first national child helpline, *Telefono Azzurro*, which had a strong focus on the protection of children, especially from physical abuse. Because of the medical and paedo-psychiatric approach of its founder, the CBM strongly emphasized the importance of connecting the protection of the child with the treatment of family relationships. This centre developed new methods of intervention and created the first Italian centre where residential care was integrated with family treatment.

This approach became a reference point for the development of Italian child protection services in the 1990s, which also saw some baseline theoretical developments. The first Italian publication on child protection was by Cirillo and Di Blasio (1986). They considered child abuse as a family problem that tends to be denied by the family. It is one that requires intervention according to a set of distinct steps: detection and assessment of harmful actions and danger; assessment of the level of protection needed for the child; protection of the child in order to stop the harm; and evaluation of both the possibility of returning their parental responsibilities to the parents, and the treatment. All these interventions were developed within the legal framework of the juvenile court, and include court orders that can impose the adoption of the child if the parents remain a risk to him or her. The whole system was founded on collaboration between the courts and local authority social services.

In the 1990s, specialized teams for abused children and child protection spread through the country. These welfare teams were set up within the framework of the public national health system, and often attached to the *consultori famigliari*. They are characterized by intervening only in the judicial context, under a court order, and are responsible for the assessment, evaluation and treatment both of the child and the parents. They are multidisciplinary and composed of social workers and psychologists. The development of a new professional awareness, together with the diffusion of public and private services, led also to the creation of a national network of professionals and services (*Coordinamento Italiano Servizi contro il Maltrattamento e l'Abuso all'Infanzia* [Italian Network of Agencies against Child Abuse and Maltreatment] (CISMAI)) that follows the principles articulated by the International Society for the Prevention of Child Abuse and Neglect (ISPCAN).

Special attention was also given in the 1990s to the phenomenon of child sexual abuse, incidences of which began to be detected, with cases being referred to the courts. Two laws were enacted to protect children from sexual abuse and exploitation: Law 66 of 1996, which established that sexual abuse was a crime against the person and not only a crime against morality; and Law 269 of 1998, which made illegal the exploitation of children through prostitution, child pornography and sex tourism. These were all defined as new forms of slavery. These laws clarified care professionals' obligations as public officers to report any suspicions of sexual abuse to the criminal court. Because child protection also embraces protection against sexual abuse, the local social services system became caught up in child protection scandals. Social workers were accused of failing in detecting such abuses; of exaggerating the facts when trying to protect children they believed to be at risk; and of exercising too much influence over such children, thereby making them focus in interviews on possible experiences of abuse. With these accusations came attacks on the specialization of the child protection teams. However, unlike some other European countries, in Italy the scandals were not used as an opportunity to explore in depth how the child protection system functioned and how it could be improved. On the contrary, they were used to feed the current political and ideological discourses, so although they influenced practice, they did so in a way that was not rational and well thought out.

In the 2000s, with the separation of the health and social care systems, especially in the North, came the withdrawal of specialized teams from the national health system and the return of their functions to local authorities. The purpose of this new arrangement was to bring the child protection teams into a closer relationship with local agencies in the community, to provide preventive interventions and, last but not least, to establish stronger control over expenditure, especially that related to children in residential care. The new local child and family services have a wide range of functions, both with respect to the judicial and the administrative protection of children, and to counselling and psychosocial support to families. Current practice is widely oriented to reducing placements in residential care, often because of cuts in spending rather than consideration of the real danger for the child. Moreover, in some areas, in order to cope with the complexity of difficult cases of child sexual abuse and other severe forms of violence, it has once again become necessary to rebuild a form of connection with health specialist agencies, with child psychiatric services and with family planning centres. The current debate is about who should provide different kinds and levels of assistance, both in social care and in healthcare.

Family policy and family values
As in other countries in Europe, the most common idea of family in Italy is that of the nuclear family: a couple with children, based on marriage as

a result of free choice between people. This idea is long standing, strongly rooted from the beginning to the second half of the nineteenth century, but is undergoing change in the light of the substantial contemporary changes occurring to family structures.

All data shows a decrease in the number of children and in the birth rate (which decreased from 1.6 to 1.4 children per woman in 2009; Italy, ISTAT 2009). This means that the number of children has decreased, and that approximately half of all children (53%) have only one brother or sister. The number of families where the parents are married and both are present has reduced; the number of single parents has increased from 6 per cent in 1981 to 9 per cent in 2001, and the number of marriages ending in separation has almost doubled, from 16 per cent in 1995 to 30 per cent in 2008.

The increase in family instability has led to a wide range of new forms of families: there are the 'blended' or 'jigsaw puzzle' families, where one or both parents have children from previous relationships as well as the current relationship. In such cases, children live with multiple parental relationships. Italian data shows that, in 2009, 6 per cent of couples were in re-constituted families, an increase of 2 per cent compared with 2005, a majority of whom (60%) are married and have children, which suggests that the birth of a child constitutes a strong drive to marry (Zanatta 2011). The most common family arrangement is an unmarried woman with a divorced man. The majority of children are born to such families. From a psychological point of view, the complexity of re-constituted families is linked to the lack of a cultural tradition to help in building these new relationships, and also because of very limited fine-tuning of the legislation.

The number of children born outside marriage is also increasing, although Italy is below the European average. In 2011, 38 per cent of children were born outside marriage, rising from 8 per cent in 1993 through to 22 per cent in 2008. This figure is higher in the North, where in some regions it reaches 30 per cent, but much lower in the South. Italian law provides for substantial equality between children born inside or outside marriage; however, there are some areas of rights that remain uncovered, such as the rules on legacies, and there is also a lexical, linguistic difference between *legitimate* children born in marriage and *natural* children born out of marriage. The European Community called upon Italy because the use of two different words is regarded as discriminatory. Moreover, the custody of children born from unmarried couples is ruled by the Juvenile Court instead of the Civil Court, as happens for the married parents.

Another important change concerns the intra-family role of men and women. With the increase in female employment (between 1988 and 2001 the economic activity rate of women increased from 40 per cent to 60 per cent), the man is often no longer the only family breadwinner, and more and more frequently men are dedicating themselves to childcare (Facchini 2008). The number of fathers who take care of children has increased from 42 per cent in 1988 to 55 per cent in 2008 (Zanatta 2011). Nevertheless, the rural tradition in Italy still maintains a role in giving importance to the ties between members of the nuclear and the extended family: not only in the affective dimension, but also in relation to the economic and social dimensions. The weight of family bonds led some scholars to speak of 'familism'. This supports the idea that the woman has the duty to care for children. While of diminishing importance over recent decades, it is still a deeply rooted value, especially in the South. The idea of family is also influenced by Catholic culture. During the 1970s, the Catholic Church strongly opposed the referendum on divorce and abortion and, more recently, it has strenuously hampered the law on assisted fertilization and the recognition of equal rights to non-married couples.

The representation of good parenting is also in transition. On the one hand, the traditional view in which the mother is responsible for the physical and emotional care of children, and the father is the repository of authority and codes of obedience, remains deeply rooted. On the other hand, profound change in the composition of families and economic changes have introduced a new image of the role of men: the care of children is commonly divided between father and mother, and the engagement of step-parents and extended families is quite frequent (Zanatta 2011). However, research shows that even if work roles and the care of children are more evenly shared, the change is partial and ambivalent: the marriage relationship still does not seem to be characterized by equality, and the management of the family's finances is not always shared. Indeed, some scholars have suggested these changes may be one of the factors contributing to an increase in domestic violence (Facchini 2008).

Having said that, overall the prevalent conception of good parenting consists of behaviour capable of nurturing children, and providing a safe and protective family environment. This process-based view of parenting, as a dynamic and adaptive process that families go through, is gaining influence. Italian culture generally seems oriented to highlight the resilience of families rather than their weaknesses and deficiencies. In the Italian professional culture, the concept of family is not related to the presence of a marriage; nevertheless it still tends to highlight deficits and deviance from norms (Fruggeri 2005).

Regarding the role of family and extended family care, Italy has a familistic welfare structure, based on the concept that the family is responsible for the wellbeing of its members. In this sense, it is suggested that the family has to be seen not only as a subject with needs, but also as a resource. This position may be criticized because it can justify the abandoning of the family, leaving it to discharge alone its duty of care to its children (Ferrario 2011). When parents are unable to care for their children, it is expected that the extended family steps in and helps. This is considered normal – a moral duty. Studies on the relational networks of families show that the extended family is the first resource that is called on for help, and indeed, if this does not happen, it is seen as a sign of problems in family relationships. The legal framework is consistent with this approach. The law on adoption provides that, before 'freeing for adoption' a child, all relatives, including those to the fourth degree, should be consulted.

Legal framework

The Italian Constitution (Article 29) recognizes the rights of the family as a 'natural society', founded on marriage and the equality between spouses ('the marriage is based on the moral and juridical equality of the spouses'), and their duty (and right) 'to support, maintain and educate their children, even if born *outside* marriage' (emphasis added). It establishes the duty of the state to protect and safeguard the family, providing measures to 'remove obstacles and support the family in the fulfilment of its duties', with particular consideration given to large families. It also establishes that parents have the 'duty to support, train and educate their children, taking into account their capabilities, natural inclinations and aspirations'; for example, they are required to send their children to school, to have them vaccinated, and not leave children unattended.

After the Second World War, Italy went through a vigorous process of modernizing its family law, with mixed results. The reforms of the divorce and separation law were issued in 1970 (Law 898), followed in 1975 by a general reform of family law (Law 151), which introduced more equality between the spouses, both with respect to children and the economic management of the family. The laws on divorce and separation, enacted in 1975 and 1987 respectively, provide that separation of married partners takes place in two stages: first the separation, and only later the divorce, with a waiting time of three years; and only divorce allows re-marriage. Both phases must be made legitimate through civil court action. The separation can be consensual when both spouses agree on the terms of the separation; or judicial, when the spouses disagree and the court decides the conditions of separation. In the presence of children, the court shall make its decisions based on 'the best interest of the child'.

Other steps in the modernization of family law were changes to the law on abortion in 1978 (Law 194), which permitted the voluntary interruption of pregnancy and established the institutions of the *consultori famigliari*, with the aim of supporting women in their choice, informing them of their rights, and supporting family planning and motherhood. More recently there have been other laws that have influenced family support provision. The already-existing parental leave for the mother was extended to the father and adoptive parents (Law 53 of 2000), so recognizing a specific role for fathers. The law on shared custody in separations (Law 54 of 2006) establishes that, in the case of divorce, the court must consider, as a priority, the custody of children to both parents instead of custody to one parent only (once mainly the mother). This law has profoundly changed divorced families: in 2008, 79 per cent of court disposals have been for shared custody, while exclusive custody went to the mother in 19 per cent of cases, compared with 80 per cent in the period before the change in the law. Laws were enacted permitting the removal of a violent person from the home (Law 154 of 2001) and establishing that stalking a spouse is a crime (Law 11 of 2009). These laws tried to govern the new forms of families, and aimed to find a balance between the protection of family unity and the protection of the rights of each individual within the family. Regarding children, the legal framework provides that intervention in family life is necessary in those cases where the safety of the child is threatened by the parents' behaviour, as well as in custody cases in separation and divorce.

There are three courts involved in family and child matters. The ordinary court in the civil division deals with the separation and divorce of spouses. The ordinary court in the criminal division deals with the prosecution of adults who commit crimes against children, such as sexual abuse or other kinds of serious maltreatment. The juvenile court is divided into three sections: the civil section, which intervenes in the relations between parents and children and regulates the separation of unmarried parents; the penal section, for minors who commit crimes (in Italy children are punishable only if they are over 14 years of age); and the administrative section, which deals with minors with behaviour problems, 'irregular in conduct and character', whose parents are absent or unable to deal with them.

The Italian legal framework that defines the whole child protection system is quite fragmented and unclear. This includes that aspect relating to the duties and responsibilities of institutions and agencies involved when a child is in danger or at risk. Different legal sources of the framework have to be restructured periodically, and the absence of a comprehensive Children Act is a critical element that is lacking in the Italian system. This has been noted by the Supervisory Committee of the *UN Convention on the Rights of the Child* (UN, OHCHR, Supervisory Committee on the Rights of the Child 2011). Having said that, the Italian Civil Code qualifies and defines negative parental behaviour, which justifies the intervention of the court, as behaviour that leads to 'serious injuries' or which is 'detrimental' to the child (Article 330). In these cases, the court can remove the parents' parental powers, order the child's removal from the family, and assign the child to the care of the local authority. It can also establish obligations to be placed on the parents.

Laws relating to foster care and adoption, enacted initially in 1983, were integrated in 2001. Italian law provides that a child can be adopted, replacing his or her biological parents with an adoptive relationship. The adoption process progresses through declaration of a 'state of moral and material abandonment' of the child by the parents; the definitions of 'abandonment' (a state of neglect) and 'serious injury' (harm) have been introduced to allow for wider margins of discretion.

According to some (Moro 2002; Ronfani *et al.* 2004), the decision to adopt these wide definitions of the thresholds for intervention was due to a belief that juvenile judges should have flexibility of action in order to respond to the individual situation of each child. This perspective is coherent with the idea of a 'reconciler' judge (Moro 2002), which implies a collaborative relationship between care professionals and judges. Nevertheless, this legal approach has been criticized by others on the grounds that it gives excessive power to the court – or to the experts and professionals who collaborate with judges in making decisions about parenting and family privacy. In recent years there has been a demand for more respect for the position of the parents; therefore the judges of the juvenile court have taken up a third-party position, distancing themselves from collaboration with children's services.

Following the Strasbourg Children's Rights Convention in 2001, Italy has introduced some rules in order to guarantee the rights of the child to be heard and to be represented in the civil process, with legal assistance. The juvenile court is a specialized court that makes its decisions collegially, with a council chamber composed of four judges, two magistrates and two lay judges who are expert in matters related to family and children. Court orders are compulsory on parents, in the sense that the failure to comply with them, or the absence of improvements in the situation of the child, can lead to the child's removal from parental authority and subsequent adoption. The intervention of the juvenile court is activated by the prosecutor's office, which receives referrals from family members or from local authorities. Children's services have a duty to conduct inquiries and any assessment requested by the attorney or the court.

Social workers have an obligation to report to the court all situations in which children are severely neglected or in a state of abandonment, as well as reporting suspected crimes against children to the criminal courts.

The obligation to report – mandatory reporting – has been the subject of discussion in relation to who is obliged to report such concerns – social workers or other professionals – and in relation to the specific wording, including the vagueness of the term 'abandoned'. Now it has been made clear that the obligation applies to all those who are 'in charge of a public service', while the definition of 'a state of neglect' remains unspecified and discretionary by choice, in order to guarantee the capacity to respond to different situations (Pocar and Ronfani 2008).

Italian law also provides for protection of minors through the criminal courts, and some behaviours are considered as crimes in the Criminal Code. These include: sexual abuse (Article 609); abuse of the means of correction or discipline (Article 571); maltreatment in the family or towards children (Article 572); and the corruption of minors (Article 573), which now are all covered under Italian law. It also provides for prosecution under the law on violation of the obligations of family care (Article 570). Finally, local authorities have the duty to intervene in emergencies (Article 403), as they have responsibility for intervening even in the absence of a court order if a child is found in an 'unhealthy or dangerous place', with subsequent verification by the juvenile court.

The state as a parent: The role of the state and the institutionalization of children

Following the Constitution, and in line with the concept of a residual welfare system, it is taken for granted that the state should intervene when children lack adequate family support. The state has responsibility for children until they reach adulthood and the age of majority, which in Italy is 18 years (and in some special cases it is provided that the child can receive assistance until they reach 21 years of age).

State care provision for abandoned children has changed greatly since the Second World War, in line with constitutional changes. This evolution can be divided into three periods. In the first period, until the end of the 1970s, children in care were housed in big institutions, accommodating hundreds of children, and managed by national bodies, either religious or secular. These children came from both poor and large families, and often from single-parent families. Placement in these cases was voluntary in that the parents requested it. In the 1980s and 1990s, there was a movement against these big 'totalizing' institutions: many studies highlighted the damage that could occur to the development of children as a result of the living conditions in large institutions. Following this, many small residential care units – *comunità educative* (educational communities) or *casa famiglia* (family homes) – commonly catering for approximately 10 children, developed within both the public and not-for-profit sector and were run by professional educators. These cared largely for children from families with severe difficulties, but they did take in children in need of protection who were removed from their homes, following a court order.

During the 1980s and 1990s there was a clear statement made about the priority being given to children being raised in family settings adequate to their needs, rather than in institutions. This was repeatedly expressed in laws on foster care and adoption. Since 1983, and especially after 2000, the use of family foster care for children in need has increased, and in 2001 a policy to close all big institutions within five years was launched.

In 2006, five years later, the number of children in care had fallen to around 25,000 children, of whom 10,000 (40%) were in foster care and 15,000 (60%) were in residential care; 50 per cent of the latter (7,500) were still in big institutions (Belotti 2009). However, this downturn did not continue. A survey carried out in 2008 (Belotti 2009) revealed that the number of children in care had increased to 32,000 children, with a notable increase in children placed in foster families (up 65 per cent, to 16,800) but with a stable trend for children in residential care in family group homes (around 15,000). This data corresponds to 3 children in every 1,000, which is less than other European countries. Belotti (2009) argues that this upward trend can be related to the weakness of the policies for prevention, and poor implementation of interventions aimed at supporting families.

Family foster care had some aspects that attracted criticism. In Italy, the underlying philosophy of family foster care is that it is a temporary measure, which should last no more than two years, and which is conceptualized as mutual support between families. In foster care, unlike adoption, it is expected that a relationship between the natural parents and foster parents should be maintained. However, these expectations about the short-term nature of placements were not confirmed by recent research which shows that placements in foster families last more than two years for most fostered children (56%) and more than four years for many children (33%). In order to respond to the different needs of children in care, besides traditional foster care, new forms of care and care support have come into being: specialized foster care and professional foster families, as well as associations of foster families and networks of foster families for mutual support. The data shows that there are a number of children for whom neither full adoption nor traditional family foster care is possible. This has opened up a debate on the establishment of a form of a 'mild' or open adoption, in which new parents adopt the child, but the possibility of maintaining a relationship with the natural parents is kept open. The debate is still ongoing.

The other significant ongoing debate is about the triangular relationship between the justice system, families and local social services. Since 2000, the duty to report child abuse, and the responsibility of the local authority for emergency protection, have been two issues about which there has been visible tension between the judicial and welfare systems. Many reports by social services have been rejected by the prosecutor's office, and some orders for urgent protection have been rejected, showing a misalignment between the criteria used by professionals and the criteria used by the judges in determining the status of risk or danger to a child and, thus, the threshold for compulsory intervention (Bertotti 2010). Those tensions are indicators of a decreasing level of consensus about the role that the state – the justice and the public welfare systems – should play in child protection: When, and in what circumstances, should the state have the right to intervene in the private lives of families? For some, the important rights to be protected are the family's rights. This indicates a reduction in the influence of state administration over the family, especially compulsory intervention by social services, and advocates leaving relationships within the family to be dealt with by the courts and judicial processes (Pocar and Ronfani 2008). Those supporting this argument also consider it necessary to achieve a greater separation between social services and the justice system, calling for a more proactive and independent role by the former in promoting the welfare of children. Social services, for their part, denounce this view, arguing that children's rights are not currently being protected and, in view of the shortage of resources, referral to the court is a way of enforcing the provision of the services needed by children. For others, the withdrawal of the state from intervention in families corresponds to a renewed defence of the family as a group, but leaving the weakest members within the family without protection. Thus, as public responsibility for the protection of children declines, the family is being abandoned in their time of need, being required to draw upon its own efforts to address its difficulties alone.

Conclusion

In welfare system studies, Italy has been included, together with Spain, Portugal and Greece, in the so-called 'Mediterranean model' welfare state (Ferrera 1998). Its key elements are identified in the political and institutional characteristics of the state: the presence of the Catholic Church with its value system, and the welfare role of the family. Italy is considered to be a familistic state, where the family is given not only a great emphasis in political speeches, but also a key role in the development of solidarity and kinship (Naldini 2003). Due to the presence of the Catholic Church's headquarters – the Vatican – within its territory, Italy has been strongly influenced by Catholic culture on moral issues relating to the family. This manifests itself in the definition of social norms and prescriptions for family behaviour, encouraging obligations and family solidarity, and seeing all forms of public intervention in social reproduction and care as 'interference', especially for children and the elderly (Saraceno 1998). The reforms of the 1970s that challenged the moral primacy of traditional family structure led to a process of democratization of the roles of family members, both in the relationships between spouses, and between parent and child. During this period a series of laws were enacted relating to family law and to the organization of welfare services. These broke with the logic of the closed nature of the institution of the family and opened it up to a range of possible interventions.

The care of children is no longer considered solely a duty of the family, especially the mother, as shown by the expansion of service organizations. The educational function of the family has been delegated to the state, at least in part, through the expansion of services such as childcare centres, kindergartens and full-time primary schools. Family planning centres, apart from being places where people can make choices with respect to their sexuality and motherhood, are places where, through multi-professional teams, it is possible to deal with relationship problems, conflict and child abuse.

Interestingly, Italy's delay in becoming aware of the problem of child abuse could be tied to the idea that children are objects owned by the family, or that motherhood – long idolized and, thus, held to be sacrosanct – could not, by definition, have any characteristics that would lead to the neglect, mistreatment and abuse of children. Admitting that the family could be prejudicial to its children involved colliding head-on with a real taboo in Italian society. In terms of intervention, once the problem was considered and discussed, Italy tried to combine the security model, typical of Anglo-Saxon countries, with the model of family support, typical of the Scandinavian countries. Alongside a commitment to recognize and diagnose risk situations, and highlight indicators that would allow a proper assessment, Italy developed programmes and services intended to work on improving care and offering family therapy (Fargion 2008).

The family was placed at the centre of social policy for the first time with the introduction of Law 328 of 2000 – a 'framework for the realization of an integrated system of social service interventions'. This expresses its true historical and innovative importance. Livia Turco (2000, p.1), the minister who presented this law in Parliament, said that welfare of families and of social policies is founded alongside, and linked to, a system of health and social security welfare whose objective is 'preventing disadvantages, opposing poverty, helping whoever is in difficulty, and improving the quality-of-life of everyone'. Article 16 gives specific importance to this approach, through valuing and supporting family responsibilities. It underlines how the protection of the rights of citizens cannot be separated from their interrelationship with their family contexts, 'as the contexts of [family] life and relationships are recognized, safeguarded and realized in their functions and potential contribution' (Manoukian 2000, p.25). Often the subjects of laws and policies have been considered in an abstract way, detached from their family context, and from the interactions that characterize their daily life, while the family has been considered as a simple background point of reference.

This shift of the focus of attention from *individuals in families* to *people in complex social contexts* moves attention from the individual as a distinct entity, to the individual as part of a family nucleus, and to the family nucleus as a form of social organization that may be hit by critical events or hardship. Two terms used in the law, 'valuing' and 'support', point out that the family is not always able to make use of its resources and competencies and may sometimes need support if it is to make use of its own resources. It is not always able to identify these resources and abilities from within itself when it requires support. Both discomfort and suffering can develop in the context of the family, and those who should have the functions of care and protection of the weaker members of the family can find themselves structuring relationships characterized by carelessness, abuse and violence.

The intention that the family should still have a central position in policies is re-asserted through the identification of certain specific functions of the family. These are both internal – education and care of its members, in times of crisis and in daily life – and external – promoting social cohesion. It is expected that families can create wider intersecting or interlocking networks providing mutual help and association in order to interact with institutional systems, also offering an opportunity to provide services themselves or participate in the evaluation of the quality of service provision. Article 16 (Law 328 of 2000) gives specific importance to this approach through valuing and promoting the support of family responsibilities; it underlines how the protection of citizens' rights cannot be separated from the state's involvement in the family context of citizens' lives, 'as contexts of life and of relationships that are recognized, safeguarded and promoted in their function and their potentiality' (Manoukian 2000, p.35).

While the centre-left government recognized the importance of state intervention in supporting families through both the integration of different functions and by giving attention to family issues, under the centre-right government the emphasis on the centrality of the family was to cover up the withdrawal of some public functions in response to the financial crisis of the welfare state. The family is now recognized only if it has a formal structure established by civil or religious marriage, ignoring the fact that the family in Italy today has a wide range of different structures. This narrow interpretation means there is a lack of recognition of many family systems, and thus introduces many problems in relation to children's rights. Moreover, family associations (such as *Forum delle Famiglie*), which represent centre-right family values, are using the centrality of the family as a justification for assigning all responsibility of the care and protection of children to the family. This disguises the residual role of the state, and its ideological position that the state should not be involved in the private family's fulfilment of its duties (Donati and Prandini 2008).

To conclude, at the moment in Italy there is no real and organized national family policy. Some interesting questions have been posed by Saraceno (2009): Who has responsibility for children in terms of their financial care and healthcare, inside and outside the family? Where are the boundaries between families' responsibilities and those of the community, and how may these be exercised? Differences in approach to child welfare policy between political parties depend largely on their goals, illuminated by the answers to the questions above. There is also the question of the relative importance of other issues: increasing child poverty; growing inequalities between those who have children and those without children; investment in human capital for the future; equality of opportunity for children; the low rates of birth and fertility; and enhancing the employment of mothers.

Different policy packages seen in Italy over recent years have created distinct and different opportunity structures for families and for fathers and mothers. Each implies different ways of understanding the respective roles of families and communities, and the roles of fathers and mothers concerning children's wellbeing. Moreover, the same policy may be argued, and be proposed, for different purposes. This is the case, for instance, with respect to provision of children's services such as preschools. These can be justified in terms of the support they provide for parents, or by reference to the care needs of children and their cognitive development.

The current financial crisis has produced very significant cuts in all social policies for children. The effects of these cuts will only be seen clearly in the future. At the same time, the problems of families are becoming more and more serious: the increase in family poverty and the increased difficulties of families maintaining an acceptable standard of living means that the needs of families are given priority over the demands of child protection. The term 'child maltreatment' has almost disappeared from public discourse, although there has been an increase in episodes of fatal family violence; attention to children decreases and society seems no longer to be able to keep a focus on them. In this light, the strong centring of policy on the family masks a real divestment of public responsibility and a return to a pre-modern vision in which the family (or the tribe) is the only place for care and for social regulation.

Faced with this withdrawal of public support, families group together with the aim of becoming *active* subjects of welfare policies. The Third Sector organizations and the National Union of Municipalities (NUM) are very much involved in a fight against the risk of a gradual erosion of the state's commitment to children. Their collective aim is to safeguard the maintenance of financial resources for children. Ten years ago, the group of organizations responsible for preparing non-governmental reports on the implementation of the 1989 UN Convention on Children's Rights was formed, and in 2012 they concluded their report denouncing dramatic cuts in resources. They asked the recently appointed National Ombudsman for Childhood to monitor the results and draw up an evaluation of the impact of the cuts. In the same spirit, the NUM has asked for the establishment of defined minimum levels of provision, and have denounced the very real risk of not being able to provide adequate social services. The challenge that Italy will face in the very near future is to rebuild a welfare system that will pay attention to equality across the country and between generations, that will be able to guarantee the inclusion of immigrant families and children, that will safeguard the rights of children threatened by poverty, and that will address the general public's low level of awareness of their plight.

References

Ascoli, U. (2010) 'Le politiche di selfare.' In M. Annick and G. Vicarelli (ed.) *Lo stato del paese agli inizi del XXI secolo* (Associazione Italiana di Sociologia). Milano, IT: Franco Angeli.

Ascoli, U. and Ranci, C. (eds) (2003) *Dilemmas of the Welfare Mix.* New York: Kluwer-Plenum.

Belotti, V. (2009) 'Introduzione.' In V. Belotti (ed.) *Accogliere bambini, biografie, storie e famiglie: le politiche di cura, protezione e tutela in Italia* (Questioni e Documenti Quaderno n. 48 del Centro Nazionale Documentazione e Analisi per l'infanzia e l'adolescenza). Firenze, IT: Istituto degli Innocenti.

Bertotti, T. (2010) 'Servizi per la tutela dei minori: evoluzione e mutamenti.' In *Autonomie locali e servizi sociali 2.* Bologna, IT: Il Mulino.

Bosisio, R. (2006) 'Il percorso dell'infanzia nel mondo dei diritti.' In F. Mazzucchelli (ed.) *Viaggio attraverso i diritti dell'infanzia e dell'adolescenza.* Milano, IT: Franco Angeli.

Caritas (2011) *Child Poverty: The State of Play in Europe.* Brussels, BE: Caritas Europa. Available at: www.caritas-europa.org/module/FileLib/stateofplay.pdf.

Cirillo, S. and Di Blasio, P. (1986) *La famiglia maltrattante.* Milano, IT: Raffaello Cortina.

Donati, P. and Prandini, R. (eds) (2008) *La cura della famiglia e il mondo del lavoro: un piano di politiche familiari* (Osservatorio Nazionale della Famiglia). Milano, IT: Franco Angeli.

Esping Andersen, G. (1990) *The Three Worlds of Welfare Capitalism.* Cambridge: Policy Press.

EURISPES (Istituto di Studi Politici Economici e Sociali) (2012) *Italy Report 2012.* Available at: www.eurispes.it.

Facchini, C. (2008) *Conti aperti: denaro, asimmetrie di coppia e solidarietà tra generazioni.* Bologna, IT: Il Mulino.

Fargion, S. (2008) 'Reflections on social work's identity: International themes in Italian practitioners' representation of social work.' *International Social Work 51,* 2, 206–219.

Ferrario, P. (2011) *Politica dei servizi sociali: strutture, trasformazioni, legislazione.* Roma, IT: Carocci Faber Editore.

Ferrera, M. (1998) *Le trappole del welfare.* Bologna, IT: Il Mulino.

Ferrera, M. (2005) *The Boundaries of Welfare.* Oxford: Oxford University Press.

Fruggeri, L. (2005) *Diverse normalità: psicologia sociale delle relazioni famigliari.* Roma, IL: Carocci.

Italy, ISTAT (Istituto Nazionale di Statistica) (2009) *Indagine multiscopo annuale sulle famiglie: aspetti della vita quotidiana.* Available at: www3.istat.it/dati/catalogo/20111216_00.

Italy, ISTAT (Istituto Nazionale di Statistica) (2011) *Italian Statistical Yearbook 2011.* Available at: http://en.istat.it/dati/catalogo/20110617_00.

Manoukian, F. (2000) 'La valorizzazione della famiglia.' *Prospettive Sociali e Sanitarie* 20/22.

Mayntz, R. (2003) 'New Challenges to Governance Theory.' In H.P. Bang (ed.) *Governance as Social and Political Communication.* Manchester, UK: Manchester University Press.

Moro, A.C. (2002) *Manuale di diritto minorile.* Bologna, IL: Zanichelli.

Naldini, M. (2003) *The Family in the Mediterranean Welfare States.* London: Frank Cass.

Pace, E. (2010) 'La geografia socio-religiosa dell'Italia che cambia.' In M. Annick and G. Vicarelli (eds) *Lo stato del paese agli inizi del XXI secolo* (Associazione Italiana di Sociologia, Mosaico Italia). Milano, IT: Franco Angeli.

Paci, M. (2005) *Nuovi lavori, nuovo welfare: sicurezza e libertà nella società attiva.* Bologna, IT: Il Mulino.

Pavolini, E. (2003) *Le nuove politiche social: i sistemi di welfare fra istituzioni e società civile.* Bologna, IT: Il Mulino.

Pocar, V. and Ronfani, P. (2008) *La famiglia e il diritto, nuova edizione riveduta e ampliata.* Roma, IT: Laterza.

Ronfani, P. (2004) *Giustizia, famiglia e cultura giuridica* (Working Paper del Dipartimento di Studi Sociali e Politici n.7/2004). Milan, IT: University of Milan. Available at: www.socpol.unimi.it/papers/2004-4-7_Paola%20Ronfani.pdf.

Saraceno, C. (1998) *Mutamenti della famiglia e politiche sociali in Italia.* Bologna, IT: Il Mulino.

Saraceno, C. (ed.) (2002) *Social Assistance Dynamics in Europe: National and Local Poverty Regimes.* Bristol, UK: Policy Press.

Saraceno, C. (2009) 'Le politiche della famiglia in Europa: tra convergenza e diversificazione.' *Stato e Mercato 85,* April, 3–31.

Turco, L. (2000) 'Una legge della dignità sociale.' *Prospettive Sociali e Sanitarie* 20/22.

UN, Office of the High Commissioner for Human Rights (OHCHR), Supervisory Committee on the Rights of the Child (2011) *Consideration of Reports submitted by States Parties under article 44 of the Convention (CRC/C/ITA/CO/3–4).* Geneva: United Nations.

UNICEF (2012) *United Nations Convention on the Rights of the Child.* Available at: www.unicef.org/crc/index_30229.html.

Zanatta, A.L. (2011) *Nuove madri e nuovi padri.* Bologna, IT: Il Mulino.

6

Romania

Contiu Şoitu and Daniela-Tatiana Şoitu

Introduction: The social, political, religious and cultural context

Child welfare has been the topic of constant debate in Romania in recent decades. Before 1990, child protection was provided under pro-birth policies founded on a punitive package of legislative measures. The negative consequences of this meant that Romania's abandoned children made the headlines of the international media in the 1990s. Efforts made to address this situation have been directed at rebuilding and modernizing the social welfare and social protection systems, with child welfare a priority. The recent economic crisis has tended to bring changes in perspective and to suggest – increasingly strongly – that the current welfare state model needs to be re-thought or replaced with something that would fit Romania's limited budget. Demographic future realities – not at all optimistic for Romania – do not leave much space for manoeuvre and make it likely that debates on the birth rate and child protection will remain in the spotlight.

Romania became a member of the European Union on 1 January 2007. It has an area of 238,391 square kilometres (ranked seventh largest in the European Union). By total Gross Domestic Product (GDP), Romania is the seventeenth largest economy in the EU and twenty-second largest in Europe. GDP per head is estimated for 2011 at 6,400 Euros. In the 2010 *Global Human Development Report*, Romania is ranked fifty-first in terms of human development, which places it in the high human development category (UNDP 2011).

Total population is approximately 21.4 million, of which 4.14 million (19.2%) are children (EC, Eurostat 2012; UNDP 2011). According to provisional data published by the National Statistics Institute (Romania, Insee 2011), Romania's stable population is just over 19 million, with the major ethnic groups being Romanians (88.6%), Hungarians (6.5%) and Romas (3.2%). Other ethnic groups larger than 20,000 include Ukrainians, Germans, Turks, Lipovan Russians and Tatars. The fertility rate is decreasing, with 1.4 births per woman in 2009. The birth rate, at 10.6 per cent in 2008, is slightly lower than the mortality rate, at 11.84 per cent, resulting in a shrinking and ageing population. After the Romanian Revolution of 1989, a significant number of Romanians emigrated to EU and other countries in search of better working conditions and study opportunities. The number of Romanians abroad is estimated to be between 4 and 12 million people (including those of mixed origin).

Romanian religious affiliations, according to the 2002 Census, are: Eastern Orthodox (86.8%), Protestant (7.5%), Roman Catholic (4.7%) and other (mostly Muslim) (1%).

The total expenditure on social protection in Romania represents a much lower percentage of GDP than the average for the EU. Thus, in 2009, only Latvia spent a lower proportion of GDP on social protection, whereas in Denmark – the highest-ranking country – the proportion was almost double (see Table 6.1). The increase in the relative importance of social protection expenditure in 2009, as compared with 2008, can be explained by reference to overall state budget cuts and the deferment of cuts in social protection expenditure until early 2010.

Romanian expenditure on families and children as given in Table 6.2 would seem to reflect an unexpectedly good situation, with Romania being above the EU average. Unfortunately, this is a statistical anomaly, as proven by the data in Table 6.3. This shows that the social protection expenditure per capita is one-third of the EU average.

Table 6.1 Expenditure on social protection as a percentage of GDP in the European region: 2000–2009

	2000	2001	2002	2003	2004	2005	2006	2007	2008	2009
Euro area (17 countries)	26.6	26.7	27.3	27.7	27.6	27.6	27.2	26.8	27.5p	29.5p
Euro area (16 countries)	26.7	26.8	27.3	27.7	27.6	27.7	27.2	26.8	27.5p	30.2p
Denmark	28.9	29.2	29.7	30.9	30.7	30.2	29.2	28.8	29.6	30.2p
Latvia	15.7	14.7	14.3	14.0	13.2	12.8	12.7	11.3	12.7	33.4
Romania	13.0	12.8	13.6	13.0	12.8	13.4	12.8	13.6	14.3	16.8

Source: Eurostat

Notes: Expenditure on social protection includes: social benefits; administration costs, which represent the costs charged to the scheme for its management and administration; and other expenditure, which consists of miscellaneous expenditure by social protection schemes (payment of property income and other). It is calculated in current prices.

p = provisional

Table 6.2 Expenditure on social benefits for families and children as a percentage of total benefits in selected countries: 2000–2009

	2000	2001	2002	2003	2004	2005	2006	2007	2008	2009
EU (27 countries)	na	na	na	na	na	7,958	7,855	8,186p	8,032p	7,989p
Euro area (17 countries)	8,450	8,319	8,427	8,403	8,344	8,157	8,051	8,166	8,080p	8,054p
Euro area (16 countries)	8,449	8,318	8,425	8,402	8,341	8,155	8,048	8,164	8,076p	8,050p
Luxembourg	16,614	15,917	16,657	17,577	17,274	16,875	16,920	16,609	19,798	17,806
Poland	4,985	4,777	4,690	4,300	4,540	4,380	4,327	4,468	4,022	3,883
Romania	11,809	12,014	12,586	11,276	12,467	13,932	14,120	12,679	10,577	10,043

Source: Eurostat

Notes: Social benefits consist of transfers, in cash or in kind, by social protection schemes to households and individuals to relieve them of the burden of a defined set of risks or needs. The social risks covered are sickness, disability, old age, survivors, family and children, unemployment, housing and social exclusion not elsewhere classified.

p = provisional

na = not available

Table 6.3 Social benefits per head of population in selected countries: 2001–2009

	2001	2002	2003	2004	2005	2006	2007	2008	2009
EU (27 countries)	na	na	na	na	466	477	505p	515p	533p
Euro area (17 countries)	470	500	509	521	529	541	570	576	594
Euro area (16 countries)	471	501	510	521	529	542	571	578	595
Luxembourg	1,507	1,733	1,959	2,069	2,051	2,164	2,160	2,739	2,537
Poland	92	96	90	97	97	101	108	103	107
Romania	83	101	93	115	144	159	173	174	185

Source: Eurostat

Notes: Social benefits consist of transfers, in cash or in kind, by social protection schemes to households and individuals to relieve them of the burden of a defined set of risks or needs.

p = provisional

na = not available

The evolution of child welfare services

For centuries, close family ties were considered a characteristic trait of the Romanian people. Fifty years of authoritarian rule have created a bleak picture, shown often in the Western media. Over 100,000 neglected, abused and disabled children were left in institutions reminiscent of those in the Dark Ages. The current situation in Romania, however, shows a very different picture from that of 40 years ago.

In the 1970s, the Romanian birth rate policy was aimed at increasing the population from 23 to 30 million. Unlike the policies of other European states, Romania pursued compliance through coercion. Thus, abortion was outlawed, and doctors that broke this injunction faced prison sentences; sex education was ignored and most methods of contraception were inaccessible; pregnancy checks were carried out in factories and workplaces; pregnant women were monitored until they gave birth; and single people over 25 and married couples that could not medically prove they had fertility problems were subject to additional taxation of up to 30 per cent of their income (Haupt 1987). Another contemporary policy that was accused of having had a negative impact on a family's ability to care for their children was that of 'urban systematization'. In designated rural and urban areas, families were moved into cramped apartments, which often lacked many required utilities. Rural–urban migration also had negative effects on traditional supportive relations within the extended family. The worst-affected aspects were the practices concerning the care for small children and disabled individuals. Accelerated payment of foreign debt and the agricultural policy were blamed for the scarcity of foodstuffs and for the quasi-generalized state of poverty. Having two working parents meant less care for children in the family. The fact that women returned to their jobs some 3–6 months after confinement resulted in an increase in the number of all-day crèches and weekly crèches with semi-residential status (Johnson, Edwards and Puwak 1993).

The social and economic situation of the state affected the ability of families to care for their young children and for disabled children and adults. Despite the provision of a range of social services, covering healthcare, education, pensions and housing, the problems associated with childrearing were solved only through institutionalization,[1] one consequence of which was that institutionalized children learned to walk and talk much later, a product of the lack of normal parental care. The tendency was to direct children towards hospitals or residential institutions whenever any problems arose in connection with their health or in their family environment because

---

1   For the period before 1990, the authors could not find any official statistics concerning the number of children cared for in institutions in Romania.

physicians were punished if a child died while under their care (Institutul mamei şi copilului 1991). Children with chronic health problems were often hospitalized indefinitely due to lack of medication and inadequate medical treatment.

Poverty and related issues are now considered to be the main cause of child institutionalization at the time. In many cases, families wanted their children, but the economic situation made bringing them up impossible. This meant that, for some families, care institutions operated like a sort of boarding school (Stephenson *et al.* 1997). Many children, however, were in institutions because of problems that amplified the effects of poverty: family abandonment; family breakdown due to separation, divorce or death; and domestic violence, with the latter usually being a phenomenon that only occurs in poor families.

The state's approach to the role and responsibilities of fathers was also a factor in the institutionalization of many children. Frequently, children were abandoned because they were the result of unwanted pregnancies or because they were not recognized by their fathers. In the 1990s, a man wishing to be relieved of any financial responsibility for raising a child needed only to give a statement asserting that he was not the father of the child. The human leukocyte antigen (HLA) test that determines genetic resemblance was not required in order to support his statement. If the mother wanted to challenge his statement in court, she would have had to have enough resources to hire a lawyer and use legal processes.

Before 1990, the social protection system was essentially a medical one. Children identified as requiring protection were often taken out of their family and admitted to an institution for diagnosis. After the diagnosis was made, a clinical decision would direct the children to the institution that best catered for the type of care chosen (Soitu 2004). These institutions were specialized, being classified as centres for dystrophic (underdeveloped infants), *leagăne* (institutions for orphaned or abandoned infants), *case de copii* (children's homes for preschool-age and school-age children), *cămine şcoală* (residential schools) and *cămine spital* (nursing homes) for those with various disabilities. As the prevailing ideology did not admit the existence of social problems, the physician – rather than a psychologist, sociologist, teacher or social worker – was the key person in determining the diagnosis and establishing the treatment. Besides, training for the non-medical social professions had gradually disappeared from universities, starting with the 1960s. For orphaned or abandoned children, the main, and often the only, form of care was institutionalization. Adoption, although practised in most socialist countries, applied to only a small number of children – the one exception being Bulgaria (Burke 1995). Most often, if parents died, grandparents or other relatives adopted their children. In the case of abandoned children, the number of adoptions was much lower.

In the 1990s, reports compiled by international organizations (such as the World Health Organization and the Helsinki Committee) mention the prevalence of children in institutions in Romania, which was twice the level of Hungary and almost five times higher than in Poland or Slovenia. During the 1990s, the number of children in foster homes reached almost 8,000 (Chakrabarti and Hill 2000).

Subsequent evolution of policies after the 1990s produced the following trends in child protection:

- an acute drop in the number of children receiving protection

- fluctuations in the number of children requiring 'Special Protection'

- a shift of emphasis from institutional care to other measures, mainly to placement in the care of a professional foster parent (an 'assistant maternal').

To illustrate these transformations, a parallel is presented between the situation at the beginning of 2002 and at the end of 2011, covering a period of approximately ten years.

The total number of children under 18 years of age receiving protective measures was approximately six million in 2002, falling to approximately four million in 2011. In 2002, 105,000 such children (1.8%) were monitored by the Specialized Child Protection Public Services, compared to 109,000 children (2.7%) in December 2011. An analysis of the types of protection measures applied reveals that there are important changes, which adds a new dimension to the increased need for protection. Prevention measures, aimed at keeping children in their family of origin, accounted for 9 per cent (about 9,700 children) of the total number of children who were monitored by Specialized Services in 2002, compared to 39 per cent (about 43,000 children) in 2011. Prevention services became very diversified, chiefly moving towards providing, for example, day centres; counselling and support centres for parents; and services for the prevention of child abandonment through family planning, and monitoring of pregnant women. The providers of prevention services came from three important categories of service providers: local councils, accredited private organizations, and public departments subordinate to the General Directorates for Social Assistance and Child Protection.

In the case of children placed in residential care, these totalled nearly 88,000 in 2002 (84% of children receiving protective measures) compared to nearly 66,000 in 2011 (61%), reflecting an important evolution in the type of care provided. Foster care now equals institutional care as the means of looking after children outside their families. The number of children in residential institutions dropped by more than half, from about 50,000 in 2002 (48%) to about 23,000 in 2011 (21%). Bearing in mind that the number of children placed in the care of relatives up to the fourth degree, or with other families and individuals, or a guardian, or given for adoption, also decreased slightly, from about 29,000 in 2002 (28%) to about 23,000 in 2011 (22%), the remaining children have been placed in the care of professional foster parents. These increased dramatically from about 8,500 in 2002 (8%) to approximately 19,000 in 2011 (18%).

This changing pattern of care was facilitated by changes in Romanian legislation, specifically Law 272 of 2004 (as amended) on the protection and promotion of children's rights. Article 60 of the law stipulates that:

> the placement of a child below the age of two can only be made in the extended or substitute family, the child's placement in a residential-type service being forbidden. In exceptional cases...placement in residential-type care of a child younger than two can be decided in situations where said child has severe disabilities, being dependent on care in specialized residential-type institutions.

The impact of this law on the number of institutionalized children is shown in Table 6.4. Less than 4 per cent of all children in institutional care in Romania are under three years of age, and less than 12 per cent are under seven years of age. The provision that this law authorizes is founded not only on the child's best interests, which is optimally promoted by family-based protection approaches, but also on economic grounds. The expense of raising a child in foster care is half that of raising the same child in a residential institution.

Table 6.4 Children by age in residential institutions in Romania: December 2011

Residential-type services	0–12 months	1–2 years	3–6 years	7–9 years	10–13 years	14–17 years	over 18	Total
Public	260	427	1,608	2,436	4,639	5,810	4,035	19,215
Private	11	42	390	717	1,195	1,018	652	4,025
TOTAL	271	469	1,998	3,153	5,834	6,828	4,687	23,240
Age cohort percentage	1.2	2.0	8.6	13.5	25.1	29.4	20.2	100

Source: Ministry of Labour, Family and Social Protection, General Department for Child Protection

After 2000, a new phenomenon began to occur. Children were being left on their own in the family home, because of their parents' temporary migration in search of employment because of economic pressures. The phenomenon became more common after Romania joined the EU in 2007. Official data indicate that about 60,000 families had at least one parent working abroad, leaving almost 87,000 children behind in Romania. Nearly 24,000 of these children (40%) have both parents working abroad. Most of them are living with relatives (related up to the fourth degree), but without state protection. Another thousand or so children are in the care of state (just over 1%). A further 50,000 children have one parent working abroad (57%), of which most are cared for by relatives, with only 1,500 (7.5%) in state care. Over 10,000 children of single parents have been left in Romania while their lone parent works abroad (12%), of whom, again, most are living with relatives, but more than a thousand are in the care of state (just over 10%). This means that the vast majority of children left behind by one or more parents working abroad are being cared for by relatives or by a parent remaining alone in Romania. Only 3,600 such children are included in the Special Protection system. About 3,500 children are in state care, of whom 520 are cared for by foster parents and 779 are in placement centres. Clearly, this is a social phenomenon that adversely affects many children growing up in Romania at the present time.

Family policy and family values

The family is considered to be the fundamental unit of society. It traditionally consists of two parents – a father and a mother – with one or more children. In the Child Protection Law (Law 272 of 2004), the meaning of the term 'family' is explained as only 'the parents and their children' (Article 4, Sub-paragraph b). Taking into consideration the social transformations of recent years, and reflecting the experience gained in providing social services and benefits to families, the essential criteria in defining a 'family' is now the shared household and residence. The recently adopted Law for Social Work (Law 292 of 2011) includes as a *family*: 'the husband and the wife, or the husband, the wife and their unmarried children who have the same domicile or residence mentioned in their identification papers, and who form one household' (Article 22, Paragraph 1); 'childless siblings who form one household and have a shared domicile or residence separate from their parents' domicile or residence' (Article 22, Paragraph 2); and 'unmarried men and women with their shared or individual offspring who live together, forming one household, if this is so recorded by the social services' inquiry' (Article 22, Paragraph 3). A *child* in Romania is an individual who has not reached 18 years of age and who, thus, cannot exercise full legal capacity (Law 272 of 2004, Article 4; Law 292 of 2011, Article 22, Paragraph 7). An *extended family* includes the child, their parents and relatives up to the fourth degree. A *single-parent family* consists of a single (unmarried) individual and the child or children he or she supports, living together (Article 22, Paragraphs 4 and 5). A substitute family, as used in child protection, consists of individuals other than those belonging to the extended family, which, according to the law, can rear and care for a child (Law 272 of 2004, Article 4, Sub-paragraph d).

Romanian literature on the family specifies its functions, which give rise to mutual rights and obligations, as providing sexual, reproductive and physical protection; as providing economic, educative and social (promoting solidarity) support; and as promoting the harmonious development of a child's personality, aimed at achieving emotional development and the development of social skills. As a social unit, the family involves a complex system of roles, both at the couple level and in the relationship between parents and children and between children. The family is considered to be the best-suited environment for transmitting values, norms and educational attitudes. The orientation of the family, and its values, depends on its social and professional status, which, in turn, depends on the level of education and on the living environment (Brinkerhoff and White 1994).

It is mainly the parents who are responsible for rearing and educating children. The Romanian phrase *'primii şapte ani de acasă'* (literally 'the first seven years spent at home' – the years before mandatory education) is invoked when describing the behaviour of a child or young person: a child or youth exhibiting offensive behaviour or disregarding social norms is judged to be lacking in those 'first seven years at home'. This perspective can also be found in social policies. According to the Romanian Ministry of Labour, Family and Social Protection's General Department for Child Protection, parents, both mother and father, are chiefly responsible for ensuring a child's development, taking into account the child's developing capabilities and participation rights.

Child protection is designed, both in terms of laws and actions, around children's rights: the rights to development, to participation and to protection. The legal representative of a child is his or her parent, or the individual appointed by law, who is responsible for exercising the rights of, and fulfilling the parenting obligations to, a child. The responsibility for rearing children and ensuring their development is primarily carried by parents, who have an obligation to exercise their rights and to fulfil their responsibilities to their children, having in mind as a priority the child's best interests (Law 272 of 2004, Article 5, Paragraphs 1 and 2).

Parent education programmes exist in Romania, mainly as temporary or short-term activities within larger projects. Publications by Romanian authors and translations from foreign authors are available to support efforts to become a better parent. One example is Kari Killen's *Barnemishandling: behandlerens dilemma* [*The Abused Child*] (Killen [1981] 1998). These training and self-help programmes can teach parents the importance of giving priority to the satisfaction of a child's basic needs before the parents' own needs; the skill of managing their own pain and frustration without reflecting it on to a child; the ability to have an empathic relationship with a child; the ability to accept that it is the adult's responsibility to satisfy a child's needs and not the other way around; and the ability to perceive a child in a realistic manner.

The principle that the child's best interests must prevail in all actions and decisions concerning children is mandatory in relation to the rights and obligations of the child's parents and other legal representatives, and any individuals in whose care the child was placed through a judicial decision. The public authorities and authorized private bodies, as well as the courts of law, must involve the family in all rulings, decisions and actions concerning the child and must support the child's care, rearing, training and education within the family. Indeed, *The National Strategy for the Protection and Promotion of Children's Rights for 2008–2013* shifts the emphasis from the protection of children at risk, to the protection of rights of all children.

Concerning child education methods, Romanian folk culture contains concepts supporting punitive interventions: the Romanian-language equivalents of 'spare the rod and spoil the child' and 'thou shalt beat him with the rod, and deliver his soul from hell'. However, the current generations of parents, both the older and the younger, are subject to numerous media campaigns directed against physical punishment.

The *Framework for Prevention and Intervention as a Multidisciplinary Team or Network in Situations of Violence against Children and Domestic Violence* was passed on 19 January 2011 (Official Gazette No. 117 of 16 February 2011). This document encourages the use of the terminology recommended by the UN 2006 World Report on Violence against Children. It proposes a number of operational definitions for the various forms of violence against children. These are used in Tables 6.5 and 6.6 to frame the data presented on rates of child abuse and neglect and to report state interventions in Romania in the first six months of 2011. The reported cases show that serious neglect is more problematic than other forms of abuse, irrespective of the setting, whether urban or rural. Nearly 4,000 of 5,550 cases of abuse (over 70%) are reported through the General Directorates for Social Assistance and Child Protection in each county. Ninety per cent of cases are handled without the authorities needing to invoke the powers of the courts. The level of prosecution of offenders is low for most forms of abuse and neglect, with the exception of sexual abuse and sexual exploitation, where levels of prosecution through the judicial system are relatively high. Girls are more prone to sexual abuse and exploitation, while boys are more often exploited for work and for crime. There are no significant gender differences in the figures for physical abuse; however, girls are more often the victims of emotional abuse. In most cases the children are recorded as receiving counselling and psychological support services (3,241 out of 5,550 cases – 58%). Medical, educational and legal services were also offered to a small proportion of the children who had suffered abuse, neglect or exploitation.

Any child temporarily or definitively lacking the protection of his or her parents is entitled to *Alternative Protection* (Law 292, Article 70), consisting of guardianship and adoption. *Special Protection* consists of placement with an alternative carer and the provision of social services aimed at having the children cared for and reared until they reach the age of legal capacity, with additional social assistance benefits being provided. Any decision to separate children from their parents, or to limit the exercise of parental rights, must be preceded by offering parents advice and counselling, and therapy and mediation. Special Protection measures are provided according to each child's individualized protection plan.

Before Romania acceded to the EU, a wide range of new measures was introduced with the aim of giving mandatory protection to children and support for families. These include having a children's hotline with mandatory minimum standards; counselling services for abused, neglected and exploited children; and community resource centres for the prevention of child abuse, neglect and exploitation. There are also new standards for emergency admission centres for abused, neglected and exploited children, as well as for case management in the protection of children's rights, and quality standards for social services protecting the victims of domestic violence.

Some interventions that have been recently introduced are multidisciplinary and also involve international child protection practice. These include intervention methodologies for exploited children, for children who are at risk of work exploitation, for children who are victims of human trafficking, and for migrant children who have been victims of other forms of violence while outside Romania. All these were developed before Romania's accession into the EU, with a visible positive impact on the system dealing with the protection of children in difficulty.

Table 6.5 Child abuse and neglect in Romania: January–June 2011

Type of case	Total cases	Urban	Rural	Number of children left behind in the family (with services provided)	Number of cases where head of DGASPC decided on emergency placement and services	Number of cases whom court decided on emergency placement through a court order	Number of cases in which the procedure for bringing the aggressor to justice was started	Number of cases still in progress	Number of closed cases
a) Physical abuse	530	251	279	390	77	4	37	270	275
b) Emotional abuse	690	433	257	559	36	4	10	401	295
c) Sexual abuse	235	88	147	188	28	1	88	148	219
d) Neglect	3,913	1,738	2,175	2,552	948	110	12	1,513	2,330
e) Exploitation for work	111	43	68	88	18	0	3	39	73
f) Sexual exploitation	23	9	14	14	5	0	8	17	11
g) Exploitation for crime	48	19	29	43	1	0	5	11	36
Total	5,550	2,581	2,969	3,834	1,113	119	163	2,399	3,239

Source: Ministry of Labour, Family and Social Protection, General Department for Child Protection

Table 6.6 Interventions by the state into child abuse in Romania: January–June 2011

Type of case	Rehabilitation services			Medical services (other than the rehabilitation ones)	Educational services		Legal counselling/ assistance
	Psychological counselling	Psycho-therapy	Other therapies		School reintegration	Career counselling and training	
a) Physical abuse	293	1	26	36	5	19	168
b) Emotional abuse	492	2	45	20	11	19	265
c) Sexual abuse	187	9	15	22	3	5	99
d) Neglect	2,152	0	204	263	121	122	1,063
e) Exploitation for work	75	0	1	6	4	0	61
f) Sexual exploitation	19	0	0	0	0	0	12
g) Exploitation for crime	23	0	3	1	1	0	17
Total	3,241	12	294	348	145	165	1,685

Source: Romania, Ministry of Labour, Family and Social Protection, General Department for Child Protection

The state as parent

The Romanian state provides for the protection of children and guarantees respect for their rights through their protection by competent public authorities (Law 292 of 2011, Article 66). If a parent or guardian abuses or neglects a child, or uses a child for public begging, requesting financial or material aid, as well as when children are victims of exploitation or trafficking at the hands of their parents or carers, then the public social assistance service of the county council (or local councils of the districts of Bucharest) must initiate actions to apply Special Protection measures. This must be done as soon as the facts of a case have been ascertained.

The provisions of the 1989 *United Nations Convention on the Rights of the Child* (UNCRC) (UNICEF 2012) – notably, Articles 19, 32, 33, 34, 35 and 36 – are well known and taken into consideration in professional circles. These are the provisions relating to protection against violence, abuse, neglect and exploitation (including sexual abuse and exploitation, economic exploitation, and the use of children for hard labour), against the illicit use and trafficking of addictive and psychotropic substances, and against child kidnapping, sale and trafficking).

The Special Protection offered to children includes the provision of social assistance benefits and social services, as well as complementary programmes and activities for the care and development of children lacking the protection of parents, whether temporarily or permanently, and of children who cannot be left in the care of their parents. Other interests that are legally protected concern their dignity. For example, the new 2011 Civil Code, Article 84, prevents civil registry officers from recording indecent or ridiculous first names that could affect the child's future. In the case of children found abandoned whose legal identity cannot be established, either because their parents are unknown, or because they were abandoned by their mothers in hospital, the family name and the first names are assigned by means of a decree issued by the local mayor of the area in which the children were found, or where their abandonment was ascertained.

The law enshrines the children's right to be brought up together with their parents, in conditions that allow for their physical, mental, spiritual, moral and social development. A special category of benefits is that of benefits for supporting families through birth, childcare and education. These include child allowances; allowances for children lacking, temporarily or permanently, their parents' protection; allowances for childcare; and employment reinsertion incentives for parents returning to work in less than one year after confinement.

State benefits in support of child welfare

It must be recognized that there are differences between the laws enacted and the social impact of those social protection measures embedded in them. Benefits have been linked to parenting behaviour in a way that is intended to make benefits work more effectively for the wellbeing and development of children. In 2011, and at the beginning of 2012, changes were introduced to the benefits that may be granted to families in difficulty. The link between benefits and responsibilities to children and the state have been made more explicit. Some of these changes are aimed at simplifying processes (such as the introduction of a single form for requesting and testing non-contributory benefits). At the same time, the civic obligations of beneficiaries are stressed (such as the duty to pay local taxes for houses and land, as well as health insurance contributions). The conditions for granting non-contributory benefits are more clearly detailed (such as for guaranteed minimum income, the heating subsidy and family support allowances).

One policy intention was to make parents in disadvantaged families more responsible for supporting their children's education. The Romanian Ministry of Education, Youth and Research recognizes the problem of children failing to attend school. In Romania, the amount granted as family support allowance is diminished by 20 per cent if the child misses ten hours of school without a reasonable explanation, with the penalty going up to 50 per cent if more than 20 hours of schooling are missed.

Children's right to health is also recognized in legislation covering all children up to 18 years of age. They are insured by the state health insurance system without having to pay any contributions. This gives them the right to have preventative and curative healthcare, which is, however, limited in certain areas of the country. For instance, consultations are free of charge, but prescribed medication is not. This causes difficulties when treating children from impoverished families, and when trying to provide decent standards of care for young single mothers from impoverished families and for young women under 18 years of age who are pregnant.

Some children of school age have difficulty in exercising their right to education. This is especially the case for those living in rural environments. The Romanian Ministry of Education has developed national programmes for facilitating access to schools, consisting of the provision of free transport, food and school stationery. In 2004, this sort of support was granted to 2.4 million children. However, despite these initiatives, 31,284 children dropped out of school in 2004, while 13,787 school-age children were not enrolled in any form of education at seven years of age (Romania, MLFSP 2007).

Children and domestic violence

Domestic violence has been identified as an issue that affects the wellbeing of children in Romania, as elsewhere. A new law for preventing and combating domestic violence was passed in early March 2012. Social services for domestic violence victims are provided in an integrated system, together with other protection measures, which include medical care through the public health insurance system, and the prevention, identification and punishment of acts of domestic violence. Currently, service planning and individualized protection plans for victims include specialist provision for services needed by the children and their families, as well as the general services that families with children can receive. Responsibility for establishing, organizing, managing and providing social services for preventing and stopping domestic violence rests with the local public administration authorities (Law 292 of 2011, Article 76). The social services provided in day centres and residential centres, which have been developed to address domestic violence, are primarily aimed not only at the victims, but also at their aggressors. There is a range of provision in residential centres for victims of domestic violence, where people may stay for short-term support. The types of social services offered through residential centres include the following (Article 77): centres for the emergency admission of domestic violence victims; recovery centres for domestic violence victims; protected housing; counselling centres for preventing and stopping domestic violence; and centres for informing people about domestic violence and raising awareness about it. Services may also be offered as daytime, non-residential services. For aggressors, Law 292 of 2011, Article 78, provides for the provision of social services through day centres, having as their objective the social rehabilitation and reintegration of offenders by providing education, counselling and family mediation measures.

Social services promoting child and family protection

Social services related to child and family protection (under Law 292 of 2011, Article 73, Paragraphs 1 and 2) have as their main objective the provision of support that ensures the quality of care, upbringing, training, development and education of children within families. The new law set out these aspirations and responsibilities. The main categories of social services identified are: services for the prevention of separation of children from their families; services for achieving a balance between professional and family life; services for children temporarily or indefinitely deprived of their parents; and support services for families in difficulty. Social assistance institutions, daycare centres or residential centres, as well as in the families' homes, in the home of the individual caring for the child or in the community, may provide these social services. The parents cover part of the expenses for these services, both those aimed at achieving balance between professional and family life, and those aimed at families in difficulty. The closure of the classic large residential institutions for children, and, to replace them, the development of support services for maintaining children in the care of their own families, has been underpinned by the creation, development and diversification of alternative services. A special emphasis has been placed on community services. Since 1 January 2005, the departments for public social assistance services in local councils have been the main actors in the development of these services. As of 30 June 2011, they provide services for over a third (35%) of the children who require such interventions, with other providers being private accredited bodies (22%), the General Directorates for Social Assistance and Child Protection, and state-level child abuse and neglect prevention services (43%).

By the end of 2006, there were already 578 'alternative to institutional care' services in operation. These include services both for young people who have had experience of being in state care, and to prevent children entering state care. Specifically, these comprise 60 maternal centres for mothers and babies, 99 day centres, 47 services for assisting and supporting young people who have grown up in residential care in placement centres, 59 centres for parent counselling and support 43 services for the prevention of child abandonment (including services provided to young people before conception), and services for pregnant women at risk of abandoning their babies (offering monitoring, support and assistance). Parents are also entitled to specialized assistance in order to care for, rear and educate their children, as well as to be informed about their rights and obligations.

There are also services for children who have experienced abuse or abandonment, or have other special needs. Specifically, there are now 38 centres for preparing and assisting children's reintegration into their families; 90 day centres for the care and rehabilitation of children with disabilities; 20 services for the guidance, monitoring and support for social reintegration in the case of young offenders; and 8 centres for assistance and support for the psychological readjustment of children with psychosocial problems. There are 11 services for assisting children in exercising their rights, including the right to the free expression of opinions; 35 services for street children; 44 centres for counselling and support in the cases of mistreated, abused and neglected children, including those who have fallen victim to domestic violence; and 24 other related specialist services. There is also residential provision for young people after they attain 18 years of age. As at the end of December 2006, placement centres cared for 6,492 young people over 18 years of age who met the legal criteria for such protection, as well as for 15,417 children aged 14 to 17 (Romania, MLFSP 2007).

Funding and overseeing service provision

There is a mixed economy of provision of services targeting children and families. Associations and foundations, including legally recognized religious organizations, can receive subsidies from the state and from the Bucharest districts, in their capacity as private providers of social services. This is to support the establishment, development, diversification and provision of a range of child and family welfare services (under Law 292 of 2011, Article 139). The state subsidies granted to non-governmental organizations (NGOs) developing social services programmes that target the elderly, the disabled, children in difficulty, victims of domestic violence and other categories of individuals with low income have led to a significant expansion of the sector's provision. In the first quarter of 2011, there were state budget-allotted subsidies to 145 NGOs and associations that had developed social services programmes in 34 counties, with an average of 15,345 users per month. Over 8,000 users were registered in the counties of Sibiu, Cluj, Bacău, Iaşi and Alba (which had 3,689 users, the highest of any county), as well as in the Bucharest Municipality (2,440 users). The amount spent on these projects was 11.5 million Lei, which is approximately 25 per cent more than in the corresponding quarter of 2010 (Romania, MLFSP 2011a, 2011b, p.21).

Responsibility for developing, providing and managing social services is divided between central and local authorities. The central public authorities are in charge of developing public policies, national programmes and strategies for regulating, coordinating and monitoring their application, as well as for evaluating and monitoring the quality of social services. The local public authorities are in charge of organizing, managing and providing social services. This provision can be outsourced to non-government sector organizations, religious institutions and other private or public individuals or legal entities. The major funding of social services (Law 292 of 2011, Article 39) aimed at families and children in need comes from local authority budget allocations, from fees paid by users and their families, and from state budget allocations.

The Romanian Strategy for Child Protection (2008–2013) emphasizes not only the primary role parents and families have in rearing, caring for and educating children, but also that society's efforts must be directed towards strengthening and supporting families in their fulfilment of their responsibilities towards children. Social assistance measures directed at families are provided to support their efforts to keep their children in the family by being better able to overcome difficult situations. This encourages the employment of parents, while allowing them to achieve a suitable balance between their professional and family lives (Law 292 of 2011, Article 67). However, when identifying the resources needed for overcoming difficult family situations, there must first be a search for support from within the child's extended family, the family's social network (such as friends, neighbours and professionals involved in the child's life, including medical practitioners, teachers or priests) and the child's community (including local authority advice agencies and primary social prevention services), and then, as a last resort, seek specialized intervention to protect and support children.

Conclusion

At least two points of reference permit the recent evolution of the child protection system in Romania to be judged as exemplary. The first is the inevitable comparison between its current state and its situation in, and before, 1990. Some of the buildings currently used by child protection institutions were in use two or more decades ago. Also, there are a handful of professionals – especially educators, psychologists and healthcare staff – who have been working continuously in such institutions in the years prior to 1990. There are young persons who, due to the fact that they are continuing their education at university level and are entitled to state protection up to 26 years of age, have experienced *leagăn* – the type of institution that was abolished in the 1990s. Despite the existence of such elements of continuity, the transformations in the child protection system have been radical.

These reforms have been concerned, above all, with a change of vision. This has shifted from an emphasis on the medical model to an emphasis on the social model. The issue is no longer ensuring that the children's physical development is 'optimal', using anatomical and physical parameters that are not always achievable, but rather a focus on the development of children's capacity to relate, within social norms, to the society in which they will find themselves as adults. This change of vision has been a major driver of the evolution of Romanian law, not only in the legislation concerning child protection, but also in the new 2011 Civil Code.

The nature and geographical pattern of available social services have also changed radically. The state has given up its monopoly on the care of vulnerable children. Despite preserving an important policy and regulatory role for itself, exercised through the local public authorities – the General Directorates for Social Assistance and Child Protection in each county – the state's activities are complementary to those offered in local communities, which became involved in the process through services funded by local councils. Private providers have also come into play through the development of both for-profit and not-for-profit organizations, whether secular or religious. This diversification of service providers has become possible due to the introduction of a system of accreditation, which certifies the observation of quality standards in each institution or provision. A minimum level of quality standards has been established for each type of social service.

One important element in achieving this was the training of human resources. This meant the emergence of new professions, the most significant one being that of foster parent – 'assistant maternal' – and the recommencement of the training of specialists in domains that had been almost dismantled in the past years. These professional disciplines include psychology, which had disappeared as a speciality from universities in the 1980s, and social work, which had languished for decades and became a profession without any purpose in a society whose ideology declared it was devoid of social problems.

There are, of course, limitations, difficulties and errors in the management and operation of the child protection system in Romania. Unlike in the 1980s, these imperfections no longer make this system a 'special case' at international level. Instead, the system is now comparable with that which exists in other countries. Limitations in provision are no longer caused by the desire to hide or deny the existence of social problems. Although serious in places, these problems have become normal problems, not extraordinary ones. They have their roots in the weakness of certain links in the system: legislation that does not anticipate, but instead reacts to, the emergence of new social realities; administrative rigidity; restricted funding; insufficient personnel with – sometimes – perfectible training and motivation; and difficulties in identifying precisely the point of balance between the need to protect children and the appropriate limits to making interventions in children's environments, in an effort not to disturb them.

The second comparison that places child protection in Romania in a favourable light is the one with other areas of social assistance, especially the protection of vulnerable adults and the elderly. The pace of child protection reform has been faster than that of other welfare reforms. It has been kept fast by the pressure put on the reform process by Romanian and international bodies. A level of funding that is more generous in comparison with the funding provided to other categories of welfare clients has supported it. The evolution taking place in child protection over the last couple of decades has had a positive impact on all social welfare domains. Child protection, thus, serves as a milestone, as a model and even as an engine for welfare reform.

References

Brinkerhoff, D.B. and White, L.K. (1994) *Sociology*. New York: West Publishing.

Burke, M.A. (1995) *Child Institutionalization and Child Protection in Central and Eastern Europe* (Innocenti Occasional Papers). Florence, IT: UNICEF Innocenti Research Centre.

Chakrabarti, M. and Hill, M. (2000) *Residential Child Care: International Perspectives on Links with Families and Peers*. London: Jessica Kingsley Publishers.

European Commission (EC), Eurostat (2012) *Population 1*. Available at: http://epp. eurostat.ec.europa.eu/statistics_explained/index.php/Population_and_population_ change_statistics.

Haupt, A. (1987) 'How Romania tries to govern fertility.' *Population Today 15*, 2, 3–4.

Johnson, A., Edwards, R. and Puwak, H. (1993) 'Foster care and adoption policy in Romania: Suggestions for international intervention.' *Child Welfare 72*, 5, 489–508.

Killen, K. ([1981] 1998) *Copilul Maltratat* [Barnemishandling–Behandlerens Dilemma]. Bucharest, RO: Eurobit.

Romania, Insee (Institut National De Statistics) [National Institute of Statistics] (2011) *Recensământul populaţiei şi al locuinţelor 2011* [Population and Housing Census 2011]. Available at: www.recensamantromania.ro.

Romania, Ministry of Labour, Family and Social Protection (MLFSP) (2007) *Strategy for Child Protection 2008–2013*. Bucharest, RO: Department of Social Services and Social Inclusion.

Romania, Ministry of Labour, Family and Social Protection (MLFSP) (2011a) *Raport statistic privind activitatea ministerului muncii, familiei şi protecţiei sociale în domeniul incluziunii sociale în semestrul 2011*. Bucharest, RO: Department of Social Services and Social Inclusion. Available at: www.mmuncii.ro/pub/imagemanager/images/file/Domenii/ Incluziune%20si%20asistenta%20sociala/raportari/Raport%202011%2030sep.pdf.

Romania, Ministry of Labour, Family and Social Protection (MLFSP) (2011b) *Situaţii e Abuz, Neglijare, Exploatare a Copilului*. Bucharest, RO: General Department for Child Protection.

Soitu, C. (2004) *Adolescenţii Instituţionalizaţi*. Iaşi, RO: AXIS Foundation.

Stephenson, P., Anghelescu, C., Stativa, E. and Pasti, S. (1997) *Cauzele instituţionalizării copiilor din România*. Bucharest, RO: UNICEF Romani.

UNICEF (2012) *United Nations Convention on the Rights of the Child*. Available at: www. unicef.org/crc/index_30229.html.

United Nations Development Programme (UNDP) (2011) *Human Development Reports: Romania*. Available at: www.undp.ro/profile_romania.php.

7

Japan

Kathryn Goldfarb

Introduction

Contemporary public discourses surrounding the Japanese family often focus on what would appear to be the family's imminent collapse, the loss of Japanese 'traditional' values, and the decline of Japanese society itself. These concerns directly relate to the ways in which families interact with society at large, and to the social and cultural expectations of the family as a social unit, and, therefore, to child welfare practices. This chapter begins with a brief portrayal of contemporary discourses surrounding the Japanese family in a period of rapid demographic change, in the context of economic stagnation that has dogged Japan since the beginning of the 1990s. It provides an abbreviated outline of contemporary child welfare practices, and their cultural and historical evolution. It then describes historical and contemporary ideologies surrounding the extended family, and relates beliefs surrounding the proper constitution of the family to practices of adoption. It also addresses the role of gender ideologies in shaping family practices, perspectives surrounding proper parenting, and the fine line between discipline and abuse, as defined within child welfare law and practice. It finally addresses several major factors that shape the form taken by child welfare practices, which depend on placement of children in children's homes (*jade yogi shiest*) and baby homes (*nyūjiin*). Although new Ministry of Health, Labour and Welfare guidelines articulate the goal of increasing family-based care and decreasing the size of institutions, two major factors continue to shape a reliance on institutional care, namely the structure and cultural expectations surrounding child guidance centres

(CGCs) (*jidō sōdanjyo*, or *jisō* for short), and the legal notion of parental rights[1] (*shinken*).

Cultural contexts for child protection in Japan

A specific set of concerns and anxieties surrounding modern social forms inevitably infuse public discourses surrounding child welfare in Japan. These centre on demographic and economic transformations, and are mainly related to the increasing incidence of nuclear families, which are perceived as cut-off from society, and economic stagnation, which has resulted in rising poverty without a concomitant boost in social welfare provision. The loss of traditional family practices, in particular, is often represented as pathology of modernity and is closely connected to changes in gendered labour practices. Conservative ideologies, however, inform a gendered division of labour within the home. These factors are centrally important to the cultural conceptualizations of the problems facing contemporary Japanese society, especially the public representation of the reasons for children being placed in protective care. In this context, it is important to note that race and ethnicity are not very salient in predominant understandings of Japanese child welfare concerns.

Japan is often described as racially homogeneous, with the categories of ethnicity, nation and state often conflated so that the Japanese nation is represented as consisting of ethnically and racially Japanese people. According to government population statistics, Japan is 98.5 per cent Japanese, 0.5 per cent Korean and 0.4 per cent Chinese. There are three major native minority groups, the indigenous *Ainu* peoples (comprising 23,782 people, as of 2006) (JFBA 2009), the people of Okinawa (formerly the *Ryukyu* Kingdom, which Japan annexed in 1872) and the *Buraku* people, who are marked by their historical association with labour practices that are considered 'unclean' in the Shinto religion (such as leatherworking and animal slaughter). Although anecdotal evidence indicates an overrepresentation of minority and immigrant children in child welfare facilities, there are no statistics on this issue.

---

1   Parental rights are broken down into two categories: custody rights, and rights to administer property. Custody rights entail the right of custody and education, the right to determine the child's residence, the right to punish the child to the extent necessary, and the right to approve the child's vocation. Administrative rights include the right to administer the child's property and the right to represent the child in a legally effective act relating to the child's property. Parental rights are held jointly if the parents are married; if divorced, parental rights must be divided, as there is no joint custody provision (Matsushima 1996).

In 2011 there were 30,594 children in Japanese in children's homes (*jidō yōgo shisetsu*), 2,968 infants in baby homes (*nyūjiin*) and 3,836 children placed with foster parents (*sato oya*) (Japan, MHLW 2011a). Children in alternative care constitute approximately 0.2 per cent of the Japanese child population. Clearly, around 90 per cent of children in need of out-of-home care are placed in children's homes and infant homes, and 10 per cent placed into foster care. Currently, the most common reasons for placement are abuse and neglect, but the category of 'neglect' comprises a vast range of parental behaviours that are shaped by marriage status, work conditions and mental and physical health. It must be highlighted that although family reunification is generally a goal, caseworkers may perceive placement in institutional or foster care as a permanent solution, while adoption is less often considered to be a viable option.

Child welfare scholars link increases in the incidence of children placed in state care with decreases in extended family residences, which provided parents with childcare resources in the form of a kinship network; with increasing incidence of nuclear families, which are said to be cut-off from the community; and with declining job security and rising poverty (Nishida 2011; Sato 2009, p.130). These characteristics are all part of broader demographic changes that are often described as pathologies of modern life. There are increasing incidences of people who are not married (43 per cent of households in Tokyo are single, non-married individuals) or who married late (the average age of marriage is 30.2 for men and 28.5 for women) (Ronald and Alexy 2011, p.13), and rising incidence of divorce. Child abuse is closely related to families' isolation from the surrounding community. This was first recognized as an issue in the 1970s (Hayes and Habu 2006), but it was only discovered by the popular press in the early 1980s, and did not gain widespread public recognition until the 1990s (Goodman 2002a, 2002b).

Many Japanese and foreign intellectuals characterized Japan's post-war economic success as a product of what they framed as 'traditionally Japanese' social and cultural structures, one of which was the concept of the extended family (see, for example, Benedict 1946; Vogel 1979; for critiques see Befu 2001; Dale 2011; Harootunian 2000). The influence of these discourses has diminished as Japan entered first into economic stagnation and then recession. Although in 2010 Japan ranked as the third largest economy in the world, after the US and China, the unemployment rates have risen to 5 per cent (2011). Companies are providing less robust welfare support, and irregular employment has increased (to 30.6 per cent in 2006) (Ronald and Alexy 2011, p.10). Despite formerly prevalent discourses framing Japan as a middle-class society (Vogel 1979), the gap between rich and poor has become significant. In 2004 Japan's relative poverty rate ranked only below Mexico, Turkey and the US out of the 30 OECD countries (Bamba and Haight 2011, p.176). The Japan Federation of Bar Associations (2009) notes that there are 'at least four million households of working poor – people who work but are unable to earn an income above social welfare payment', comprising 'ten per cent of all Japanese households'.

Japan's population in 2011 was 126.5 million (US, CIA 2011). The Japanese Statistics Bureau projects that by 2105 Japan's population will have declined to 44.6 million, with only 3.9 million children under 14 years of age (Japan, SB 2011). Japan's decreasing birth rate is, thus, another cause for social and economic concern. Only 13.2 per cent of the total population is under 14 years of age (Japan, SB 2011). Ochiai (1997, pp.39–40) points out that despite government pro-birth rate efforts in the 1920s and 1930s, the birth rate in Japan had already begun to decline prior to the Second World War. There was a brief birth rate increase immediately after the war, presaging an eight-year decline beginning in 1949, after which the birth rate levelled. A second decline began in the mid-1970s and continues today. The oft-cited '1.57 shock' of 1989, the year the declining birth rate received sudden public attention, marked the beginning of panicked demographic predictions, with some that posited the eventual extinction of the Japanese nation. As of 2011, the birth rate fell to 1.21 (US, CIA 2011). The birth rate for married women has remained around 2.2 over the past three decades, and thus 'the decrease in fertility is almost totally due to an increase in women of reproductive age not getting married and not having children' (Goodman 2002a, p.13). The illegitimacy rate in Japan remains around 1 per cent, a result of liberal abortion policies and strong social stigma against pre-marital births (Hertog 2009).

On the other side of Japan's demographic transition, life expectancies have increased from around 52 years at the time of the Second World War (Goodman 2002a), to an average of 82 years in 2011 (US, CIA 2011). The average life expectancy in 2011 was 79 years for men and 86 years for women, the fifth highest in the world (US, CIA 2011). One-third of the population is projected to be over 65 years of age by the year 2040 (Ronald and Alexy 2011, p.12). Interestingly, the emergence of Japan as an ageing society took only 24 years, while similar shifts in many Western countries took four times as long (Ochiai 1997; Ronald and Alexy 2011).

The combination of decreasing fertility and increasing longevity indicates, for the future, an extension of the current economic problems with increasing burdens of eldercare, a decreasing tax base and an insufficient labour supply, exacerbated, some would claim, by the Japanese government's concomitant resistance to liberalized immigration policies

(Arudou 2009; Goodman 2002a; Ochiai 1997; Roberts 2002). These trends are a challenge to a state whose welfare regime is characterized by 'low social expenditures, low benefit levels, priority for spending on education' and an understanding that the government's role is that of 'regulator' rather than 'provider', along with 'subordination of public welfare to economic growth and development and, on the other [hand], reliance on the family' and the private sector (Walker and Wong 2005, pp.9, 18). Although in the immediate post-war period of economic growth the Japanese government slowly increased welfare spending in a manner consistent with Western welfare expenditure growth, as Japan entered its low economic growth era, the Japanese government was apparently convinced that 'the Welfare State had become a disadvantage to the competitiveness of other advanced capitalist countries' (Gould 1993, quoted in Kono 2005, pp.199–200). At this point, discourses surrounding welfare became focused on the excesses of Western welfare states that encouraged public welfare dependency (Goodman 2002a), and on the contemporary Japanese-style 'welfare society', based on low state social expenditures and a reliance on the family to care for its members (Kono 2005). Goodman (2002a, p.16) points out that the term 'welfare society', distinct from 'welfare state', emphasizes the presumed source of help: the family, the community and the company. Neoliberal policy discourses, specifically those surrounding the ideal of self-responsibility (*jiko sekinin*) and the requirement of the family to care for its members, reinforce an image of a citizenry that cares for itself largely independently of state support. Indeed, the requirement that the family care for its own is enshrined in the Civil Code (Minamikata, Shigeru and Hiroko 1999).

But with the contemporary perception that the family is no longer capable of caring for its own, this welfare model seems, correspondingly, insufficient to the task, and there have been increasing calls for more state provision (Ronald and Alexy 2011). From a child welfare perspective, multiple factors indicate the emergence of new welfare needs: the increasing numbers of children who require protective care, particularly in cities; children's homes and temporary care facilities in CGCs often being full to capacity; and an increase in the reported incidence of abuse and neglect (Sato 2009, p.130). However, because the Japanese welfare provision has, over the past four decades, depended heavily on family care and provisioning by private and non-governmental organizations (NGOs), there seems to be little sense that the government *should* provide welfare services (Kono 2005). There is also a corresponding sense that the services the government does provide are neither comprehensive nor of a high quality, and thus private and community-based welfare services are perceived to be preferable. Over 90 per cent of Japanese children's homes are privately run, many through social welfare NGOs (*shyakai fukushi hojin*). By multiple standards – child to staff ratios, size of the overall institution, quality of the physical buildings, and the professional qualifications of the staff – private children's homes are considered to provide higher quality care than institutions run by the government, a situation that reinforces the value given to non-governmental welfare provisioning (Goldfarb 2012; Goodman 2001; Hinata Bokko 2009).

History of child welfare services in Japan

During the early years of the Meiji period (1868–1912), the Japanese central government made its first nation-wide efforts to provide social welfare services. Indeed, prior to this era, there was no national administration. In the past, religiously motivated individuals and groups provided charitable aid locally, and the first national ordinance addressing social welfare in 1874 focused on the importance of 'self-help and family care rather than any state responsibility' (Takahashi 2003, p.96). Some private organizations were provided with limited imperial funds, 'given as an act of imperial mercy' (Takahashi 2003, p.96). In 1917, what would become the system of voluntary welfare commissioners, the contemporary *minsei-iin seido*, began in the Okayama prefecture and gradually spread to Osaka and other cities, until it was integrated into law in the 1930s (Goodman 1998b; Takahashi 2003; Takahashi and Hashimoto 1997). Later welfare initiatives, such as the 1938 Social Welfare Law, similarly authorized some government financial support to be given to private or voluntary welfare organizations. The dependency of non-governmental services on state funding, and the state's use of non-governmental organizations, continues today. Goodman (1998b) has pointed out the potential conflicts of interest in the government's funding of voluntary welfare organizations. Although the efficacy of the untrained *minsei-iin* commissioners – voluntary welfare commissioners – has been questioned, they are often of high status in their communities and sit on local governing boards. Goodman also notes that they 'were behind successful attempts in 1951 to block government proposals to introduce professional social workers, arguing that these would simply be duplicating the work that they were already doing' (1998b, p.149).

In inter-war Japan, there were more than 6,700 private welfare organizations, but by the wartime 1940s the number had decreased by more than half, although they were still responsible for the bulk of welfare provisioning (Takahashi 2003, p.99). The post-war American occupiers were concerned with the lack of clarity between public and private service providers, and part of the welfare laws that were immediately put into place, including the 1947 Child Welfare Law, were aimed at implementing explicitly governmental services, which the occupiers framed as the right of the citizenry (Garon 1997; Takahashi 2003). The immediate severe post-war economic problems, coupled with vast numbers of children orphaned because of the war, promoted a wide variety of local and governmental responses. Post-war surveys indicated that there were 123,504 double orphans in Japan, around 90,000 children who needed some sort of care, and 1,800 children who needed to be placed in children's homes (Takahashi 2003, p.265; Yoshizawa 2007, p.10).

The foster care system was established in 1948, and was modified 60 years later to incorporate the provision of childrearing allowances to foster parents (2008 Child Welfare Law). New children's homes were built and pre-existing buildings were given to the service of housing the vast numbers of children in need of care. Some of these orphanages were funded by religious charities and wives of servicemen stationed in Japan. They called for the introduction of adoption programmes, based on private networks of religious organizations and individual mediators. Adoption from Japan to the US emerged in the 1950s, and continues today, with around 40 or 50 documented adoptions each year (Hayes and Habu 2006). Hayes and Habu (2006, p.81) point out that these numbers are likely to under-represent the prevalence of intercountry adoption from Japan, in part because there is no central body governing adoptions in general, and in part because intercountry adoption is defined as adoption that takes place when one of the adopters is foreign. There are no reliable government statistics on the practice. Further, the Japan Federation of Bar Associations has critiqued intercountry adoption as expressing a failure on the part of the Japanese government to care for its own people.

Religious communities continue to play an important role in child protection regimes. The majority of Japanese people self-identify with one or both of Shintoism (84%) and Buddhism (71%), with Christianity being self-identified by just 2 per cent. Although most people (even Japanese Christians) practise some Shinto and Buddhist rituals, very few consider themselves to be highly religious. However, despite the low reported level of religiosity in Japan, religious organizations and philosophies play significant roles in Japanese child welfare. A disproportionate number of foster parents are Christian or adherents of a minority religious sect, *Tenri-kyo*. Christian and Buddhist private children's homes are common, with the former begun, and in many cases, administered, by foreign missionaries.

In accordance with the 1947 Child Welfare Law, CGCs were established by prefectural and city governments, with the explicit objective of supporting child welfare through consultation and assessments (Amino

2007, p.24). At the time, there was no focus on CGCs intervening into, or addressing, child maltreatment, which was not yet recognized as a social problem (Bamba and Haight 2011; Goodman 2002b). In fact, as Goodman (2002b, p.133) points out, although child abuse was recognized as a problem in *other* countries, 'the majority of Japanese, including many professionals in child welfare, believed that there was no, or virtually no, child abuse in Japan'. Many factors contributed to this perception, particularly a perception of the strength of family and community ties, which included ties to neighbourhood police, volunteer welfare workers (the *minsei-iin*) and teachers, all of whom were presumed to be able to easily notice and report problems of abuse (Goodman 2002b).

In the early 1970s, the issue of abandoned infants, most commonly found in train station coin lockers, became a cause for government concern. Child abuse and maltreatment gradually began to be recognized as a potential social issue. It was only in the 1990s, however, that child abuse was 'discovered' as a social pathology (Goodman 2002b). Although in the early 1990s parental rights were widely seen as 'virtually inviolable, and a child was seen by and large as the property of the parent', Goodman recounts, 'by the end of the decade, the idea of children being endowed with their own rights had gained enormous ground'. The perception that parents are incapable of abusing their children had transformed into a perception that child abuse is 'virtually endemic' (Goodman 2002a, p.21). NGOs sprung up in the 1990s, such as the Association for the Prevention of Child Abuse, which started a telephone hotline. The trend spread. There are now over 40 NGOs that offer counselling and advice. Bamba and Haight (2011, p.183) note that these services do not actually investigate or intervene into families, which encouraged potential abusers to make free use of the services provided. The 2000 Child Abuse Prevention Law increased public awareness of child abuse; created clear definitions of abuse (as physical, sexual and psychological abuse) and neglect; and stated that anyone suspecting abuse is required by law to place a report. Between 1999 and 2009 the annual number of incidences of CGC involvement in potential or actual abuse cases increased by 3.8 times, to 44,211 cases (Japan, MHLW 2010b), probably the result of awareness-raising efforts. However, many scholars also maintain that the real incidence of abuse has also increased over time, particularly given the contemporary economic slump.

Abuse occurring within child welfare facilities has, of late, received explicit government attention, in part because of the advocacy activities of private organizations. The 2005 Minimum Standards for Child Welfare Facilities stipulated provisions that explicitly prohibited the abuse of children by staff members in children's homes, and required the provision of a method to address children's complaints (UN, OHCHR, Supervisory Committee on the Rights of the Child 2009). The 2008 Child Welfare Law also included, for the first time, 'abuse within institutions' under the category of 'child abuse'. However, the Japan Federation of Bar Associations remains concerned that 'cases of corporal punishment and abuse at child welfare facilities have not decreased', and criticizes the measures taken by the government, including the fact that complaint boxes for children are provided within and managed by the institutions themselves (JFBA 2009).

Adoption 'for the sake of the child' was established as a guiding principle in Japan in 1988. Up until then, 'regular adoption' (*futsū yōshi engumi*) had long been used mostly to adopt adults into families, primarily for the purpose of keeping alive a family name, passing down responsibilities for ancestor worship, for inheritance of property or business, and succession. When children are regularly adopted they are usually related to their adopter. Under 'regular adoption', the adoptee maintains legal ties with both birth parents and adoptive family (Bryant 1990; Paulson 1985). The 'special adoption' (*tokubetsu yōshi engumi*) system was created in response to the activities of an obstetrician, Kikuta Noboru, who had for many years been arranging unauthorized infant adoptions between women with unintended pregnancies and couples who could not have their own children. Although Kikuta was disbarred from medical practice after his activities were discovered in 1973, he was vocal in supporting a new adoption system. Kikuta's activism was informed not only by his work as an obstetrician, but also by an awareness of the increasing incidence of infant abandonment – the 'coin-locker babies'. Kikuta felt that women with unintended pregnancies who had exceeded the timeframe for abortion were coerced into abandonment because there was no adoption system that would not leave a stigmatizing mark on the birth mother's family registry (Kikuta 1981; see also Hayes and Habu 2006; Hertog 2009; for detailed analysis of issues surrounding family registries, see Krogness 2011). The new 'special adoption' system was framed 'for the sake of the child', in distinction to the family-oriented (or feudal) 'regular adoption'. Because the child's legal ties are severed from the birth family, it is possible that 'special adoption' has protective capacities: the family court must approve all 'special adoptions', and it is possible that 'special adoption' can be used to place vulnerable children into adoptive families. However, because the family court tends to uphold the rights of the biological parents, the 'protective' capacities of 'special adoption' are mostly untapped (Hayes and Habu 2006), although as Suzuki (2011) points out, the 'regular adoption' for youth who have been fostered, which often occurs around the time a young person turns 18 years old and must leave foster care, *does* probably have a protective function. Further, there is still a designation in the family registry of both adoptive parents and birth mother, which does not protect her from social stigma surrounding illegitimate birth and adoption, which still remains present in Japanese society (Hayes and Habu 2006; Krogness 2011).

'Special adoption' can be arranged, free of charge for adoptive parents, by government CGCs, or by a scattering of private or semi-autonomous organizations, doctor associations, religious groups or private arrangements (Hayes and Habu 2006). There is no overarching system of regulation. It can be difficult for prospective adopters to obtain information. At the time of writing, only one CGC in Japan – the Aichi prefecture CGC in Kariya – arranges the adoption of newborns; other CGCs arrange adoption of older children, many of whom have spent time in a baby home or children's home. There are no reliable statistics on 'special adoption', but it has been estimated that there are around 500 each year.

Japan ratified the 1989 *UN Convention on the Rights of the Child* (UNCRC) (UNICEF 2012). Lawmakers are said to have believed that the Convention was not in conflict with current child welfare law, but the continuing dialogue between the Japanese government and the United Nations regarding Japan's implementation of this Convention, in addition to the Japanese Federation of Bar Associations' alternative reports to the UN, would indicate otherwise (Freeman 1996; JFBA 2009; Matsushima 1996; UN, OHCHR, Supervisory Committee on the Rights of the Child 2009). Japan's ratification has brought the Civil Code under review once more, and made apparent the tensions between the UN Convention's perceptions of child rights and Japanese legal protections for the rights of biological parents.

The notion of 'external pressure' (*gaiatsu*) from an international community has long been a factor in Japan for the development of welfare policy (Goodman 1998b; Kono 2005; Matsushima 1996), and Japan's engagement with the UNCRC seems to be a major force behind the current emergence of new child welfare policies and practices. In recognition of the UNCRC's principles on alternative care, and increasing public awareness of developmental and attachment disorders in institutionalized infants, the Japanese government's most recent policy statement on future directions in child welfare focuses on providing a household-like atmosphere for out-of-home care, which includes foster care, small-group homes, unit-care within children's homes, and a new system of 'family homes' established in 2009 (Japan, MHLW 2011a). Contemporary objectives for children in need of out-of-home care, as outlined in the 2010 Vision for Children and Child-rearing, are to eventually increase foster care and 'family-home' placements to one-third or more, a rate similar to that of Germany, Belgium or Hong Kong. In this long-term plan, another one-third of children would be placed in small-scale group homes of around six children administrated by three children's home staff; and the final one-third would be placed in children's homes of 45 children or fewer, broken up into smaller units, each with 6–8 children.

Other important drivers in contemporary child welfare policy are abuse scandals and pressure from NGOs, most particularly the Japanese Federation of Bar Associations (Fujiwara 2001), non-profit advocates and research groups. Movements to establish systems for the support of foster and adoptive parents have emerged in light of high-profile abuse cases in foster care. For instance, in both the 2002 *Utsunomiya* case, in which a mother fostering with a view toward adoption killed a three-year-old girl, and a 2009 case in Osaka, in which a foster mother sexually abused and gravely injured a five-year-old girl, neither foster carer had received adequate support from the CGC. Neither of the foster families was given adequate information about the foster child's potential behavioural problems or the resources that would allow them to receive respite care or support. In both cases, the foster mother contacted the CGC, intimating that she had begun to act in an abusive manner towards the child, and in neither case did the CGC perceive this as a serious call for help (Hayes and Habu 2006; Murata 2011).

Abuse cases within children's homes, so far, do not seem to have acted as much of a policy driver, although there have been suggestions that caregivers in institutions should be required to hold professional certification (Bamba and Haight 2011, p.188). However, pressure from NGOs and bar associations *has* resulted in concrete action to address abuse cases on an individual basis. The Japanese Federation of Bar Associations (JFBA 2009) notes:

> There are no public statistics on abuse within child welfare facilities, but according to the Association for Intolerance of Child Abuse in Institutions, a private sector organization…misconducts and rights violations were allegedly occurring in 15.5 per cent of children's homes nationwide…

Forty-three per cent of abuses are related to corporal punishment and 24 per cent to sexual abuse. Even if repeated reports are made about an institution, local governments can be slow to investigate. This was the case of the Onchōen children's home in the Kanto area, where physical and sexual abuse by staff (including the son of the Director) continued for over ten years before the Director was sanctioned and removed, at least in part due to the interventions of a private advocacy group (Onchōen Children's Support Group 2011; see also Hayes and Habu 2006, p.127; JFBA 2009).

Tsuzaki, an outspoken critic of the contemporary child welfare system's extensive use of children's homes, argues that abuse within children's homes rarely attains public attention, unless a child dies (2009, p.134).

Some potential policy drivers are success cases. Government initiatives to increase foster care placements might well have been encouraged by the achievements of individual cities in increasing placements and developing robust support services for foster caregivers. For example, the city of Fukuoka increased foster care placements from 7 per cent in 2003 to 21 per cent in 2009 (JaSPCAN 2010). Finally, self-advocacy groups have begun to bring the voices of youth in care to the government level (Hinata Bokko 2009).

Family policy and family values

Although the adoption of unrelated young children occurs in only small numbers in contemporary Japan, 'regular adoption' has been and remains quite common. The extended family (*ie*) system was instated during the 1868 Meiji Restoration. Sweeping efforts were made to bring a fragmented national body together, and the *ie* system located every individual within a family line, which was documented within a family registry system. The Emperor was considered the paternal figure of the nation, and each family line was thus seen as 'a miniature of society' as a whole (Paulson 1985, p.13). After the Second World War, the American occupiers abolished the *ie* system because they believed that its logic supported nationalistic sentiment. The 1948 Civil Code thus removed mention of the *ie* as a legal entity, as well as the stipulation of primogeniture, which was perceived as undemocratic. The 1947 Family Registration Law also limited family units to two generations. However, adoption law remained unchanged. Although even today public opinion generally seems split regarding the degree to which the *ie* mentality remains salient, the numbers of 'regular adoptions' remain high. Further, although primogeniture is no longer a legal rule, Paulson (1985) indicated that 70 per cent of surveyed families in cities and 80 per cent in villages chose the eldest son as the family successor (p.375). Paulson speculates that the lack of social services in Japan may play a key role in these practices, which reinforce the role of family in providing care (p.378). People sometimes also adopt, thus stipulating an inheritance, in exchange for childcare (Bryant 1990).

So if 'regular adoption' is historically common, why do people so rarely make use of the 'special adoption' system? The phrase 'You don't know from which horse the bone came' (*doko no uma no hone ka wakaranai*) is sometimes cited to explain the undesirability of a person of unknown origin, and thus perhaps with 'bad blood', as a marriage partner or a family member in general

(Goodman 1998a). 'Regular adoption', on the other hand, is generally pursued to adopt adults, the children of kin or the child of a spouse. In the past, a wide variety of people might have been considered for adoption – a servant, concubine, apprentice or employee. But as nuclear residence patterns became more common, and household appliances reduced the need for domestic assistance, notions of who may be incorporated into the family have become narrower (Ronald and Alexy 2011, p.5; see also Goldfarb 2012; Ochiai 1997). According to Japanese ethnographers Yanagita and Ariga, fostering, itself, has a 'traditional' counterpart that is no longer practised – ritualized quasi-parent relationships a child might have with different members of the community: 'All those "parents" took their place beside the biological ones, watching over the child and contributing to his or her development' (Yamamura 1986, pp.32–33). Adopting an unknown child whose past, and thus future, is perceived to be uncertain is seen by many as strange and risky, and can still inspire stigma or discrimination. Further, advances in reproductive technologies give couples with infertility problems the possibility to have their own biological child, which some researchers argue has, itself, become a coercive norm (Shirai 2010). Thus the contemporary notion of 'family' in Japan has narrowed over the past century, and is now often discussed in terms of blood relatedness or genetic inheritance.

As family and residence practices changed, so did perceptions of gender roles and expectations surrounding parenting. Ochiai (1997) ties the economic boom of the Taisho Period (1912–1926) to the emergence of a new middle class that moved to city suburbs, and clearly separated work and home, and public and private. By the mid-Taisho and early-Showa (1926–1989) periods, Ochiai (1997, pp.31–33) judges that a large portion of the population had sufficient income for wives to stay at home. By the end of the Second World War, housewives were 'the overwhelming majority', and women who differed from this new norm felt 'socially inferior' (Ochiai 1997, p.35). Academic discourses supported the notion of the nurturing housewife and mother, like the psychological theories of *Takeo Doi*, who posited that 'giving and receiving deep, indulgent love formed the basis of all significant relationships in Japan' (Holloway 2010, p.36). The perception that women should stay at home with their children and give them constant attention until the child turns three years old is commonly referred to as the 'myth of three years' (*sansai shinwa*).[2] But mythic or not, the concept is still prevalent: Holloway discusses the results, from four different surveys carried out from 2003, that indicate that between 60 per

---

2   This concept is expressed by the colloquial saying '*mitsugo no tamashii hyaku made*', which can be translated as 'the child is father to the man'.

cent and 83 per cent of respondents believe that 'mothers should stay at home with their children during the first three years of life' (2010, p.34; Takahashi 2003). Social expectations for motherly devotion remain so high that childrearing neurosis and childrearing anxiety (*ikuji fuan*) have become public health concerns and are believed to contribute to child maltreatment (Arimoto and Murashima 2007; Holloway 2010; Ochiai 1997). Public policies attempting both to ameliorate the declining birth rate and to address issues of child abuse have represented these gendered expectations as 'nontraditional' values imported from North America and Europe in the 1960s, and make explicit the benefits of men being involved in childcare (Goodman 2002a, p.19; Roberts 2002). Critics of public policies focused on childcare provisioning note that corporate practices must first be altered, in order to change gendered expectations of childrearing.

Gender-defined 'role perfectionism' is tightly connected to family ideologies in Japan, as well as to problems of child welfare. The concept of role perfectionism relates, first, to issues of parenting and the gendered division of labour. As Morrone and Matsuyama (2010, p.374; see also JaSPCAN 2010, p.174) note:

> Underlying both the father's decision to stay at work and the mother's decision to oversee the house and children is the strong cultural notion that one should be devoted to only one thing at a time, and that this devotion must be 100%.

Further, as Hertog's nuanced research has shown, if a woman cannot provide an optimal environment for a child, she may believe it preferable – and in the child's best interest – to abort. 'According to my interviewees,' Hertog writes, 'abortion quite often seemed less morally questionable than giving birth to an illegitimate child' (2008, p.210; see also Hardacre 1997, p.72; Hertog 2009). Goodman analyses public perceptions of *oyako shinjyu* (the suicide of a parent in which the parent also kills the child), which is rarely socially understood as child abuse or murder. The term *shinjyu* itself 'connotes a double suicide committed out of love' (Goodman 2002b, p.138). Hertog's analysis of the social pressures of role perfectionism, and the cultural value of having a normative family, bring increased nuance to Goodman and others' interpretation that *oyako shinjyu* reflects the belief that a child is 'an extension of, rather than separate from, the parent' (2008, p.139; see also Matsushima 1996; Yamamura 1986).

Parents' proper disciplining of their children is understood to have a formative role in the child's developing personality. Hendry describes the role of discipline (*shitsuke*) as shaping the child for the child's benefit: the term *shitsuke* (躾) is a compound of the characters body (身) and beauty (美), and thus the concept of discipline can be glossed as 'to beautify the body', or to constitute the body of the child with the manners necessary to be a member of society (1986, p.11). Physical discipline is often understood as 'an integral part of turning Japanese children into adult members of Japanese society', and until recently its use was legally accepted at schools and in child welfare institutions (Goodman 2002b, p.142). Parents are still legally entitled to use corporal punishment for disciplinary purposes (Minamikata *et al.* 1999), and the notion that guardians are entitled to inflict physical punishment may be one of the reasons corporal punishment still seems to be common in children's homes (Goodman 2002b, p.143; JFBA 2009). Isolation of a child, ignoring a child or putting the child out of the house, particularly at night, are other disciplinary methods that Hendry analyses as socially effective because 'the child is being ostracized by the people from whom it can normally expect benevolence; it is being separated from the "inside group" to which it belongs' (1986, p.111). Hendry also mentions threats, supernatural sanctions and ridicule as ways of socializing a child into 'ordinary' behaviour (1986, p.114). Holloway's survey of contemporary disciplinary practices yields scolding, and when her respondents were asked to identify a disciplinary behaviour that was most common, one-third mentioned spanking or other corporal punishment, while less than 15 per cent mentioned threats and isolation (2010, p.130).

Child abuse in Japan is categorized as either physical, sexual or psychological abuse, or neglect (Japan, MHLW 2011b). Contemporary social standards shape the legal distinctions between appropriate discipline and child maltreatment, and the threshold for removing parental rights (Minamikata *et al.* 1999). The removal or suspension of such rights can result from neglect 'without legitimate reason'; wrongful exercise of the parental right to administer the child's property; and 'gross misconduct', measured against current social norms, when detrimental to the child's welfare (Minamikata *et al.* 1999). When child maltreatment is suspected, CGCs may, according to Bamba and Haight (2011, p.179):

> (1) take temporary protective measures to safeguard the child without parental consent, (2) enter a private household to investigate the allegation, (3) apply for a court order to remove the child to a place of safety without parental consent, and (4) apply for the deprivation of parental rights by a family court.

After investigating and developing a plan for intervention, a CGC may provide services to the family or remove the child. In the case of removal, the child may be placed in temporary care within the CGC building, or be placed in a children's home, a medical facility or in foster care (Bamba and Haight 2011, p.180). It is extremely rare that parents would have their parental rights removed by court order. Bamba and Haight cite 2007 statistics, in which 40,639 cases of child maltreatment were brought before CGCs, and out of those cases, CGC staff members appealed to the family court for termination of parental rights in only four cases, only one of which was approved (2011, pp.180–181). Parental rights can be restored through an application to the family court, but these processes are considered very serious (Matsushima 1996, p.129).

The child in state care

Children's homes in Japan (*jidō yōgo shisetsu*) are distinguished from orphanages (*kojiin*) because they are not institutions for orphans, but rather social welfare institutions that house children whose parents cannot care for them, including abandoned children (2.2%) and those parents whose location is unknown (2.0%). In fact, only 8.6 per cent of children in Japanese children's homes and 2.1 per cent of babies in infant homes lack both parents. Baby homes (*nyūjiin*) care for babies from birth to around two years of age. After that age, a baby is either transferred to a children's home; efforts are made to reunite the baby with his or her parents; or the baby is placed into adoptive or foster care, a less likely outcome (reasons for which are discussed below). Although the age of majority in Japan is 20 years, alternative care is terminated at 18 years of age, unless an extension until the age of majority is obtained. Additionally, if a child completes compulsory education (middle school) but does not go on to high school, that child must leave the children's home or foster care. Independent-living support facilities may be available for such adolescents.

The Ministry of Health, Labour and Welfare (2011b) presents survey results indicating the reasons for placement in institutional or foster care. Notably, the survey does not mention placement by court order, which occurs very rarely. In 2008, there was only one case in which an abusive parent lost custody under a family court ruling (Tsuzaki 2011). Most commonly, CGC caseworkers negotiate with parents to have children placed in out-of-home care because the parent has been shown to be neglectful or abusive. In another Ministry of Health, Labour and Welfare survey (2010a), which allowed for only one answer in describing the reasons for placement, the most predominant reasons were abuse from either mother or father and neglect. However, a more detailed examination of the survey results presents a picture highly dependent on parental gender roles. The most prevalent reasons for placement specifically identify problems with the mother: her neglect (11.7%), her mental illness (10.1%), her abuse (8.5%), her abandonment (5.9%) or her hospitalization (4.8%). Father-specific reasons were: his abuse (5.9%) or his work and job (5.6%). Non-gender specific factors were: economic (7.6%), general refusal to care for the child

(4.4%) or parents' divorce (4.1%). The same survey notes that 53.4 per cent of children in Japanese state care have experienced some form of abuse, but most practitioners would note that this figure should be higher, because almost all children in state care have experienced at least some degree of neglect in their families of origin. These survey results reveal two important issues. Single parents often have difficulty caring for their children, both because of financial instability and workplace expectations for long working hours, especially for men; and a lack of childcare services with flexible hours. There is no dual custody agreement in the case of divorce, so divorced parents face the same childcare barriers as a single parent.

When children are placed in out-of-home care, the objective is generally to reunite the family, but because of a lack of social welfare services supporting parental needs, institutional and foster care often become long-term placements; the average stay in a children's home is 4.6 years, with a small percentage of children (5.2%) living in institutional care for over 12 years. Here is an imagined case with fairly typical characteristics: A couple has four children, and they divorce, leaving two children under paternal custody, and two under maternal custody. The father works long hours and leaves the two children, who are three and five years of age, home alone during the day, preparing rice balls every morning for their meals. Community members report to a local CGC that two young children have been seen playing alone in a neighbourhood park, or perhaps a convenience store clerk discovers these children repeatedly shoplifting snacks and toys. In collaboration with CGC staff, the father's siblings, who are unable to take care of the children, encourage the father to have the children placed in an institution, where he can visit them on his day off. In a case like this, the children might be able to return to the father's home when they become older and spend longer hours in school and are more capable of caring for themselves. However, in many cases, children are placed in institutional care even though there is no likely prospect of family reunification. Sixteen per cent of children in children's homes and 20 per cent of babies in infant homes have no contact with their parents (Japan, MHLW 2010a).

As of November 2010, there were 569 children's homes and 121 baby homes in Japan. The majority of children's homes accommodate between 40 and 60 children, and in response to government calls to provide more household-style care, larger homes are sometimes broken into smaller units, which are called *shōkibo gurūpu kea* (458 locations). A 2009 initiative to create family homes, each run by three caregivers who may or may not be foster parents, resulted in 53 family homes by February 2010 (Japan, MHLW 2010a). There are also small-scale group homes, which are run by children's homes but situated within a community, usually housing around six children and usually in a normal house (*chiiki shōkibo jidō yōgo shisetsu*) (190 locations). Additionally, there are short-term medical treatment institutions for emotionally and psychologically disturbed children (*jyōsyo shōgaiji tanki chiryō shisetsu*) (32 institutions); institutions to support independent living, specifically for youth with behaviour and delinquency problems (*jidō jiritsu shien shisetsu*) (58 institutions); dorms for single women and their children (*boshi seikatsu shien shisetsu*) (270 institutions); and homes for youth who have finished middle school (compulsory education in Japan) but have not gone on to further education, or have left children's homes and require support in order to live independently (*jiritsu shien hōmu*) (54 institutions) (Japan, MHLW 2010a). Finally, as of November 2010, there were four shelters run by NGOs that house teenagers in emergency situations who are ineligible for entry into any of the above-mentioned institutions; more shelters are expected to be established in the future (JFBA 2009; JaSPCAN 2010).

Approximately 10 per cent of the children in Japanese state care are placed in foster homes, although the Japanese government's 2010 Vision for Children and Child-rearing specifies the goal to increase foster care placements to 16 per cent by 2014, and eventually to 30 per cent. The current foster care system divides foster parents into three different types: kinship foster parents, foster parents with the intent to adopt, and foster parents without the intent to adopt. The latter category is broken into a further sub-category for 'specialist' foster parents, who receive training beyond that of normal foster parents in order to care for children with special needs stemming from disability, behavioural problems and/or a history of abuse (Japan, MHLW 2010a). The separation of foster parents with and without the intent to adopt was a strategic move made in 2008, in an attempt to clarify the difference between foster care and adoption. Prospective adoptive parents working through CGCs are required to register first as foster parents, and this may be part of the reason these distinctions are unclear. CGC caseworkers often complain that prospective foster parents are overly particular in specifying the type of child they would consider, which may be the result of lingering confusion regarding the differences between fostering and adoption. This is also one explanation for the large gap, in November 2010, between the numbers of families registered as foster parents (7,808) and the numbers of foster parents who have a child placed with them (2,727) (Japan, MHLW 2010a). However, children that are eligible for foster care often have no contact with their birth parents, which effectively makes foster care similar to adoptive care. As found in a 2008 survey, 71.9 per cent of children in foster care had no contact with their birth parents (Japan, MHLW 2010a). Additionally, foster parents hoping to adopt are often convinced to take in a child who is not eligible for adoption, but who they end up raising as their own child (Goldfarb 2012; Hayes and Habu 2006). Hayes and Habu cite a 1997 opinion survey of CGC staff: 'Only 4% of the respondent CGCs were willing to take the initiative to go to court to remove the custody right from birth parents so that the children could be adopted by foster parents' (2006, p.150). While adoption is not a common permanent plan, children's homes or foster care are often long-term placements (Hayes and Habu 2006).

Two major factors shape the form taken by child welfare services in Japan: the structure of Japan's CGCs, and the legal notion of parental rights (*shinken*), as interpreted by CGCs and family courts. At the time of writing, there are around 200 CGCs in Japan, although new centres continue to be established. They address all manner of issues surrounding child welfare, including school bullying, disability, truancy, delinquency, parenting concerns, child abuse, adoption and arranging placements for children in out-of-home care. CGC caseworkers hold an average of 107 cases at any given time (JaSPCAN 2010, p.46). CGCs are government offices, and as such, around 40 per cent of officers even within the child welfare division are general administrative officers with no training in child welfare; another 20 per cent have qualifications in some area of human service (such as teaching, public health, childcare or child welfare), and the remaining 40 per cent are educated in social welfare (Bamba and Haight 2011, p.181). There are no professional qualifications in social work in Japan, however, so an education in social welfare is not equivalent to a professional degree. Government officials in Japan are generally transferred to different offices every three to five years, ostensibly to give them a broad sense of the issues affecting diverse areas. Thus an officer who is not a specialist in child welfare might be first placed in the water sanitation department, and in the next rotation transferred to a CGC. This transfer system is additionally difficult in a profession that depends on building rapport with clients and maintaining long-term files tracking children's placements. News of an imminent transfer can come suddenly, and neither caseworkers nor clients can necessarily count on a continuous relationship (Goldfarb 2012).

Many CGC buildings also contain temporary emergency care facilities for children who are removed from their parents or are waiting for placement in a more permanent location. These facilities are known for being overcrowded, and it is difficult to provide sufficient supervision and support for the wide variety of children and youth who might be placed in temporary care. Violence among the children and youth placed in these facilities is an endemic problem (Bamba and Haight 2011; JaSPCAN 2010; JFBA 2009). Children placed in emergency temporary care cannot attend school for the duration of their placement, which can last for over a year in exceptional cases, because there are not enough staff to accompany children to school, and because children are often placed in institutions far from their former neighbourhoods. Youth who have experienced placement in temporary care described the experience as traumatic and isolating, as they had no contact with their friends (Nishida 2011).

CGC workers' job requirements often place them in a difficult position. They are required to develop rapport and consult with their clients, but they are also charged with investigating potential child-maltreatment cases and petitioning the family court for suspension or termination of parental rights. Takashi Sato (2009), a caseworker in the Kanagawa prefecture, writes compellingly about the tensions caseworkers perceive between these two roles. Based on a national survey of CGC staff, Sato summarizes the majority opinions that CGC workers' jobs are social work positions, which includes negotiation with parents, and should not include the enforcement of restraining orders, demands that parents appear at the CGC with the child, or forceful investigations of residences. CGC staff feel the need for police and legal support and the active involvement of family courts in restricting parental contact with children (Sato 2009, p.139). In complicated cases requiring law enforcement involvement, caseworkers worry that conflicts with clients will 'impede subsequent social work interventions' (Bamba and Haight 2011, p.182). Indeed, up until now, placement decisions even in cases of child abuse have been predominantly negotiated between CGC staff and the child's parent. Because CGC caseworkers tend to believe that parents will feel threatened by the possibility of foster care placement, most caseworkers suggest institutional placements right away, even for infants (Goldfarb 2012; Hayes and Habu 2006). Illustratively, although the Aichi prefecture CGC in Kariya is heavily involved in providing adoptive placements for newborns, there are no CGCs that aggressively place infants in foster care. A research team investigating this issue presented their findings at the Japanese Society for the Prevention of Child Abuse and Neglect Conference in 2010. Although infant-home representatives recognized that placing infants in foster care might have benefits from an attachment perspective, they were sceptical that birth parents would agree to foster placements, and were concerned that foster caregivers would refuse infants with illness or disability. The research team's survey of foster parents yielded many enthusiastic responses, although there were concerns with having the proper equipment to care for an infant, the need for institutionalized support, and the necessity to encourage young and energetic people to become foster parents (JaSPCAN 2010, p.176). Finally, even when CGCs are involved in abuse cases, the above reasons contribute to the possibility that they will not adequately intervene. The JFBA (2009) notes that, in 2005, CGCs were already involved in almost 20 per cent of the known abuse cases that resulted in the child's death.

CGC staff members have the legal right to make placement decisions without the consent of a child's biological parents. When a birth parent *explicitly* protests, the CGC officer must receive a family court order to place a child in alternative care, which must be for a period of less than two years, although this term can be extended with family court approval (JFBA 2009). In order for the family court to renew the period of placement, the JFBA (2009) notes, CGCs must have maintained active involvement in the case; this may be problematic since many CGCs consider placement in children's homes or foster care to be the conclusion of a case. The JFBA (2009, paragraph 165) suggests, in this context, that:

> The Government should give consideration to an effective system whereby the judicial system is involved in guidance of the persons with parental authority following order of a child's placement in an institution. This might take the form of a legal system which would include, for example, orders for persons with parental authority to undergo counseling or treatment by the family court.

These stipulations are currently not in place.

The practice of making placement decisions without explicit permission is important in the context of CGC officers' desires to maintain the good will of birth parents. If a child is abandoned, the parents' whereabouts are unknown (*yukuefumei*) or the parent never visits a child in a children's home, a proactive children's home staff member or caseworker may decide that it would be in the child's best interest to place him or her in foster or adoptive care. However, many CGC staff are reluctant to pursue such an option without a signature from the birth parent approving the placement, as this action would seem like an inappropriate encroachment on the parent's rights (Goldfarb 2012). That a CGC officer must receive a family court order if the parent explicitly protests against a placement is also problematic, because CGC staff are aware that family courts are likely not to terminate parental rights or make a decision that disfavours a parent. Because of this, CGC staff are more likely to negotiate with the birth parent and hope that the birth parent will allow the child to be placed in, and remain in, a children's home.

A 2011 revision to the Civil Code addresses this issue as it applies to children who have been recognized as abused by their parents.[3] This new revision, implemented on 1 April 2012, has major effects for the rights of abusive parents. First, parental rights can be *temporarily* suspended for a period of two years, subject to renewal, but rights will be reinstated if the parent exhibits evidence of improvement. This revision emerges out of recognition that CGC caseworkers are reluctant to pursue the *full* removal of parental rights in addition to placing the child in alternative care, which would 'seem to cut the tie between the parent and child' (Japan, MHLW 2011b). This revision also may be targeted at family courts known for conservatism even in cases of child abuse and neglect: 'Court willingness to accept evidence of abuse may be too limited to obvious signs of physical injury, with other ways of establishing the truth, including forensic interview methods, left unexplored' (Hayes and Habu 2006, p.128).

In abuse cases where parental rights have *not* been temporarily suspended, this revision prohibits the parent from using the weight of parental rights to make unreasonable demands. Examples given include the parent withholding approval for the child's medical treatment, removing the child from school against the child's wishes, or making any other unreasonable demands of the children's home or foster parent (Japan, MHLW 2011b). This latter example probably refers to the parent demanding that the child be taken home again, although the vagueness of the wording may give CGC officials latitude to negotiate and may not completely protect a child from being removed from alternative care by the parent.

Finally, this revision encourages the assignment of a legal guardian for a child whose parents have lost parental rights. In the past, it was common for only children with inheritances to be assigned a legal guardian. This revision makes it easier to assign a guardian, with presumably the intended effect of increased use of the guardian system. Guardians can now be multiple persons, and can also be the welfare organization that runs a children's home, which would be expected to maintain activities as a guardian after the child leaves care (Japan, MHLW 2011b).

Conclusion

Efforts to address child maltreatment in Japan often rhetorically frame the child as 'belonging' to society at large rather than 'belonging' (*mono*) to the child's parents (JaSPCAN 2010; Morioka 1986). This form of

---

3   A distinction is drawn between parents who are deemed to be abusive, and those who are unable to maintain their children, and thus are not considered suitable caregivers, for whatever reason, but have not been deemed abusive.

representation articulates with concerns regarding the power of parental rights in law, anxieties regarding the isolation of private homes, and traditional framings of the child as an extension of the family or parent. But, despite a decade and a half of engagement with the UN as Japan attempts to meet the stipulations of the UNCRC, the importance of child *protection* through social mechanisms may have become commonly known, but the idea of the child as a rights-bearing individual is still less salient. Thus, growing recognition of child abuse does not necessarily imply increased recognition of child rights, and child welfare policies still focus on vague references to the 'best interests of the child' or the child's 'wellbeing'. The actual *content* of 'child rights' remains undefined within the Child Welfare Law itself (JFBA 2009). Further, although legal and policy initiatives increasingly engage with the concept of child rights, sometimes explicitly referencing the UNCRC or other UN initiatives (Japan, MHLW 2011a), there remains a significant gap between laws and policies, and enforcement in daily practice. This chapter has described the complexity of child welfare practices in Japan, which have been shaped by a multitude of interconnected factors: ideologies surrounding the family as a social and cultural form; concepts of gender roles and norms surrounding parenting practices; bureaucratic and institutional structures; and culturally and legally ingrained concepts of parental rights. Although legal and policy changes are certainly key in altering child welfare practices, this chapter argues that fine-grained cultural analysis is necessary in order to fully understand both the stakes of contemporary welfare practices, and the wide variety of beliefs and values that must be considered in any reform effort.

References

Amino, T. (2007) 'Jidō fukushihō 60nen no ayumi' ['Progress made in 60 years of the child welfare law']. In S. Takahashi (ed.) *Nihon no kodomo katei fukushi: Jidō fukushihō seitei 60nen no ayumi [Japan's Child and Family Welfare: Progress Made in 60 Years after the Legislation of the Child Welfare Law]*. Tokyo, JP: Akashi Shoten.

Arimoto, A. and Murashima, S. (2007) 'Child-rearing anxiety and its correlates among Japanese mothers screened at 18-month infant health checkups.' *Public Health Nursing 24*, 2, 101–110.

Arudou, D. (2009) 'Demography vs. demagoguery: When politics, science collide.' *Japan Times*, 3 November.

Bamba, S. and Haight, W.L. (2011) *Child Welfare and Development: A Japanese Case Study*. Cambridge: Cambridge University Press.

Befu, H. (2001) *Hegemony of Homogeneity: An Anthropological Analysis of Nihonjinron*. Melbourne, AU: Transpacific Press.

Benedict, R. (1946) *The Chrysanthemum and the Sword: Patterns of Japanese Culture*. Cleveland, OH: Meridian Books.

Bryant, T.L. (1990) 'Sons and lovers: Adoption in Japan.' *The American Journal of Comparative Law 38*, 2, 299–336.

Dale, P. (2011) *The Myth of Japanese Uniqueness*. London: Taylor and Francis.

Freeman, M. (1996) 'Introduction: Children as Persons.' In M. Freeman (ed.) *Children's Rights: A Comparative Perspective*. Aldershot, UK: Dartmouth Publishing.

Fujiwara, S. (2001) 'The role of lawyers and bar associations in the promotion and protection of the human rights of children.' Paper presented at the 12th Presidents of Law Association in Asia (POLA Conference, Christchurch, New Zealand).

Garon, S.M. (1997) *Molding Japanese Minds: The State in Everyday Life*. Princeton, NJ: Princeton University Press.

Goldfarb, K. (2012) *Fragile Kinships: Family Ideologies and Child Welfare in Japan* (unpublished PhD dissertation). Chicago, IL: University of Chicago, Department of Anthropology.

Goodman, R. (1998a) 'A Child in Time: Changing Adoption and Fostering in Japan.' In J. Hendry (ed.) *Interpreting Japanese Society: Anthropological Approaches* (2nd ed.). New York: Routledge.

Goodman, R. (1998b) 'The "Japanese-Style Welfare State" and the Delivery of Personal Social Services.' In R. Goodman, G. White and H. Kwon (eds) *The East Asian Welfare Model: Welfare Orientalism and the State*. New York: Routledge.

Goodman, R. (2001) *Children of the Japanese State: The Changing Role of Child Protection Institutions in Contemporary Japan*. Oxford: Oxford University Press.

Goodman, R. (2002a) 'Anthropology, Policy and the Study of Japan.' In R. Goodman (ed.) *Family and Social Policy in Japan*. Cambridge: Cambridge University Press.

Goodman, R. (2002b) 'Child Abuse in Japan: "Discovery" and the Development of Policy.' In R. Goodman (ed.) *Family and Social Policy in Japan*. Cambridge: Cambridge University Press.

Hardacre, H. (1997) *Marketing the Menacing Fetus in Japan*. Berkeley, CA: University of California Press.

Harootunian, H. (2000) *Overcome by Modernity: History, Culture, and Community in Interwar Japan*. Princeton, NJ: Princeton University Press.

Hayes, P. and Habu, T. (2006) *Adoption in Japan: Comparing Policies for Children in Need*. New York: Routledge.

Hendry, J. (1986) *Becoming Japanese: The World of the Pre-School Child*. Manchester, UK: Manchester University Press.

Hertog, E. (2008) 'The worst abuse against a child is the absence of a parent: How Japanese unwed mothers evaluate their decision to have a child outside wedlock.' *Japan Forum 20*, 2, 193–217.

Hertog, E. (2009) *Tough Choices: Bearing an Illegitimate Child in Contemporary Japan*. Stanford, CA: Stanford University Press.

Hinata Bokko (2009) *Shisetsu de sodatta kodomotachi no ibashyo 'Hinata Bokko' to shyakaiteki yōgo* [*A Place to Belong for Children who were raised in Institutional Care: Hinata Bokko and Social Protective Care*]. Tokyo, JP: Akashi Shoten.

Holloway, S.D. (2010) *Women and Family in Contemporary Japan*. Cambridge: Cambridge University Press.

Japan Federation of Bar Associations (JFBA) (2009) *The Japan Federation of Bar Associations' Report on the Japanese Government's Third Report on the Convention on the Rights of the Child and the Initial Reports on OPAC & OPSC*. Available at: www.crin.org/resources/infodetail.asp?id=22436.

Japan, Ministry of Health, Labour and Welfare (MHLW) (2010a) 'Shyakaiteki yōgo no genjyō to torikumi no hōkōsei ni tsuite' ['Present conditions and initiatives in social protective care']. Paper presented at the 56th National Foster Parent's Convention, Tokyo, 11 November.

Japan, Ministry of Health, Labour and Welfare (MHLW) (2010b) 'Jidō gyakutai bōshi taisaku ni tsuite' ['Measures to prevent child abuse']. Paper presented at the 16th annual Japanese Society for the Prevention of Child Abuse and Neglect (JaSPCAN) Conference, Tokyo, 27–28 November.

Japan, Ministry of Health, Labour and Welfare (MHLW) (2011a) *Investigative Commission Report on Issues Concerning Children's Homes and Social Welfare* (30 June). Available at: www.mhlw.go.jp/english.

Japan, Ministry of Health, Labour and Welfare (MHLW) (2011b) *Jidō gyakutai kankei no saishin no hōritsu kaisei ni tsuite* [*About the Latest Revisions to Law Related to Child Abuse*]. Available at: www.mhlw.go.jp/seisaku/2011/07/02.html.

Japan, Statistics Bureau (SB) (2011) *Statistics.* Available at: www.stat.go.jp/english/data/index.htm.

Japanese Society for the Prevention of Child Abuse and Neglect (JaSPCAN) (2010) 'Nihon kodomo gyakutai boshi gakkai' ['Japanese Society for the Prevention of Child Abuse and Neglect']. Paper presented at the 16th annual JaSPCAN meeting, 27–28 November.

Kikuta, N. (1981) 'Nihon no kogoroshi wo kangaeru: Kodomo no kōfuku yorimo oya no sekinin wo jyūshi suru nihon shyakai' ['Considering infanticide in Japan: Japanese society that considers a parent's responsibility more important than a child's wellbeing']. *Keizai oūrai,* August, 200–213.

Kono, M. (2005) 'The Welfare Regime in Japan.' In A. Walker and C. Wong (eds) *East Asian Welfare Regimes in Transition: From Confucianism to Globalisation.* Bristol, UK: Policy Press.

Krogness, K.J. (2011) 'The Ideal, the Deficient, and the Illogical Family: An Initial Typology of Administrative Household Units.' In R. Ronald and A. Alexy (eds) *Home and Family in Japan: Continuity and Transformation.* London: Routledge.

Matsushima, Y. (1996) 'Controversies and Dilemmas: Japan Confronts the Convention.' In M. Freeman (ed.) *Children's Rights: A Comparative Perspective.* Aldershot, UK: Dartmouth Publishing.

Minamikata, S., Shigeru, M. and Hiroko, T. (1999) 'Japan.' In W. Pintens (ed.) *International Encyclopaedia of Laws: Family and Succession Law, Japan Supplement.* The Hague, NL: Kluwer Law International.

Morioka, K. (1986) 'Privatization of Family Life in Japan.' In H. Stevenson, A. Hiroshi and H. Kenji (eds) *Child Development and Education in Japan.* New York: W.H. Freeman.

Morrone, M.H. and Matsuyama, Y. (2010) 'Japan's parental leave policy: Has it affected gender ideology and child care norms in Japan?' *Childhood Education 86,* 6, 371–375.

Murata, K. (2011) 'Satooya ni yoru gyakutai jiken wo kangaeru futatsu no saiban wo bōchyō shite' ['Considering foster care abuse cases upon attending two court hearings']. *Satooya dayori 87,* 14–17.

Nishida, Y. (2011) *Jidō yōgo shisetsu to shyakaiteki haijyo* [*Children's Homes and Social Exclusion*]. Tokyo, JP: Kaiho Shyuppannsya.

Ochiai, E. (1997) *The Japanese Family System in Transition.* Tokyo, JP: LTCB International Library Foundation.

Onchōen Children's Support Group (2011) *Jidō shisetsu no jidō gyakutai* [*Abuse within Children's Homes*]. Tokyo, JP: Akashi Shoten.

Paulson, J.L. (1985) *Family Law Reform in Postwar Japan: Succession and Adoption* (PhD Dissertation, University of Colorado at Boulder). Arbor, MI: University Microfilms International.

Roberts, G. (2002) 'Pinning Hopes on Angels: Reflections from an Aging Japan's Urban Landscape.' In R. Goodman (ed.) *Family and Social Policy in Japan*. Cambridge: Cambridge University Press.

Ronald, R. and Alexy, A. (2011) 'Continuity and Change in Japanese Homes and Families.' In R. Ronald and A. Alexy (eds) *Home and Family in Japan: Continuity and Transformation*. London: Routledge.

Sato, T. (2009) *Jidō sodanjyo no genjyō to kadai: Jidō gyakutai taiō to taisei seibi* [*The Contemporary Conditions and Challenges at Child Guidance Centres: Response to Child Abuse and Organizational Structure*]. Tokyo, JP: Sōdo Bunka.

Shirai, C. (2010) 'Reproductive technologies and parent–child relationships: Japan's past and present examined through the lens of donor insemination.' *International Journal of Japanese Sociology 19*, 1, 19–35.

Suzuki, H. (2011) 'Jidō sodanjyo ga kanyo shita yōshi engumi ni kan suru ankēto no hōteki bunseki' ['Legal analysis of adoption undertaken by child guidance centres']. *Hikakuhō zasshi 45*, 1, 291–301.

Takahashi, M. (2003) 'Care for Children and Older People in Japan: Modernizing the Traditional.' In A. Anttonen, J. Baldock and J. Sipila (eds) *The Young, the Old and the State: Social Care Systems in Five Industrial Nations*. Cheltenham, UK: Edward Elgar.

Takahashi, M. and Hashimoto, R. (1997) 'Minsei i'in – between public and private: A local network for community care in Japan.' *International Social Work 40*, 303–313.

Tsuzaki, T. (2009) *Kono kuni no kodomotachi: Yōhogo jidō shyakai-teki yōgo no nihon-teki kōchiku; otona no kitoku keneki to kodomo no fukushi* [*This Country's Children: Constructing Social Care for Children in Need of Care; The Vested Interests of Adults and Children's Welfare*]. Tokyo, JP: Nihon Kajyo Syuppan.

Tsuzaki, T. (2011) 'Minpō kaisei to higyakutaiji no shyakaiteki yōgo: Jidō fukushi no shiten kara' ['Revisions to the civil code and social care for abused children: From a child welfare perspective']. *Hōritsu Jihō 83*, 7.

UNICEF (2012) *United Nations Convention on the Rights of the Child*. Available at: www.unicef.org/crc/index_30229.html.

United Nations, Office of the High Commissioner for Human Rights (OHCHR), Supervisory Committee on the Rights of the Child (2009) *Consideration of Reports Submitted by States Parties under Article 44 of the Convention on the Rights of the Child: Japan*. Available at: www2.ohchr.org/english/bodies/crc/docs/co/CRC.C.JPN.CO.3.pdf.

US, Central Intelligence Agency (CIA) (2012) *CIA World Factbook*. Available at: https://www.cia.gov/library/publications/the-world-factbook.

Vogel, E. (1979) *Japan as Number One: Lessons for America*. Lincoln, NE: iUniverse.com, Inc.

Walker, A. and Wong, C. (2005) 'Introduction: East Asian Welfare Regimes.' In A. Walker and C. Wong (eds) *East Asian Welfare Regimes in Transition: From Confucianism to Globalisation*. Bristol, UK: Policy Press.

Yamamura, Y. (1986) 'The Child in Japanese Society.' In H. Stevenson, H. Azuma and K. Hakuta (eds) *Child Development and Education in Japan*. New York: W.H. Freeman.

Yoshizawa, E. (2007) 'Kodomo katei fukushi no 60nen wo furikaette' ['Reflections on 60 Years of Child and Family Welfare']. In S. Takahashi (ed.) *Nihon no kodomo katei fukushi: Jidō fukushihō seitei 60nen no ayumi* [*Japan's Child and Family Welfare: Progress Made in 60 Years after the Legislation of the Child Welfare Law*]. Tokyo, JP: Akashi Shoten.

8

India

Selwyn Stanley

There can be no keener revelation of a society's soul than the way in which it treats its children.

Nelson Mandela[1]

Introduction: The social, political, religious and cultural context

India, the world's largest democracy, is a country rich in diversity in terms of population, geography, climate and cultural heritage. Its roots lie in the ancient Indus valley civilization. Its history is one of cross-cultural contact with several ancient societies that have enhanced its vibrancy and variety in terms of culture, race, ethos, religion, caste and language. It is the world's seventh largest country by area. With six major religions (Hinduism, Islam, Sikhism, Christianity, Buddhism and Zoroastrianism) and 18 official languages, innumerable dialects and tribal languages, it is a union of 28 states and 7 territories. Its current population at 1.21 billion makes it the second most populous country in the world after China, constituting over 17 per cent of the world's population, with one in six people on the planet living there. About 72 per cent of that population lives in about 638,000 villages and the rest in about 5,480 towns and urban agglomerations across India. The population density is 382 people per square kilometre.

With a population growth rate of 1.58 per cent, India is expected to overtake China's population by 2030, when it is predicted to have more than 1.53 billion people. More than half of India's current population is under 25 years of age, and more than a third is under 18 years of age. India

---

1   Nelson Mandela made this statement in his summary of the first year of the Nelson Mandela Children's Fund (www.ppseawa.org/Bulletin/02Aug/children.html).

has the largest child population in the world, with 158.8 million children being six years of age or younger (13% of the total population) (India, Ministry of Home Affairs 2011). Almost three-quarters of them live in rural areas, the rest in urban conglomerations. The overall population in India has grown by nearly 18 per cent during the last ten years. While the rural child population has decreased by about 7 per cent, the urban child population has increased by about 10 per cent.

Despite the current unprecedented economic boom, India is plagued by social problems, such as poverty, illiteracy and unemployment.

The family in India

The family is defined by the UNCRC as a unit of two or more persons united by ties of marriage, blood, adoption or consensual unions, generally constituting a single household, and interacting and communicating with each other. Though this definition of the family is rapidly changing, particularly in urban areas, it is the accepted social norm, valid in Indian society even today. The family in India is fairly well developed in terms of its identity, with strong bonds amongst its members, and it is based on a range of kin-extensions. Loyalty to the family and family honour are cherished values, almost sacrosanct for family members.

Family structure in India has a plurality of forms that varies with class, ethnicity and individual choices. The normative family composition types in India are the extended or joint family, and elementary or nuclear family. In many rural areas, where the traditional joint family system is still very strong, a child grows in the company of his or her own siblings, cousins and grandparents, and several generations may be living under the same roof. In most urban areas, however, the nuclear family is becoming the norm: couples and their unmarried children. They are generally financially independent of other families. In tribal societies, kinship structures are still strong, and community care of children is common, especially during difficult times, such as migration and natural calamities.

The major religious communities in India have their own separate set of laws that govern matters of marriage, divorce, succession, adoption, guardianship and maintenance. These laws have been left untouched by government, unless the demand for change comes from within those communities. The type of family life an Indian child experiences is, therefore, shaped by where they are born, and the religious and ethnic group into which they are born.

The 'spare the rod and spoil the child' dictum is very much an ingrained feature of the collective consciousness in India. Harsh disciplinary practices are very much in vogue within families and even in schools, through caning and other forms of corporal punishment. This is the case even though there are legislative sanctions in place against physical abuse. This attitude to child discipline seems to cut across caste, religious and class divides, and appears to be linked to the cultural idea that children and women are expected to be subservient to men. This inherently patriarchal ideology permeates the entire social fabric. Further, the notion of family honour ensures that matters relating to incest, domestic violence and child abuse, while widely prevalent, are considered taboo for discussion and tend to remain closely guarded family secrets.

The state does not usually interfere in family matters, unless they are in violation of the law. Even then there is only intervention when specific cases are lodged with the police by concerned parties. This tends to be more the exception than the norm, as neighbours usually treat such abuses as internal family affairs, and thus not really their concern. They would prefer not to get embroiled with their neighbours' affairs or with the harshness of the criminal justice system. For this reason, the state does not play a visible, or proactive, role in matters of family abuse, and will not intervene in a manner that would happen in many European countries by, for example, separating children from their family to ensure their protection.

Vulnerable children in India

All children are considered to be at risk for exploitation, abuse, violence and neglect (Childline India Foundation 2012). Though age is one component, vulnerability is also measured by the child's ability to self-protect or to get help from people who can provide protection. A child's vulnerability comes from various factors that hinder a child's ability to function and grow normally.

UNICEF identifies specific groups of Indian children as being vulnerable. These include children who are (Childline India Foundation 2012):

- subjected to violence

- in the midst of armed conflict or associating with armed groups

- affected by HIV/AIDS

- without birth registration

- engaged in under-age labour

- forced into early marriage

- in conflict with the law

- being used for commercial sexual exploitation

- female and subjected to genital mutilation

- the victims of human trafficking.

This highlights the many varied and serious difficulties that impact on the safety and wellbeing of Indian children. Poverty is a common factor in the causation of many of these problems, while others relate to specific cultural and religious values, such as the rejection of girl children.

Survival and the girl child

The patriarchal, patrilineal and patrilocal[2] nature of Indian society places women in a position subordinate to men. The double jeopardy of gender and young age places a girl child in a unique position of vulnerability. This is reflected in statistics of infant and child mortality, leading to a skewed gender ratio with respect to child sexual abuse, and the under-representation of girls at all levels of education.

The sex ratio of children under six years of age is a matter of special concern. The 1991 Census reported a ratio of 945 girls per 1,000 boys, which a decade later had dropped to 927 girls per 1,000 boys, and has since fallen to 914 girls per 1,000 boys in both rural and urban areas, according to the most recent statistics (India, Ministry of Home Affairs 2011). Mumbai, India's commercial capital, has a ratio of 874 girls per 1,000 boys, one of the lowest in the country, while Jhajjar district in the northern state of Haryana could be the capital of female foeticide, with a ratio of 774 girls to 1,000 boys (Patnaik 2011). The Government of India, in its 2001 report to the UN Committee on the Rights of the Child (2003), acknowledged that, of the 12 million girls born every year, three million (25%) do not survive to see their fifteenth birthday. About one-third of these deaths occur in the first year of life. It is estimated that every sixth female child death is directly due to gender discrimination.

Discrimination against the girl child manifests itself even before birth in the form of foeticide, based on prenatal sex determination tests (amniocentesis). This is a phenomenon widely prevalent in urban areas and practised by wealthier, better-educated, middle-class families, who view a girl child as a financial liability and burden, and who are able to afford the prenatal tests and desired medical intervention. The enduring magnitude of the problem is evidenced by statistics that show for example that, in 1984 in Bombay, out of the 8,000 abortions that took place, 7,999 of them were of girls (Gangrade 1988). It is estimated that between three and six million female foetuses were aborted from 2000 to 2010, and that between

---

2   A family system in which the bride moves to live with the family of her husband (editors' note).

1980 and 2010 there could have been as many as 12 million abortions of girls in India (Jha *et al.* 2011). Being a second daughter is even more risky for girls. Jha *et al.* (2011) report that the birth ratio of girls to boys fell by 0.52 per cent a year between 1990 and 2005 when the first child was a daughter, but there was no decline in the ratio among couples whose first child was a son. The prevalence of selective female foeticide in various parts of the country has led the Government of India to attempt to curtail this phenomenon by closing down several sex-detection clinics, particularly in North India, following legislative sanctions and the enactment of the 1996 Pre-Natal Diagnostic Techniques Act.

Female infanticide is another risk faced by girls. This has been reported in several rural areas in some states, including Rajasthan, Uttar Pradesh and Tamil Nadu. The girl child is murdered soon after birth by being neglected and abandoned. Often crude methods – such as feeding her with un-husked rice grains that puncture the windpipe, poisoning, or smothering her with a wet blanket – are resorted to by families wanting to get rid of unwanted girls. The magnitude of the problem prompted the State Government of Tamil Nadu to introduce in Salem district in 1992 a 'cradle baby scheme' with a view to eradicating female infanticide. This enabled families, as an alternative to female infanticide, to abandon their unwanted female children anonymously in cradles available in certain centres, to be brought up by the state. According to newspaper reports, the introduction of this scheme has led to an increase in that state's girl child sex ratio at birth (SRB) from 942 to 946 live female children per 1,000 live male births in 2001 as compared to 2011 (*The Hindu*, 2012). So far 3,200 girls and 582 boys have been rescued under this scheme, of whom 2,088 girls and 372 boys were adopted within the country and 170 girls and 27 boys were adopted in foreign countries (*The Hindu*, 2011).

At the root of discriminatory practices towards the girl child in India is a mindset ingrained by sociocultural and religious factors, one that places higher value on having sons. It is underpinned by an implicit cultural expectation that adult sons will provide economic support for their parents, and take care of them in their old age. A male heir may also be preferred in order to keep family property or a business within the family. In contrast, a daughter may represent a substantial economic burden, as parents often have to pay an exorbitant dowry to get her married. The money spent on bringing up a son is considered to be an investment and that spent on a daughter a waste, as she will, one day, move after marriage to her husband's family. Girls are devalued not only because of economic considerations but also because of sociocultural factors, such as the belief that a son extends the lineage, enlarges the family tree, provides protection, safety and security to the family, and is necessary for salvation, as he alone can light the funeral pyre and perform other death-related rites and rituals (Tandon and Sharma 2006).

Gender-based discrimination in the allocation of resources persists and has even increased, even when their availability is not a constraint (Kishore 1993). A substantial body of research documents that couples with a strong son preference may provide less food or poorer healthcare to their daughters, a practice that contributes to the increased child mortality rate of daughters (Clark 2000). Daughter devaluation is tied to patrilineal kinship structures in which systems of descent, marriage and inheritance work to produce and reinforce the subordinate position of women, thereby generating a desire not to produce female children. Families in such societies have many incentives to strategically avoid having daughters through abortions or neglect (Gill and Mitra-Khan 2009).

Child marriage

'Premature pregnancy and motherhood are an inevitable consequence of child marriage. Girls under 15 are five times more likely to die during pregnancy and childbirth than women in their twenties' (UNICEF 2007a). According to the NFHS-III survey conducted in 2005–2006 (IIPS and Macro International 2006), 47.3 per cent of women between 20 and 24 years of age were married by 18 years of age. Of these, 2.6 per cent were married before they turned 13 years of age, 22.6 per cent were married before 16 years of age and 44.5 per cent were married when they were between 16 and 17 years of age. The official statistics probably do not reveal the true picture. It is estimated that, in some northern states, nearly 80 per cent of the marriages are among girls under 15 years of age (Gupta 2005).

Various underlying sociocultural factors perpetuate this practice, such as traditional gender norms, the high value of virginity, parental concerns surrounding premarital sex, and the financial pressure of dowry and poverty (Amin, Chong and Haberland 2007). The deep-rooted cultural mores that abet child marriage led to the gang rape of Bhanwari Devi[3] by upper-caste men in 1992 in a hamlet in Rajasthan, where she was employed as a *Sathin* (a grass-roots worker in a Women Development Project of the Rajasthan Government). Her 'punishment' followed her opposition to the practice of child marriage prevalent in her village. Although on the wane, several instances of child marriage are still reported from many parts of the country, particularly from the northern states.

---

3   For more details see www.hrsolidarity.net/mainfile.php/1994vol01no01/1935.

Some of the harmful consequences of child marriage for girls are the segregation of children from their family and friends and from their community and peers, as well as the loss of educational opportunities. Adolescent girls placed in child marriages are often deprived of basic healthcare and health information, and achieve extremely low educational attainment (Amin *et al.* 2007; Bruce 2007; Mathur, Greene and Malhotra 2003). Early marriage negatively affects girls' social networks, decision-making power and ability to negotiate with partners – all of which influence health and wellbeing (Bruce 2007). It is also reported that married adolescent girls tend to have higher rates of HIV infection than their sexually active, unmarried peers (Clark, Bruce and Dude 2006).

Legislative imperatives have been put into place to deal with this issue of child marriage. Under the 1929 Child Marriage Restraint Act, those promoting or engaged in the act of marrying under-age boys and girls were liable for punishment. However, the new spouses were not liable for any punishment in law, and the marriage, despite either or both parties being under the prescribed age, remains legally valid and enforceable, since non-recognition of such marriages would imply that any offspring would be illegitimate. This would have consequences for the children, who would carry a stigma that the law seeks to avoid. Subsequently, the 2006 Prohibition of the Child Marriage Act came into effect. Under this Act, the parties to an under-age marriage were given rights to get their marriage declared void. In such cases the girl's right to maintenance from her former husband is protected, until she remarries. The punishment for encouraging or facilitating or solemnizing such marriages has also been increased.

Child labour

A common sight in India is that of children as young as six years of age rummaging through garbage in order to collect recyclable material. These children usually rise before dawn and carry their heavy load in a large bag over their shoulder. They can often be seen on their hands and knees, alongside pigs and dogs, searching through rubbish heaps. Child labour is harmful to children's health and impedes their physical, mental, spiritual, moral and social development. Children who work are not only subject to the strains and hazards of their labour, but they are also denied the education or training that could enable them to escape the poverty trap in which they find themselves.

Child labour in India is a complex problem, one that is rooted in poverty and perpetuated because it is cheap and, thus, profitable for unscrupulous employers. It is a violation of a child's right to protection from economic exploitation, and from performing work that is likely to be hazardous or which interferes with his or her education. Children are forced to work by economic necessity (coming from large families living in poverty) and greed (employers making profits by employing children and paying them a pittance). According to the 2001 Census, there were 12.7 million economically active children of between 5 and 14 years of age, a rise from 11.3 million working children in 1991 (India, Ministry of Home Affairs 2001). Children can be poorly paid, easily exploited and bullied into obedience, so being forced into working long hours doing any type of work. They can be kept in a state of fear and are unable to organize themselves against exploitation in the way that adults can (Caesar-Leo 1999). The commonly accepted notion is that employers of children are helping to reduce poverty by providing them with jobs and, thereby, providing economic relief for their families. Thus, the fear is that eliminating child labour would result in the closure of certain industries. This helps, in part, to fuel the demand for child labour.

The urban unorganized (informal) sector accounts for a large number of children employed in work settings as domestic workers; as helpers in restaurants, shops, canteens and garages; as hawkers and street-side vendors; as porters, shoe-shine boys, sweepers and rag-pickers; and as prostitutes, drug peddlers, beggars and petty criminals. Children in India are employed in many industries listed as hazardous by the 1986 Child Labour Act.[4] They are also employed in non-hazardous industries, although any form of child labour that interferes with a child's normal growth and development in varying degrees or restricts a child's access to education is hazardous (Caesar-Leo 1999). Many of these children work in harrowing circumstances with excessively long hours of work, for low remuneration, with a constant exposure to unhealthy and unsafe working conditions, resulting in long, and sometimes permanent, separation from their families, and in physical abuse and often cruelty (Digwaney et al. 1988). Accidents and debilitating injuries may force children out of work, many of whom, in the absence of education or vocational skills, may resort to begging and criminal activities as a means of sustenance. The lack of information on the vast, unorganized sector of the economy that employs the majority of children, and under-reporting in industries where child labour is regulated, keep the issue and the real numbers involved hidden from official view, and thus official statistics.

Exploitation of female children for cheap labour is a common feature of Indian society. It is hard to get accurate statistical information about female child labour since many girls are engaged in active labour disguised

4   The 1948 Factories Act defines hazardous processes as any process or activity where the raw materials, finished products, wastes or effluents cause health impairment or result in pollution of the general environment.

as household chores, and the kind of work girls undertake is less visible than that of boys, such as agricultural work, domestic work, care of younger siblings, and working in home-based trades such as beedi (indigenous leaf-rolled cigars) rolling.

Bonded child labour compels children to work in conditions of servitude to pay off a family debt. The debt that binds them to their employer is incurred not by the children themselves, but by their relatives or guardians, perhaps to pay for the costs of an illness, provide a dowry to a marrying child, or to help put food on the table. The children who are sold to these bond masters work long hours over many years in an attempt to pay off these debts. But, due to the very high rates of interest charged, and the abysmally low wages paid, they are usually unsuccessful. As they reach maturity, the employer, in favour of a newly indebted and younger child, may release some of them. Many others will pass the debt-repayment obligation on, intact or even higher, to a younger sibling, back to a parent or even to their own children (Human Rights Watch 1996).

The phenomenon of bonded labour is closely linked to the problems of surplus labour, unemployment, under-employment, inequitable distribution of land and assets, low wages, distress migration, social customs and a plethora of broader socioeconomic issues. Many of these children are pledged to employers in agriculture and, to name a few industries, the carpet, brassware, glass, leather, gemstone and silk industries. Legislative efforts to curb this practice have met with mixed success, and the problem continues to thrive because of the poor implementation of sanctions, official apathy and the pervasive extent of the problem. Section 374 of the Indian Penal Code prohibits unlawful compulsory labour and holds that whoever unlawfully compels any person to labour against one's will shall be punishable with imprisonment of up to one year, or a fine, or both. As early as 1954, India ratified the International Labour Organization's 1930 Forced Labour Convention (ILO Convention No. 29) and in 1975 The Bonded Labour System (Abolition) Act came into effect, which loftily proclaimed that: 'On commencement of this Act the bonded labour system shall stand abolished and every bonded labourer shall stand freed and discharged free from any obligation to render bonded labour.' In addition, the 1933 Children (Pledging of Labour) Act calls for penalties to be levied against any parent, middleman, or employer involved in making or executing a pledge of a child's labour. The penalty imposed on parents for violating this law is a mere 50 Rupees, while that imposed on middlemen or employers is 200 Rupees,[5] an amount that is hardly punitive enough, even by Indian standards, to serve as an effective deterrent.

---

5   A Rupee is approximately US$0.02 at the time of writing (editors' note).

Street children

Nearly 29 per cent of the population of India now lives in urban areas, leading to a dramatic growth of slums and shantytowns. It is estimated that there are 11 million children living on the urban streets of India, with 420,000 street children living in the six metropolitan cities (Butterflies 2003). Myers (1989, p.127) has classified street children into three broad categories: those who are primarily working children who still have more or less regular family connections; those who see the street as their home, thereby seeking shelter, food and a sense of family among companions, for whom family ties exist but are remote and their former home is visited infrequently; and those who are 'runaways', who have been abandoned and are, thus, entirely on their own in terms of not only meeting their basic material survival needs but also ensuring their psychological survival.

The phenomenon of street children is a manifestation of disturbing and abusive life experiences (Mathur, Rathore and Mathur 2009). They are children caught in the cycle of poverty and degradation, ill health and exploitation. The majority come from slums – urban pockets characterized by high levels of illiteracy, drug use, strained parent–child relationships and unemployment (Abdelgalil et al. 2004). Almost all street children are victims of poverty, parental alcoholism, large family size, the death of one or both parents, or strained relationships with step-parents (Mehindru 1998). Homeless and 'runaway' children often come from disruptive or dysfunctional families with problems like maternal depression, parental alcoholism, inter-familial stress, a history of violence and abuse (Rew 2002), marital discord (Dadds et al. 1993) and domestic violence (Buckner and Bassuk 1997). These problems compel children to come to the streets to earn a little money in the unorganized sector in urban cities (Manihara 2002). A history of conduct problems (Rotheram-Borus 1993), poor scholastic performance and high dropout rates is common among Indian street children (Bose 1992). Life on the streets is no better. Studies have reported a high rate of physical and sexual abuse (Mathur and Rathore 2006; Whitbeck, Hoyt and Bao 2000), emotional abuse (Ringwalt et al. 1998) and neglect (Dadds et al. 1993) of street children. Several studies have shown that abused and neglected children develop a heightened sense of vulnerability; suffer anxiety, anger and fear; and have low self-esteem (Emery 1989; Parke 1977; Whitbeck et al. 2000). Further, commercial and other exploitation result in harm to such children's survival, health, personal development and sense of dignity (Mathur et al. 2009). On the streets, these children survive and protect themselves to a certain extent by forming groups or cliques (Awad 2002), which develop their own territory or hierarchy. These groups often have a leader who sometimes exploits the younger children and persuades them to engage in petty theft, prostitution and drugs (Butterflies 2003).

Any visitor to India will remember the distressing scenario of children begging on the streets, often carrying infants in their arms to evoke sympathy. Organized gangs who exploit them have deliberately maimed some. While India does have an anti-beggary law and laws to deal with child labour, enforcement is poor and protection for child beggars is minimal.

Child trafficking

Trafficking in women and children is a contemporary form of slavery, like indentured labour. India is a source, transit and destination country for human trafficking for sexual and labour exploitation. The gendered nature of trafficking, as well as its age specificity, derives from the historical context of laws, policies, customs and practices that justify and promote the discriminatory treatment of women and girls and prevents the application of the entire range of human rights and constitutional laws to women and girls. In a country notorious for its dismal human rights record (e.g. custodial rapes and deaths, and atrocities by the armed forces and the police), it is not surprising, then, that the violation of human rights of women and children subjected to trafficking hardly evokes more than cursory attention. The sociocultural context, the powerlessness of the victims and the ineffective machinery (politics, policy and police) together collude to make this activity increasingly profitable to the unscrupulous mafia that runs a well-oiled system to perpetuate this trade, often in nexus with politicians and the police.

A study by UNICEF found that children in India were trafficked for prostitution and sex work, forced marriage, domestic work, agricultural labour, construction work and work in, for example, the carpet and garment industries, begging, camel jockeying and the illegal adoption trade; they are also victims of organ harvesting (Sanghera 1999). Deterioration in the availability of food, together with an increase in organized crime and increased opportunities for moving people from place to place, have also heightened the level of threat to children and young women.

Child health challenges

Clearly, while some of the most serious challenges to children's welfare and survival in India are a direct result of poverty (including those linked to abuse and neglect), many others are the result of scarcity of resources, especially food and healthcare. India faces a huge malnutrition crisis (UNICEF 2011). A global hunger index ranked India sixty-seventh out of 84 countries on indicators that include child malnourishment, child mortality and calorie deficiency (International Food Policy Research Institute 2010). Twenty-eight per cent of infants born in India have low birth weight. The percentage of children under five years of age who are underweight is almost 20 times as high as would be expected in a healthy, well-nourished population and almost twice as high as for children in sub-Saharan African countries (IIPS and Macro International 2006). Forty-five per cent of children under five years of age are stunted (low height-for-age), more than for all of sub-Saharan Africa (UNICEF 2009). Seven out of ten young children are anaemic (IIPS and Macro International 2006).

Infant and child mortality rates remain very high among marginalized groups such as Scheduled Castes and Scheduled Tribes.[6] These make up 25 per cent of the rural population but 42 per cent of the poor (Farrington and Saxena 2003). Millions of Indians still suffer from chronic undernourishment and severe micronutrient malnutrition, especially women and children and people of Scheduled Castes and Scheduled Tribes (UN Economic and Social Council 2006). Muslim children have the highest rate of stunting and second-highest rate of being underweight (Childline India Foundation 2012). More than two million children die every year from preventable diseases, such as measles, which remains the biggest killer.

UNICEF (2008) estimates that India has 220,000 children infected by HIV/AIDS and that an estimated 55,000 to 60,000 children are born every year to mothers who are HIV positive. Without treatment, these newborns stand an estimated 30 per cent chance of becoming infected during the mother's pregnancy, labour or after six months' breastfeeding.

There are almost no services for children with mental health issues. Children with disabilities and mental disorders are stigmatized and hence have little access to health facilities (Childline India Foundation 2012), although policies have been formulated to address this deficit.

Reduction of infant and child mortality is a key governmental priority, which has taken steps to strengthen existing health systems by increasing the number of health workers, preventing newborn deaths through home-based medical visits and increasing children's access to immunization.

6   The term Scheduled Caste (now also called *Dalits*) was adopted in 1935 by the British in India, when the lowest-ranking Hindu castes were appended to a schedule to the Government of India Act for the purpose of constitutional safeguards and other benefits. Historically, they were considered to be underprivileged and marginalized, and this classification entitles them to positive discrimination ('reservation') in government jobs, and in gaining entry into educational institutions, as well as to other socioeconomic benefits. This is underpinned by the notion of upliftment and social mainstreaming. Articles 341 and 342 of the Constitution of India define which communities are included in the list of Scheduled Castes and Scheduled Tribes, the members of which constitute, respectively, around 15 per cent and 7.5 per cent of the population of India (India, Ministry of Home Affairs 2001).

Education, gender and children of scheduled groups

The Constitution of India has enshrined the right to education as a fundamental right. While enrolment levels propelled by the flagship *Sarva Shiksha Abhiyan* (Education for All) Project show an increase in child participation in education, levels of retention in schools remain a matter of concern. In a society in which many children are living in poverty, access to education is intimately linked with cultural values about which children should be supported in education. The percentage of students who stay in school until fifth class was recently estimated to be 62 per cent. Although showing improvement, the enrolment of girls is still below that of boys, and girls' dropout rates increase at the higher levels of education. Children belonging to Scheduled Castes and Scheduled Tribes continue to have lower enrolment and higher dropout rates (India, Ministry of Home Affairs 2001).

With one upper primary school for every three primary schools, there are simply not enough upper primary schools even for those children who complete primary school (UNICEF 2007b). Continuing cultural discrimination against girls plays a crucial role in determining which children go to school. Of India's 700,000 rural schools, only one in six have toilets, deterring girls, especially, from going to school. The persistence of class and caste differences and the prevalence of child labour further complicate this scenario.

There is a wide caste and class divide in terms of facilities and quality of education, as well as a rural–urban divide (Bhakhry 2006). As with the healthcare system in India, two options are available. One is private education, generally attended by children from the middle and upper classes. The second option used by the majority of the population is educational provision run by the states, which is either free or largely subsidized. Most of these schools are in rural and tribal areas, lack even basic infrastructure and facilities, have poorly paid teachers, evidence low teaching standards and have a poor performance record. Further, the disadvantage of little or no academic support at home, due to the generally low levels of education of family members, is a key issue in contributing to high dropout rates and poor scholastic achievement (Bhakhry 2006).

Poverty, economic transition and the plight of children

The dismal plight of the majority of children that emerges from harsh socioeconomic realities is obvious, whether it manifests as poor health and nutritional status, educational deprivation or as issues such as child labour or practices such as female infanticide. Poverty is the crucible that grinds these hapless children to an existence where many of their needs, often very basic ones, go unmet. They are victims of their parents' plight and of problems such as illiteracy, unemployment, low wages and exploitation faced by adults, which have drastic consequences for any children born to them.

UNICEF (2009) observes that, despite robust economic growth, India has failed to provide basic healthcare for its poorest children. Furthermore, the report underscores the effect of the rising trend of privatization in the health-service sector. As more and more public services are privatized and the government's share of the health budget diminishes, public facilities become more run down. Vast inequities in income, geography, gender and ethnicity are obstructing children from surviving or thriving. It may be appropriate to quote from the United Nations Economic and Social Council (2006, p.2), to conclude this section:

> Starvation deaths have not been fully eradicated, nor has discrimination against women and against lower castes, corruption, impunity and a wide range of violations including forced labour, debt bondage and forced displacement (destroying people's access to productive resources) remain serious obstacles to the realization of the right to food. In the current transition to a more liberalized, market-oriented economy, the poorest are disproportionately bearing the costs, with undernourishment rising as public spending on rural development and social programs is being cut back. With falling agricultural wages, increasing landlessness and rising food prices, food insecurity is growing particularly in rural areas. Recent economic growth is generating employment mostly in high-tech sectors that will not be able to absorb the loss of livelihoods from the agriculture on which two thirds of Indians still depend.

An overview of the major national policies for children

The disadvantage faced by children in India is reflected in the fact that it was only in 1974, 27 years after independence, that the Government of India promulgated its first National Policy for Children. It was, however, a step in the right direction. This policy declaration focused on several issues facing children, and offered a framework to begin to deal with them. It described children as 'supremely important assets' and acknowledged the crucial role that the voluntary sector could play in ameliorating issues causing distress to millions of children around the country. Government has the key role in the safeguarding and development of children in terms of comprehensive healthcare and nutrition programmes. Education was to be a priority and it envisaged that children should have free and compulsory education until 14 years of age. It acknowledged that there was a need for children to be protected from abuse, cruelty and exploitation, and that those from marginalized backgrounds should receive special attention. It recognized the need for legislative enactments to safeguard the interests of all children, particularly those from marginalized sections of society, and the need for all governmental policies and programmes to ensure that the best interest of the child is always a top priority. In a significant step, it called for the constitution of a National Children's Board to be in charge of planning and upholding the rights of children and for promulgating policies and programmes relating to child welfare.

Education

An important milestone pertaining to educational reform came with the National Policy on Education in 1986 (revised in 1992). This focused on acheiving universal access and enrolment, universal retention of children up to 14 years of age, and better quality of educational provision. It stressed the need for education to be based on values that are in tune with cultural norms around what constitutes good educational provision and the desirability of promoting local languages in education. It sought to improve training and evaluation standards, to overhaul the educational system at the national, state and local levels, and to have greater community involvement in the educational system at various levels.

Child labour

A key issue on the national agenda has been child labour. This was addressed through the 1986 Child Labour (Prohibition and Regulation) Act, and the launch of the National Child Labour Project. The aim was to eliminate employment of children under 14 years of age in hazardous occupations by 2010. This has been a goal that has been elusive, yet it has set in process a country-wide mechanism to consciously deal with the issue. A multi-pronged strategy has emerged that includes stricter legislative enforcement and harsher punitive measures for employers of children, and measures for the rescue and rehabilitation of such children. Formal and non-formal educational initiatives have been undertaken in areas where child labour is prevalent, through the creation of special schools and setting up child labour rehabilitation-welfare centres, achieved by enlisting the support of voluntary organizations. The *Sarva Shiksha Abhiyan* Project has been launched to promote the working child's access to education. Project schools aim to prevent children from working in hazardous industries, mainstreaming them into the formal education system, and offer stipends, nutritional services and health services to children. An important effort has been to provide supplementary income-generation programmes for their families. Media campaigns and other public awareness programmes are also being undertaken to curb the malaise of child labour.

All parents aspire for a life of comfort and contentment, for themselves and their children; one where needs are met and there is more to spare. Parents who put their children into labour are no different. The deprivation, grinding poverty and abysmal living conditions of the majority of families, and the harshness of that reality, puts parents in a situation where sending children to work is a necessity rather than an option. A couple of more working hands provide a better rationale than having to feed a couple of hungry mouths. For others, the plight of these children and their parents is seen as an issue of poverty and being born poor, perhaps attributed to their karma. The overwhelming poverty and its visible manifestations, such as beggary, squalor and the deplorable conditions seen in urban slums, all to a certain extent de-sensitize and de-personalize the situation for people who see it all, day in and day out. The family that employs a child for domestic help will probably use the justification that they are 'helping' the poor and that the child servant in their house is at least well fed and cared by them.

Child health, poverty and nutritional poverty

The National Nutrition Policy of 1993 outlined a series of measures relating to the alleviation of nutritional poverty, with a focus on women and children in particular. It focused on providing nutritional information, including low cost–high nutrition dietary practices. It emphasized monitoring children's nutrition, and that of adolescent girls and pregnant mothers. Poverty alleviation programmes, and a functional public distribution system to ensure that poor families are capable of buying food, are important strategies suggested by this policy. The need relates to the alleviation of protein-energy malnutrition, anaemia and deficiencies in children relating to iodine, vitamins (particularly vitamin A) and low birth weights. One outcome sought was the establishment of a national nutrition council, the issuance of guidelines for state governments, and a proper monitoring of children's nutritional status. It also highlighted the importance of expanding the integrated child development services (ICDS) special nutrition programme and other nutritional schemes such as the Wheat Based Nutrition Programme.

The National Health Policy (NHP) was updated in 2002 to take account of new health issues, such as HIV/AIDS. Some of its policy goals include increasing the use of public health facilities to more than 75 per cent by 2010, and increasing government health expenditure from 0.9 per cent to 2 per cent of GDP by 2010. As people are not using publicly provided health services because they do not provide patients with essential drugs, there is a need to improve delivery of essential treatments through increased central government funding.

The Policy Framework for Children and AIDS in India (2007) sought to address the needs of children infected with, or affected by, HIV/AIDS, to be achieved by integrating services targeting them within the existing development and poverty-reduction programmes. The four key strategies are prevention of parent-to-child transmission, primary prevention among adolescents, paediatric AIDS treatment, and the protection and care of children and families affected by AIDS.

The National Charter for Children (2003) reiterates the commitment of government to child welfare and protection. It recognized the right of every child to survival, life and liberty, and the need for government to protect these rights. It provides an overview of the various needs of children relating to nutritious and adequate food, physical and mental health, safe drinking water and environmental sanitation and hygiene, as well as leisure, recreation and opportunities for cognitive development. It acknowledges the responsibility of government to provide for the minimum needs and security of every child as well as to ensure their protection from all forms of abuse, especially mentioning girl children and other marginalized children from Scheduled Caste and Scheduled Tribe communities.

The National Plan of Action for Children (2005) outlines goals, objectives and strategies to promote child welfare and protection under the four categories of child survival, child development, child protection and child participation. The section on child development deals with early childhood care and education, emphasizing, among other things, the need for registration of all births and good parenting skills. The third section, on child protection, defines categories of vulnerable children: children experiencing neglect and abuse, children in conflict with the law, children at risk of sexual exploitation and child pornography, child trafficking, child labour and children affected by HIV/AIDS. Rehabilitation strategies and reintegration into mainstream society are emphasized, particularly in relation to children with disabilities, homeless children, street children, destitute children and orphan children. Issues relating to pornography and sexual exploitation, child labourers and children who come into conflict with the law have also been recognized. The final section on child participation emphasizes the need to promote awareness about child rights and providing children with appropriate channels through which to voice their concerns. It calls for provisions to involve children in planning and decision making relating to programmes designed for them. It discusses the importance of state budgeting, taking into consideration the actual population of children, and the proper implementation and monitoring of programmes relating to children.

This section has shown that there are numerous policies targeting children: the limitation on progress is not a lack of policies, but rather the problem of earmarking scarce resources to realize their aims. This is exacerbated by problems of bureaucracy, including red tape, corruption and apathy, which limit their implementation. The Eleventh Five-Year Plan aimed to address this set of challenges.

The Eleventh Five-Year Plan for Children (2007–2012)

The most recent Five-Year Plan for Children recognizes the rights of children regardless of class, caste, religion, ethnicity, region of origin and gender. It takes forward, more vigorously, the agenda of child rights and inclusive growth. This it does by further strengthening legislation and expanding delivery systems, for example, through the universalization of services for nutrition and support for the development of children up to six years of age; the introduction of free compulsory education for children between 6 and 14 years of age; and the launching of schemes for the protection of vulnerable children, such as those in difficult circumstances, working children and victims of trafficking. The Plan lays down six specific targets:

- Raise the sex ratio for the 0–6 age group to 935 girls to 1,000 boys by 2011–2012, and 950 to 1,000 boys by 2016–2017.

- Ensure that women and girl children comprise at least 33 per cent of direct and indirect beneficiaries of all government schemes.

- Reduce the infant mortality rate from 57 to 28 per 1,000 births, and the maternal mortality rate from 3.01 to 1 per 1,000 live births by 2012.

- Reduce malnutrition among children aged three years or younger to half its present level by 2012.

- Reduce anaemia among women and girls by 50 per cent by 2012.

- Reduce dropout rates at the level of primary and secondary schooling by 10 per cent for both girls and boys by 2012.

The first half of the period covered by the Eleventh Five-Year Plan saw the introduction of new schemes to tackle the issues of the sex ratio, trafficking and child protection. The steps being taken to attain inclusive growth as per the goals set out in the Plan are clearly visible;[7] and efforts are being made to accelerate this progress.

---

7 For example, the conditional cash transfer scheme (*Dhanalakshmi, Ujjawala*) to address the issue of trafficking, the Integrated Child Protection Scheme (ICPS) and the Rajiv Gandhi National Crèche Scheme (RGNCS).

An overview of major schemes for child welfare and protection

The Ministry for Women and Child Development is the apex national body that oversees the implementation of programmes targeting women and children. These include *Shishu Greh*, a scheme that seeks to promote in-country adoption and to provide support for the institutional care and protection of infants and children up to six years of age who have been abandoned or orphaned, or rendered destitute. Nearly 6,000 children have been placed in adoption through *Shishu Greh* in 18 states. This scheme has now been merged with the recently launched Integrated Child Protection Scheme (ICPS), a centrally sponsored scheme (CSS), with a view to providing a safe and secure environment for the overall development of children in need of care and protection, as well as children in conflict with the law and in difficult circumstances. The scheme also oversees investigation of actions that lead to abuse, neglect, exploitation, abandonment and separation of children.

The services financed under the ICPS include emergency outreach services through Childline, a unique scheme being run by the government through an NGO partner, which provides transitional open shelters for children in need in urban and semi-urban areas; cradle baby reception centres for abandoned children; family-based non-institutional care through sponsorship; and foster care, adoption and after-care. In addition, institutional services, such as shelter homes, children's homes, observation homes, special homes and specialized services for children with special needs, are also provided under the scheme. Grants-in-aid are provided to several NGOs for offering innovative interventions, such as creating a child-tracking system that includes a website for missing children. Interventions are being planned for advocacy, public education, communication and training of all child protection personnel.

Childline also provides a 24-hour, toll-free telephone outreach service linking children in need of care and protection to organizations run by government departments, as well as by civil society agencies. Modelled on Childline in the United Kingdom, it currently operates in 83 cities and towns across the country, with 190 collaborative, support and nodal partners, and services over two million calls a year. Under the ICPS, Childline services are to be extended to the entire country in a phased manner. Childline is dependent on a set of state- and district-based structures and services to rehabilitate the child. The government is continuously strengthening these structures, so as to ensure child protection, notably the state child protection societies and the district child protection societies. Inter-departmental coordination and integration at the field level is also being strengthened to ensure that children can be rescued and rehabilitated in time, and that prosecution is initiated against perpetrators of crimes against children. Prosecutions are carried out by the police force, which deals with a wide variety of offences. There is no dedicated police force that deals specifically with crimes against or involving children. Childline ensures the proper documentation of all children rescued, so as to facilitate their rehabilitation and restoration where possible, and to provide data for the compilation of a comprehensive national database on child protection.

The comprehensive scheme for the prevention of trafficking, and the rescue, rehabilitation, re-integration and repatriation of victims of trafficking and commercial sexual exploitation – *Ujjawala* – was launched in December 2007. This focuses on preventing trafficking through social mobilization and community involvement in child safety, and through the rescue and rehabilitation of its victims.

The integrated programme for street children provides shelter, nutrition, healthcare, education, recreation facilities and services to protect targeted children against abuse and exploitation. Its target group is children without homes and family ties: street children, and other children especially vulnerable to abuse and exploitation (such as children of sex workers and children of pavement dwellers). The strategy is to develop awareness and provide support to build the capacity of the government, NGOs and the community at large to realize the rights of the child enshrined in the 1989 *United Nations Convention on the Rights of the Child* (UNCRC) (UNICEF 2012) and in the 2000 Juvenile Justice (Care and Protection of Children) Act. Ninety per cent of the costs of services under this programme are provided to NGOs working for the welfare of street children to fund services such as education, vocational training, shelter, healthcare, nutrition, sanitation and hygiene, safe drinking water, recreational facilities and protection against abuse and exploitation.

The scheme for welfare of working children in need of care and protection was launched in 2005–2006 and lends support to projects in urban areas not already covered by existing schemes. It provides support for the development of child workers, especially those with no or ineffective family support (such as the children of pavement dwellers, drug addicts and children living in slums, on railway platforms and along railway lines); and children working in shops and *dhabas* (road side eateries, which employ a substantial population of child labour).

The plight of girl children merits high priority in the government's scheme of things and several welfare programmes focus exclusively on this vulnerable sector of the society. *Dhanalakshmi* provides insurance cover across seven states. This scheme seeks to change the mindset about girls being a liability by providing a set of staggered financial incentives for families to encourage them to retain the girl child and educate her. It provides cash transfers to the family of the girl child (preferably the mother) on fulfilling certain specific conditions related to the girl child: at the time of birth and registration of birth; through *Sarva Shiksha Abhiyan* during immunization; on enrolment and retention in school; and, if unmarried, upon reaching 18 years of age. Various programmes aim to promote the development of girl children through improved education and nutrition.[8]

The midday meal scheme in India is the largest school meal programme in the world, covering an estimated 139 million children (Young Lives 2010). It was extended in 2007 to children in the upper primary stage of education in 3,479 areas designated educationally backward blocks (EBBs). Approximately 17 million additional children are expected to be included in this scheme, which now provides hot cooked food of good nutritional quality. Following a Supreme Court ruling in 2001, all state governments were mandated to introduce cooked school meals, and by 2003 most states had started providing school meals. Crucially, in 2004 a Supreme Court order made it mandatory to provide midday meals during summer vacations in drought-affected areas. This was an important intervention, as drought has affected large sections of India's rural population (Young Lives 2010). The scheme aspires to feed five million children by 2020 and has won accolades globally for its coverage, success and benefits to low-income families.

Conclusion

This chapter has provided an overview of major concerns relating to child welfare and protection in India. It has looked at issues related to trafficking, child labour, child marriage and vulnerable children (exploitation and abuse among girl children, and children on the streets); and to education

---

8   The Rajiv Gandhi scheme for the empowerment of adolescent girls promotes self-development, nutrition and health status, literacy, and numerical and vocational skills among girls aged between 11 and 18 years. The national programme for education of girls at the elementary level provides support for the development of a model girl child-friendly school, with more intense community mobilization and supervision of girls' enrolment in schools. The programme provides bridging and remedial teaching to girls as well as additional incentives, such as uniforms. The *Kasturba Gandhi Balika Vidyalaya* (KGBV) was launched in 2004 to set up residential schools at upper primary level for girls belonging predominantly to Scheduled Castes and Scheduled Tribes, Other Backward Castes and minority communities. This scheme has now been merged with the *Sarva Shiksha Abhiyan* scheme, which aimed to address the educational needs of children aged between 6 and 14 years.

and healthcare. Social policies and legislative safeguards to ameliorate the plight of children in distressing circumstances in relation to these issues have also been highlighted. The role of socioeconomic and cultural factors in sustaining discriminatory and oppressive attitudes towards children and women leading to their abuse, neglect and exploitation have also been discussed.

Most of the social problems plaguing India, and those impinging on women and children in particular, can be seen as rooted in its three major demons of poverty, population and illiteracy. The administration of a pluralistic country, which is both diverse (culturally, religiously, linguistically, economically and politically) and geographically widespread, is, in the best of times, not an easy task. Difference and diversity result in discrimination and oppression, particularly for vulnerable women and children. This is further compounded by a heritage that harbours notions of caste and gender superiority.

Admittedly, while the scenario presented comes across as being bleak and worrying, it is certainly not one that is entirely without hope. This is true, in particular, because of the dynamism of voluntary sector organizations. These are playing a proactive role in highlighting various maladies, generating public awareness and campaigning for the rights of the oppressed and the marginalized, achieved through their focus on aspects relating to human rights, social justice and empowerment. The burgeoning middle class, with its increasing levels of literacy, social awareness and economic prosperity, is a key stakeholder in this scenario. The fourth estate has an important role to play in terms of highlighting the plight of vulnerable children and in shaking officialdom out of its stupor by turning the spotlight on corruption in high places, bureaucratic apathy and administrative incompetence. The policies and legislations are all there, all thoughtfully envisaged and scrupulously crafted. Lacking is the wherewithal, and the political will, to implement them with conscientiousness. Until this happens, the plight of the majority of India's children will be one mired in abuse, suffering and despair.

References

Abdelgalil, S., Gurgel, R.G., Theobald, S. and Cuevas, L.E. (2004) 'Household and family characteristics of street children in Arecaju, Brazil.' *Archives of Disease in Childhood 89*, 817–820.

Amin, S., Chong, E. and Haberland, N. (2007) *Programs to Address Child Marriage: Framing the Problem* (Population Council, Brief No. 14). Available at: www.popcouncil.org/pgy.

Awad, S. (2002) 'The invisible citizens roaming the city streets.' *Educational Review 54*, 105–113.

Bhakhry, S. (2006) *Children in India and their Rights*. New Delhi, IN: National Human Rights Commission.

Bose, A.B. (1992) 'The disadvantaged urban child in India' (Innocenti Occasional Papers: The Urban Child Series 1, 47–52). Florence, IT: UNICEF Innocenti Research Centre.

Bruce, J. (2007) *Child Marriage in the Context of the HIV Epidemic* (Population Council, Brief No. 11). Available at: www.popcouncil.org/pgy.

Buckner, J.C. and Bassuk, E.L. (1997) 'Mental disorders and service utilization among youths from homeless and low-income housed families.' *Journal of American Academy of Child and Adolescent Psychiatry 36*, 890–900.

Butterflies (2003) *A Dossier on Children and Children's Rights: A Compilation of 10 Years of Writing on Child Rights. My Name is Today: Children in News, 1* (Annual Report). New Delhi, IN: Butterflies Foundation.

Caesar-Leo, M. (1999) 'Child labour: The most visible type of child abuse and neglect in India.' *Child Abuse Review 8*, 2, 75–86.

Childline India Foundation (2012) *Publications.* Available at: http://childlineindia.org.in/publications.htm.

Clark, S. (2000) 'Son preference and sex composition of children: Evidence from India.' *Demography 37*, 1, 95–108.

Clark, S., Bruce, J. and Dude, A. (2006) 'Protecting young women from HIV/AIDS: The case against child and adolescent marriage.' *International Family Planning Perspectives 32*, 2, 79–88.

Dadds, M., Braddock, D., Cuers, S., Elliot, A. and Kelly, A. (1993) 'Personal and family distress in homeless adolescents.' *Community Mental Health Journal 29*, 413–422.

Digwaney, M., Dogra, S., Vidyasagar, R. and Gupta, R. (1988) *Children of Darkness: A Manual on Child Labour in India.* New Delhi, IN: Rural Labour Cell.

Emery, R.E. (1989) 'Family violence.' *American Psychologist 44*, 321–328.

Farrington, J. and Saxena, N.C. (2003) *Food Insecurity in India.* London: Overseas Development Institute. Available at: www.odi.org.uk.

Gangrade, K.D. (1988) 'Sex determination – A critique.' *Journal of Social Change 18*, 3, 63–70.

Gill, A. and Mitra-Khan, T. (2009) 'Explaining daughter devaluation and the issue of missing women in South Asia and the UK.' *Current Sociology 57*, 5, 684–703.

Gupta, G.R. (2005) 'Forum on child marriage in developing countries.' Remarks to the US Department of State's Forum on Child Marriage in Developing Countries (No. 3) (14 September 2005).

Human Rights Watch (1996) *Human Rights Watch World Report 1996 – India.* Available at: www.unhcr.org/refworld/docid/3ae6a8aa20.html.

India, Ministry of Home Affairs (2001) *India Census 2001.* New Delhi, IN: Office of the Registrar General and Census Commissioner.

India, Ministry of Home Affairs (2011) *India Census 2011.* Available at: http://censusindia.gov.in/2011-common/censusdataonline.html.

International Food Policy Research Institute (2010) *The Challenge of Hunger: Focus on the Crisis of Child Undernutrition.* Available at: www.ifpri.org/sites/default/files/publications/ghi10.pdf.

International Institute for Population Sciences (IIPS) and Macro International (2006) *National Family Health Survey (NFHS-3) 2005–06, India: Key Findings.* Mumbai, IN: IIPS.

Jha, P., Kesler, M.A., Kumar, R., Ram, F. *et al.* (2011) 'Trends in selective abortions of girls in India: Analysis of nationally representative birth histories from 1990 to 2005 and census data from 1991 to 2011.' *The Lancet 377*, 1921–1928.

Kishore, S. (1993) '"May God give sons to all": Gender and child mortality in India.' *American Sociological Review 58*, 2, 247–265.

Manihara, N. (2002) *Street Children?* Available at: www.skcv.com.

Mathur, M. and Rathore, P. (2006) 'Children in Twilight: Abuse and Trauma in the Lives of Street Children in Jaipur City, India.' In *Abstract, Nineteenth Biennial Meeting of the International Society for the Study of Behavioural Development.* Melbourne, Australia.

Mathur, M., Rathore, P. and Mathur, M. (2009) 'Incidence, type and intensity of abuse in street children in India.' *Child Abuse and Neglect 33*, 907–913.

Mathur, S., Greene, M. and Malhotra, A. (2003) *Too Young to Wed: The Lives, Rights, and Health of Young Married Girls.* International Centre for Research on Women. Available at: www.icrw.org.

Mehindru, B. (1998) 'Exploratory Study on the Institutionalized Abandoned Children.' In *Children in Difficult Circumstances: Summaries of Research.* New Delhi, IN: National Institute of Public Cooperation and Child Development.

Myers, W. (1989) 'Alternative Services for Street Children: The Brazilian Approach.' In A. Bequela and J. Boyden (eds) *Combating Child Labour.* Geneva, CH: International Labour Organization.

Parke, R. (1977) 'Socialization into Child Abuse: A Social Interactional Perspective.' In J.L. Tapp and F.J. Levine (eds) *Law, Justice and the Individual in Society: Psychology and Legal Issues.* New York: Holt, Rinehart and Winston.

Patnaik, P. (2011) 'India's census reveals a glaring gap: girls.' *The Guardian*, 25 May. Available at: www.guardian.co.uk/global-development/poverty-matters/2011/may/25/india-census-alarming-sex-ratio-female-foeticide.

Rew, L. (2002) 'Characteristics and health care needs of homeless adolescents.' *Nursing Clinics in North America 37*, 423–431.

Ringwalt, C., Greene, J., Robertson, M. and McPheeters, M. (1998) 'The prevalence of homelessness among adolescents in the United States.' *American Journal of Public Health 88*, 1325–1329.

Rotheram-Borus, M. (1993) 'Suicidal behavior and risk factors among runaway youth.' *American Journal of Psychiatry 150*, 103–107.

Sanghera, J. (1999) *Trafficking of Women and Children in South Asia: Taking Stock and Moving Ahead.* New Delhi, IN: UNICEF Regional Office South Asia and Save the Children Alliance South and Central Asia.

Tandon, S.L. and Sharma, R. (2006) 'Female foeticide and infanticide in India: An analysis of crimes against girl children.' *International Journal of Criminal Justice Sciences 1*, 1, 3–13.

The Hindu (2011) '"Cradle baby" scheme to be extended.' *The Hindu*, 24 July. Available at: www.thehindu.com/news/states/tamil-nadu/article2290679.ece.

The Hindu (2012) 'Girl child sex ratio at birth increasing in Tamil Nadu.' *The Hindu*, 22 February. Available at: www.thehindu.com/todays-paper/tp-national/tp-tamilnadu/article2918313.ece?css=print.

UN Committee on the Rights of the Child (2003) *Government of India Status Report* [2001] (CRC/C/93/Add.5, 16 July). Available at: www.childlineindia.org.in/India-and-UNCRC.htm.

UN Economic and Social Council (2006) *Economic, Social and Cultural Rights: The Right to Food* (Report of the Special Rapporteur on the Right to Food). Available at: www.refworld.org/cgi-bin/texis/vtx/rwmain?page=search&docid=45377b1b0&skip=0&query=right%20to%20food%202006.

UNICEF (2007a) *State of the World's Children Report 2007*. Available at: www.unicef.org/ sowc07/report/report.php.

UNICEF (2007b) *Child Poverty in Perspective: An Overview of Child Wellbeing in Rich Countries* (Innocenti Report Card 7). Available at: www.unicef-irc.org/publications/pdf/ rc7_eng.pdf.

UNICEF (2008) *The State of the World's Children 2008*. Available at: www.unicef.org/ sowc08/docs/sowc08.pdf.

UNICEF (2009) *The State of the World's Children 2009*. Available at: www.unicef.org/ sowc09/docs/SOWC09-FullReport-EN.pdf.

UNICEF (2011) *The State of the World's Children Report 2011*. Available at: www.unicef.org/ sowc11/docs/SOWC11-FullReport-EN.pdf.

UNICEF (2012) *United Nations Convention on the Rights of the Child*. Available at: www. unicef.org/crc/index_30229.html.

Whitbeck, L., Hoyt, D. and Bao, W. (2000) 'Depressive symptoms and co-occurring depressive symptoms, substance abuse and conduct problems among runaway and homeless adolescents.' *Child Development 71*, 721–732.

Young Lives (2010) *The Impact of the Midday Meal Scheme on Nutrition and Learning* (Policy Brief). Available at: www.younglives.org.uk.

9

Kazakhstan

Nazgul Assylbekova and Anuarbek Kakabayev

Introduction

The Republic of Kazakhstan (henceforth Kazakhstan) is a country that bridges Central Asia and Eastern Europe. By land area (2.7 million square kilometres), it is the ninth largest country in the world. It is sub-divided into administrative-territorial units, including 14 regions, a city of national significance (Almaty), the capital city (Astana), 175 districts (including 15 districts in the cities), 86 major cities at the regional and district level, and 7,066 settlements (comprising 35 villages and 7,031 *auls*[1]).

Kazakhstan is a unitary state with a presidential form of government. The elected head of state is President Nursultan Nazarbayev (in office since 1991). State power in Kazakhstan includes the legislative power, exercised by the parliament; executive power, exercised by the government, which consists of the central authorities (Ministries, Departments and Agencies) and local authorities (*Akimats*); and judicial power, exercised by state courts (the Supreme Court and local courts).

The economic context

The economic context for the delivery of services to children and families has changed very rapidly over the last decade. Kazakhstan's economy is growing rapidly, unemployment is dropping, poverty is less prevalent, and an increasing share of Gross Domestic Product (GDP) is being spent on social services. Since independence, sustained economic growth has been the basis for the emancipation of private initiative and entrepreneurship in the form of public–private partnerships (PPPs) and active foreign trade, both attracting direct investment. During the period from 2001 to 2010 the share of per capita GDP in PPPs increased almost threefold, reaching

---

1   Extended family group or small group of families living together (editors' note).

2.4 million Tenge[2] (KZT). Average per capita public expenditure in 2010 is estimated at 744,000 KZT, which is 6.3 times higher than in 2001 (118,500 KZT). For 10 years the level of private income has been increasing against a backdrop of increasing national prosperity. Average monthly per capita income increased by 5.3 times, now estimated to be 40,473 KZT.

Table 9.1 Expenditure on social services in Kazakhstan: 2007–2010

Public expenditures (millions KZT)	2007	2008	2009	2010
GOVERNMENT BUDGET				
Education	480,696	641,060	746,477	797,414
%	17.0	16.9	17.6	16.9
Healthcare	299,381	363,210	450,893	551,326
%	11.2	10.7	12.0	12.4
Social assistance and social security	502,381	622,017	758,308	905,273
%	18.8	18.3	20.3	20.3
Culture, sport, tourism and information	122,210	163,969	173,618	227,564
%	7.5	6.9	8.1	5.1
NATIONAL BUDGET				
Education	127,700	168,210	215,560	236,392
Healthcare	100,830	115,581	176,800	367,185
Social assistance and social security	462,667	566,194	695,931	835,497
Culture, sports and information	62,964	87,461	104,389	135,389
LOCAL BUDGET				
Education	352,996	472,850	530,917	579,648
Healthcare	262,852	320,762	386,553	330,352
Social assistance and social security	44,789	61,874	86,123	97,381
Culture, sport, tourism and information	73,778	108,493	108,183	129,795

2   The exchange rate for the US dollar is fixed at 150 Tenge (editors' note).

In recent years, expenditure on social services has been increasing (see Table 9.1). The share of expenditure of the total government budget in 2006 was 41 per cent; by the end of 2010 it was more than 50 per cent of GDP.

The positive dynamics of economic development, despite the unstable position of the global financial system, has had a beneficial effect on the level of poverty. Since 2001, the proportion of the population with incomes below the official subsistence level has been reduced by a factor of 7.2, and at the end of 2010 there were just over one million people (7%) living below this subsistence level. While continuing on an aggregate downwards trend for both urban and the rural areas, significant regional variations are apparent in the extent of poverty.

The rate of employment is increasing: from 90 per cent in 2001 to 94 per cent in 2010. The unemployment rate has almost halved: from 10 per cent in 2001 to 6 per cent in 2010. Significantly, the level of youth unemployment has fallen from 19 per cent in 2001 to 5 per cent in 2010, and the average duration of unemployment fell over that period from 15 to 9 months. Average monthly wages have grown by a factor of 4.5 in the last decade, while there is still a significant differentiation between income in industrial and other occupations. In 2010, the lowest wages, as before, remained in agriculture.

The child population of Kazakhstan

The population of Kazakhstan in 2011 was 16.4 million people, of whom 8.5 million (52%) were females, 7.9 million (48%) were males and just over 4 million (27%) were children aged 16 years and younger. Children and young people make up an increasing proportion of the population of Kazakhstan. Over the last five years, the younger generation (those aged 29 years and younger) has grown to occupy just over 50 per cent of the total population. As of 1 January 2011 the number of children 18 years of age and younger was more than 5 million (about 30%), including 2.5 million girls (48%) and 2.6 million boys (52%). There has been an increase in the number of children aged four years or younger of more than 300,000 (see Table 9.2).

In Kazakhstan, a majority of the population (54%) live in urban areas. But due to the larger size of rural families, more children live in rural areas, outnumbering urban children by approximately two to one.

Table 9.2 The number of children in Kazakhstan: 2007, 2009–2011

Age	All population			
	2007	2009	2010	2011
0	318,159	347,404	351,920	362,630
1	297,598	305,865	346,688	351,459
2	275,150	289,109	305,841	346,814
3	269,761	269,847	289,237	306,168
4	244,938	266,643	270,026	289,463
5	223,923	245,116	266,795	270,342
6	217,295	232,737	245,327	267,071
7	217,359	221,669	232,952	245,596
8	211,338	224,050	221,949	233,273
9	218,930	217,806	224,243	222,211
10	216,588	223,989	218,023	224,527
11	227,343	225,280	224,118	218,271
12	249,898	243,083	225,488	224,386
13	269,491	258,451	243,222	225,710
14	272,169	277,924	258,598	243,416
15	281,659	284,778	277,876	258,716
16	293,220	298,724	284,767	277,958
17	302,202	310,231	298,819	284,945
18	312,660	327,783	310,027	298,803

Children will play a vital role in the future social, economic and physical development of Kazakhstan. The welfare of children, and their quality of life, are key indicators of a healthy environment, good governance and sustainable development. Children are the most vulnerable category of citizens. They need special legal and social support to create the most favourable conditions for their full development. The wellbeing of children in Kazakhstan should be a top priority in the preparation of strategic plans for national development.

Kazakhstan recognizes childhood as a key stage in a person's life based on the principles and priorities of preparing children for a full life in society. Childhood is under state protection, for which there are consistently implemented mechanisms and forms of children's rights. The protection of children's rights is the subject of a specific Law on the Rights of the Child in the Republic of Kazakhstan.

Legal and treaty developments and children's welfare in Kazakhstan

Kazakhstan ratified the 1989 *UN Convention on the Rights of the Child* (UNCRC) (UNICEF 2012) in 1994. A programme was developed based on obligations arising from these international norms regarding the protection of children. This defines the main directions of state policy on the protection of the rights and interests of children, and establishes a comprehensive system of measures to ensure social and legal guarantees for children in all circumstances. The implementation of the programme helped to maintain and develop social priorities, enabling children in all categories to have equal access to education, quality healthcare and sanitation, protection from all forms of neglect, cruelty and exploitation, and the right to rest, leisure, cultural activities and to live a creative life.

In accordance with Article 4 of the UNCRC, Kazakhstan has adopted legislative, administrative and other measures to implement the standards defined by that Convention. Legislation to protect children and promote their rights appears in many areas of the emerging legislative framework for family policy in Kazakhstan. Between 2002 and 2011, many laws were adopted relating to the rights of the child, including legislation covering state youth policy; social, medical and educational support for children with disabilities; state benefits for families with children; the health and social rehabilitation of drug addicts; the prevention and control of smoking; the prevention of juvenile delinquency; the prevention of child neglect and abandonment; the establishment of children's villages and youth homes; a healthcare system; the prevention of iodine deficiency disorders; and military duty and military service.

One progressive piece of legislation for ensuring the rights of the child was the adoption of the Law on Marriage and Family. This establishes, in accordance with the standards of the UNCRC, a child's right to live and grow up in a family, and to have protection of their right of expression, their property rights and the right to restoration of their interests in the event of any breach of them, as well as to protect the rights and interests of children who are without parental care.

Kazakhstan has been active in expanding its international commitments to the protection of important dimensions of children's need for protection from harm. The state has recently ratified such significant UN Conventions as the Convention on Recovery Abroad of Maintenance; the Optional Protocol concerning Trade of Children, Child Prostitution and Child Pornography; the Optional Protocol concerning Participation of Children in Armed Conflicts; and the Convention on the Fight Against Human Trafficking and Prostitution (including its Final Protocol); as well as the International Labour Organization's Convention on the Minimum Age for Employment and the Convention concerning the Prohibition and Immediate Action for the Elimination of the Worst Forms of Child Labour.

State policies protecting the legitimate rights and interests of children have been incorporated into programmes as they relate to education, healthcare, poverty alleviation, migration, demographic development and the rehabilitation of disabled people.

The National Commission of the President of the Republic of Kazakhstan on Family and Gender Policy includes a section that covers 'family problems'. This addresses the protection of the rights and legitimate interests of children when addressing solutions to family problems.

In January 2006, a resolution of the government created the Committee on Protection of the Rights of Children within the Ministry of Education and Science. The main objective of this Committee is the realization of state policy on the protection of the rights and legitimate interests of children. Its concerns also include prevention of social orphanhood.[3]

Non-governmental organizations and child welfare in Kazakhstan

Non-governmental organizations (NGOs) have a significant role to play in providing services for children in Kazakhstan. There are 221 NGOs dealing with children's issues. More than 40 have signed memorandums, contracts and cooperative agreements with the government. They have, with the help of international and national experts, jointly implemented projects; conducted case studies; held forums, conferences, round tables, workshops and training events; and convened meetings on ways of addressing problems facing children. Their areas of involvement include penal policy and practice, welfare of social orphans, access to healthcare and the development of civil society.

In June 2011, a tripartite Memorandum of Cooperation was signed between the Ombudsman, the United Nations Children's Fund in Kazakhstan and the Representatives of the International Prison Reform Organization of Central Asia, whose goal is to train NGOs to monitor the respect given to children's rights in childcare centres.

---

3   This is an abandoned child with a living parent or parents (editors' note).

From 2007 to 2010, the Ministry of Education and Science, in cooperation with NGOs, carried out 24 social research projects, and developed and published more than 80,000 collected papers. They also created four movies, 14 video clips on the rights of children for the information of children and adults, and two animated movies on the theme 'What should I know?'

Ten of the fourteen regions now have 'schools' to prepare citizens who want to take orphans into their families to be foster parents.

The major cities of Karaganda and Zhambyl, in South and East Kazakhstan, and the capital, Astana, have seven new family centres for services and family support.

In October 2009 the IVth Civil Forum took place in Astana. Representatives of state authorities, NGOs and businesses attended. It made recommendations and suggestions for further work on the effective implementation of Phase II of the project for the development of civil society in Kazakhstan in the coming years.

In 2009–2011, the BOAT Foundation allocated more than 190 grants nationwide, totalling more than 600 million KZT, to support projects on social services for children and youth. Putting investments into local services and non-profit organizations, the Foundation strengthened and influenced a partnership role between NGOs, families, communities and local authorities for the improvement of life of children, youth and their families. In addition, the BOAT Foundation has more than 13,000 young student beneficiaries living in the Kyzylorda, Akmola and Almaty areas. More than 300 scholars – young people from the lower-income strata – are training in Kazakhstan under these educational grants.

State services for children and families

There is a system of free medical care and specialist paediatric services for children. Law 446 of 2005 approved a list of types of diseases and the categories of the population who qualify for outpatient treatment. Under this scheme certain medicines and special foods for children and nutritional therapy are provided for free.

There are also services for children when parents divorce. The principle of ensuring the 'best interests of the child' is the primary concern in the divorce of parents. When children are left without parental support, support is available through the social care system, including their placement in various institutions and provision for their care.

To promote children's rights, 5,777 schools (two-thirds of all schools) have, since 2010, provided hot meals for 1,741,822 students (70 per cent of all students). Of these, one-third receive free hot meals. Eighty per cent of children who receive free hot meals are from families defined as 'needy', and just under half were primary school pupils. All primary school children in the cities of Astana, Almaty, Aktobe and in the Karaganda regions have free hot meals provided for them. This represents a substantial increase in investment in the quality of nutrition. Between 2005 and 2010, public expenditure on catering for students from poor families increased five-fold: from 518.5 million KZT in 2005, to 2.9 billion KZT in 2010.

A child's right to leisure, recreation and cultural activities is implemented through a network of extra-curricular organizations. The 'home school' offers a space for children and youth to be creative, and is the base station for young technicians, naturalists, children's music, sports schools, art schools, clubs, sports, recreation, tourist camps and other activities. The state has also intensified the process of familiarizing children with art through the creation of appropriate conditions in educational institutions: high schools, grammar schools and secondary schools with advanced teaching in art, line and drawing classes.

At present, Kazakhstan has 541 extra-curricular organizations, of which 208 (38%) are based in the countryside. There are about 700 domestic clubs, 5,500 gyms and more than 9,000 sports fields. Despite this, the coverage of extra-curricular organizations for school-age children is only 11 per cent across the country, including only 6 per cent in rural areas.

There are still challenges to achieving free school education and the benefits associated with it being available to all children. The right to education is affected by the availability of schools: 76 per cent of school-age students are living in settlements where there are still, as yet, no schools.

Children in Kazakhstan who are needy and in need of protection

Kazakhstan is trying to help children from needy families. The President of the Republic himself chairs the National Commission on Family and Women's Affairs. In 2010, the education authorities identified about 150,000 needy families with more than 300,000 children. Children, and their families, quite often face problems in accessing quality education, healthcare and other major social services. Spending on them is increasing, including spending on projects to try to get more children from the most deprived backgrounds into education. Education is an important means by which the state is attempting to offer support to such children, including those without parents. Now, to assist in guarding the interests of children, there will be support from the Norwegian government, which has become the main donor of the UNICEF project for strengthening the system of child protection.

According to sub-paragraph 4 of Article 8 of the Law About Education, the state fully or partially compensates the maintenance costs of citizens needing state assistance during their education. In 2010, the 'Road to School' project helped 374,655 children from socially deprived backgrounds, at a cost of 1.7 billion KZT. Funds are set aside by the state to promote universal education for disadvantaged students, at a cost totalling 5.5 billion KZT, or 1.7 per cent of the cost of schools.

There are also educational grants for orphans. In the 2008–2009 educational year, 510 orphan children were identified for educational grants, compared with 444 in 2010–2011 and 463 in 2009–2010.

In Kazakhstan, at both the regional and national levels, there are many programmes operating for the protection of the rights of children, and for the prevention and struggle against various forms of violence concerning children. For example, in 2011 the government's 'Children of Kazakhstan' project came to an end, at a cost of 10.5 million KZT, while ongoing projects include 'Cities Friendly to Children' and 'The Road to School'.

Law enforcement authorities regularly carry out spot-checks under the 'children in a Night City' programme. In all areas of the country, departments for the protection of the rights of children have been created. A national telephone hotline started some years ago. There are supportive telephone lines based on the workplace, city and regions.

State investment in child welfare:
The continuing challenge

The care of children left without parental support has been a policy issue in Kazakhstan. The Ministry of Education and Science is responsible for financial support for those citizens of Kazakhstan who take on the care of such children. In addition, it is working on the prevention of child neglect and the abandonment of minors. Over the duration of the project 'Care', it provided financial assistance to more than 134,000 children in socially unprotected (high-risk) circumstances, at a cost of about 330 million KZT. The 'Road to School' project provided financial assistance to 252,000 children of poor families, at a cost of over 1.6 billion KZT. As a result, the number of homeless street children has decreased by about half.

Currently, the protection of the rights and legitimate interests of children who have no parental care is entrusted to their state-appointed guardians and those who have custody of children through placement. As the Kazakhstan Commission for the Affairs of Minors and Protection of their Rights has only an advisory status and role, there is no permanent effective regional body to protect the rights of the child and really improve the welfare of children at risk.

All these measures and provisions have still not solved all the problems of children in Kazakhstan. They cannot, however, continue to remain unnoticed or ignored. To carry out effective fruitful work in protecting children's rights requires more human and financial resources, in order to cope with the high level of demand for such services. Child welfare authorities, because of their limited capacity, cannot cope with the volume of problems presented. In addition, there is no coherent plan of action by central and local authorities. Regional departments and state agencies have agreed to cooperate with international NGOs, as the Kazakh NGOs only take part in child welfare matters with great reluctance. Across the country hundreds of professional NGOs render social services to help such children and their families to overcome problems and to improve their living conditions. However, very often at the end of the grants, the work of the international NGOs is terminated. Therefore, it is very important that the process of providing social services for needy and vulnerable groups of children and youth becomes both continuous and viable.

Despite some achievements in protecting the rights and interests of children, currently not all children in all situations and categories have the opportunity to enjoy fully their rights. At the beginning of 2011, there were 5.3 million children under 18 years of age, but the number of specialists in their care and protection amounted to only 191 experts: an expert for every 27,738 children. World practice suggests the number of specialists required in child welfare is determined by calculating a specialist for every 5,000 children. The specialists' role needs to include establishing effective inter-agency coordination, and ensuring the appropriate supervision of educational institutions. The experts' representatives in the field would be the child welfare authorities, which need to be resourced so as to be able to develop effective mechanisms to improve the quality of life of those children not currently receiving a service and creating the right conditions for their development.

The lack of a uniform system of data collection and continuous monitoring means it is not possible, at present, to regularly monitor and evaluate the results of the state's efforts to satisfy the norms of the UNCRC and the effectiveness of the social welfare provision available. The introduction of a mechanism for such continuous performance monitoring and control would be a useful contribution to achieving universal coverage of children's rights declarations.

The question of access to education for children remains an open one. In Kazakhstan, between 2005 and 2010, the spread of access to preschool education increased by 17 per cent, but it still only covers 40 per cent of eligible children, whereas in most developed countries coverage reaches

90–100 per cent. One issue is that of the annual growth of the population. The increase in the annual birth rate has averaged between 5 and 7 per cent in recent years, which increases the demand for preschool places and creates an ongoing increase in the cost of providing them. In addition, in three regions – South Kazakhstan, Kyzylorda and Zhambyl – and in the cities of Almaty and Astana the child population is growing by 11 per cent, due to both increases in the birth rate and inward migration. There are 100 places in nursery schools, on average, for every 111 children in the cities; however, there are only 100 places for every 120 children in rural areas. In urban areas, there are kindergarten places for one in three children, but in rural areas there are only places in kindergarten for one child in twenty. The development of low-cost forms of preschool education is an area for reform of early childhood education.

Children with disabilities as children in need

There is a high level of child disability in Kazakhstan. According to the Kazakh Statistics Agency, in January 2011 there were 147,700 children with disabilities, of whom 111,400 (75%) were of school age. Of these, 51,000 (46%) were living at home and enrolled in special education institutions, 9,000 (8%) were in special schools and 2,000 (2%) were attending college. The most prevalent features of childhood disability are congenital malformations (33%) and nervous system diseases (24%).

To ensure the more effective access of children with disabilities to education provision, 103 special remedial educational organizations were set up from 2006. These are only able to accommodate just under one-quarter of the total number of eligible children, with an enrolment of 17,030 children (15% of school-age disabled children). Despite the fact that the special education system has been consistently expanded, not all disabled children in need have access to it. Currently in schools there are about 65,000 disabled children being educated who do not receive timely assistance from appropriately qualified professionals. Only in 766 of the many hundreds of schools in Kazakhstan are there secondary schools with special classes that can create the conditions needed for intellectually disabled children. They are only able to accommodate the needs of about 700 such children. There is also an acute shortage of textbooks and teaching aids, and special teaching aids for children with hearing, vision, musculoskeletal system and speech problems.

There is still an as yet unmet need to develop and implement measures to support special education programmes to train staff on issues related to disability, and to develop the approaches to education that are appropriate for children with disabilities, so as to enable them to actively and equally participate in cultural life. This includes the identification of gifted children with disabilities, for example children with special abilities in arts and sports. Children with disabilities living in residential institutions have limited access to information resources, such as modern editions of books, periodicals and access to the Internet. They do not attain useful levels of computer skills, nor do they have the opportunity to learn a foreign language.

A continuing significant problem associated with raising children with disabilities is the way it limits the child's mother's possibilities for work, because employers will not recruit women with high childcare demands because of the need to create specific employment conditions for them.

Children and health issues

One of the most pressing problems is the health status of adolescence (12–18-year-olds). The social significance of this problem is linked to the need of this group of adolescents to prepare for their careers, and for establishing a family. The right to healthcare for all children and adolescents is provided for by the following measures: recent improvements in the legislation related to child health, covering advocacy and promotion of healthy lifestyles, health checks for both children and parents, and the prevention of childhood diseases. Healthcare is an area in which significant additional investment has been made. In the five years to 2010, the share of expenditure on GDP on healthcare increased dramatically from 2 per cent in 2006 to 8 per cent in 2010.

Despite these efforts, each year there are about 4.7 million health cases involving children under 18 years of age. The primary causes of childhood illness are the violation of sanitary norms and rules, the lack of nutritional supplements, and poor nutrition in schools. As a result of the annual preventive medical examinations of adolescents, it has been established that more than 53 per cent have significant health problems related to diseases of the digestive system, the eyes, musculoskeletal system, respiratory system and the nervous and endocrine systems. Almost one in five school children under 14 years of age suffer such illnesses.

There remains a high child mortality rate from accidents, injuries and poisonings: 200,000 accidents and injuries to children under 14 years of age are reported annually, of which 1 per cent result in disability. Kazakhstan has only limited medical personnel, and has an inadequate material and technical base in its children's healthcare organizations. In this regard, it is necessary to develop and implement additional measures to enhance the safety and security of the life and health of school-age children. The priority need of children is to have socially oriented healthcare services. Healthcare should be provided on the basis of the required standards of care, determined by the needs of the child, not the amount of money allocated to deliver the services.

On 1 January 2010, more than 19,000 young people were registered as having juvenile behaviour problems. Young people's health is being adversely affected by their risk-taking behaviour, such as teenage drinking, smoking and drug use. There were over 54,000 officially registered drug users, of whom more than 3,700 (about 7%) were aged between 14 and 17 years. Of particular concern is the lack of measures for the prevention of behaviours that are dangerous to the health and lives of adolescents. Actions to prevent teenage behaviours that are dangerous to life and health need to be systemic in nature. What is needed are implementable targeted actions designed to attract the attention of, and motivate, the community to understand and address this problem. Government policy on children is implemented in the context of economic and political reforms. There are many ongoing positive developments in Kazakhstan. There are measures to improve the situation of children in society in many important respects. Despite this, challenges remain if Kazakhstan is to reduce the negative role the family can play for many children, since a growing number of parents are leading an anti-social way of life, affecting their children's care, development and life chances.

Parental behaviour and child neglect and abandonment

Being born to a young unmarried mother is a problem for some children. This often entails a child being abandoned, perhaps because his or her mother may be unwilling, or unable, to care for him or her. The incidence of illegitimate births at the beginning of 2010 was 70,000. A significant proportion of the mothers involved were under 20 years of age (nearly 40%) and, more worryingly, under 16 years of age (almost 19%).

Divorce is an issue that affects an increasing number of children. This situation has the effect of reducing the role of the family in the moral and spiritual formation of the child, and parental responsibility for childrearing. Financial and housing difficulties may also follow, particularly for young families, and the lack of interaction between schools, families and society leads to a weak propagation of family values and family education.

The problem of social abandonment of children remains a serious one. On 1 January 2011, there were over 51,000 abandoned children, of whom more than 31,000 (61%) lived with caregivers' families, including those in children's villages with family-type accommodation and care, and in family-type homes; just under 1,900 (4%) were in foster care; and more than 18,000 (35%) were in orphanages and boarding schools on full state support, of whom 29 per cent (just over 15,000) were social orphans with living parents (some of whom are unknown to the child as they were foundlings, some are seriously ill and some have been deprived of parental rights or are in prison for long-term sentences), and 6 per cent (3,000) were orphans whose caregiving parent or parents are dead. Overall in the orphanages and boarding schools there were 18,198 juveniles in residence.

The problems for adolescents range from unemployment among teenagers, to the lack of after-school support facilities. The network of youth and sports clubs is under-developed; there are gaps and weaknesses in the organization of summer camps, recreational activities and recreation areas. One problem that is especially acute is attracting older teenagers to engage actively in socially useful activities, so as to reduce their anti-social behaviour. The development of supplementary education and after-school extra-curricular activities, for children in all age groups, is crucial to strengthen their emotional and physical capacities. Based on the principle that priority must be given to preparing children for a full life in society and to developing their capacity for socially meaningful and creative activities, it is necessary to continue to develop a network of recreational centres and public children's associations, and to provide access for all children to culture and recreation facilities. This would involve working closely with the NGOs.

Violence against children is a pressing social problem. This includes various forms of child exploitation, child neglect and child and family homelessness. Annually, there are identified about 10,000 homeless and street children. Public authorities are paying more attention to the need to identify and prevent acts of violence against children, but the resources available to eradicate this problem are not fully utilized. According to the results of a survey conducted in 2010 by the Association of Sociologists and Political Scientists of the Republic of Kazakhstan, 60 per cent of children experience violence from peers, 25 per cent from teachers and 15 per cent from their parents. Under Article 137 of the Criminal Code, the 'failure to carry out parental responsibilities for the upbringing of minors, and child abuse' carries criminal liability, and, according to the Ministry of Internal Affairs, 370 parents were prosecuted between 2006 and 2009.

Adoption is another issue. According to the available statistics, Kazakhstanis adopted 3,277 children in 2008, and non-Kazakh foreign nationals adopted 733 children, of whom 335 (46%) were adopted by Americans, 149 (20%) by Spaniards and 59 (8%) by Belgians. It should be noted that adoption visas for prospective adopting parents are no longer available. A code, currently in draft form, contains a special chapter that sets adoption standards for the foreign adoption of Kazakhstani children. Adoption overseas is only possible if the prospective parents come from countries that have ratified international conventions that set expectations about the protection of the rights and interests of children. Agencies dealing with adoption ensure that adopters from abroad meet the required standards of the authorized adoption body, in order to protect the rights and interests of adopted children.

International experience shows that there is a need for a single integrated system of managed care for children and families and for an updating and expanding of the range of services to support children in all categories of need. In some countries (such as Russia, Czech Republic, Latvia, Romania, Bulgaria, Albania, Denmark and Sweden) new ways of working with children and families – 'social patronage' and centres of social services for families and children – have been created. These services are aimed at providing social, psychological, medical and legal assistance to children and families in all sectors of society. It is hoped that, in the future, such international experience will be applied in Kazakhstan.

The future of Kazakhstan, in the context of globalization and the large-scale socioeconomic change, depends on children being prepared for their future life by education, training and physical and spiritual development. However, despite the passage of a whole set of new laws, mainly related to advancing the rights and interests of children, there are still child welfare and protection problems and unresolved issues. Currently, various national ministries are working to protect children's rights from different perspectives. Thus, in the education system, there are 722 residential organizations for children, including orphans and children left without parental care, accommodating 79,674 children. In the healthcare system, there are 26 children's homes, accommodating 2,105 children. In the social protection system, there are 19 houses that are homes for children with disabilities, accommodating 1,294 children. In the law enforcement system, there are 18 centres for the temporary isolation and rehabilitation of juveniles, accommodating 9,883 children. These organizations are intended to achieve a common goal: to preserve and strengthen the physical and moral wellbeing of children. They are different, however, in the way they undertake this task. They all provide social, medical, legal and other services, but each does so according to its own specifics and particular approaches inherent to their organizations. The lack of common approaches and coordinated actions means that they cannot realize, for many and varied reasons, the rights of children who need out-of-home care.

Phasing out institutional residential care in favour of other forms of care is a necessity for the successful social adaptation of these children. Research shows that in many countries of Europe long-term residency of children in these institutions has been replaced by an approach to their care that maintains them initially in short-term placements in special institutions (shelters), followed by either reunion with their family or the transfer of caring responsibilities to foster carers. The drastic reduction in the use of orphanages throughout Europe has prompted a change of view on children's rights in society. It has increased the emphasis placed on the value of education in hospital-based facilities and on the value of family education. There is now little confidence on the part of society on the value of residential care for children without parental care, based on evidence of the poor outcomes achieved by this form of care.

One effective mechanism for implementing this process of dismantling care in large institutions is the strategy of placing students from boarding schools with families; another is to change institutions to create conditions that are closer to those experienced in a family setting. However, at present no definite rules have been agreed on the appointment and payment of guardian allowances for the maintenance of such children, which hinders transfer of the children to alternative family caregivers. It also requires an improvement of the legal framework to protect the interests and rights of children, including when they can leave care arrangements. At present only 13 per cent of children living in orphanages and boarding schools have been assigned alternative housing on leaving.

Another possible mechanism for the reduction of the number of larger residential organizations would be to expand the system of patronage. This is a form of alternative care that is provided in conjunction with education services.

Conclusion

Serious challenges face Kazakhstan in its endeavour to provide support and protection for children and young people at risk, or otherwise in need. Analysis of the current state of childhood in Kazakhstan suggests that progress requires the adoption of comprehensive measures to counter the impact of negative events and pressures on children and adolescents, such as youth unemployment and differential access to education and family support. This will involve carrying out fundamental institutional and structural reforms. It will also involve developing further public education and training on the protection of the rights and interests of all children, so as to advance their quality of life in a way that is consistent with, and take account of, the current socioeconomic and political situation in Kazakhstan.

References and further reading

It must be noted that very little is written about child and family welfare and services in Kazakhstan in English, and the Kazakhstani references that follow are mostly published in Russian or Kazakh.

Baymukanova, M.T. (2005) 'Family Counselling as a Method of Social Work with Families.' In *Proceedings of the Republican Scientific-Practical Conference: 'Actual Problems of Training for Social Work in the Republic of Kazakhstan.'* Karaganda, KZ: Ministry of Education and Science.

Kazakhstan Statistics (2012) *Publications.* Available at: www.stat.kz.

Kholostova, E.I. (2006) *Social Work with Families: A Tutorial.* Almaty, KZ: Publishing and Trading Corporation 'Dashkov K'.

Sarsenova, Zh.N. (2004) *Social Work: A Tutorial.* Almaty, KZ: Kazakh University.

Solodyankina, O. (2007) *Raising a Child with Disabilities in the Family.* Moscow, RU: Arctic Press.

UNICEF (2012) *United Nations Convention on the Rights of the Child.* Available at: www. unicef.org/crc/index_30229.html.

Zhanazarova, Z.Zh. (2003) *Social Work with Families: A Textbook for Students in Human Sciences Faculties of Higher Educational Institutions.* Almaty, KZ: Kazakh University.

10

The Middle East

Alean Al-Krenawi and Dennis Kimberley

Justice is the soul of the universe.

Omar Khayyam, 1048–1131

Introduction

Within the context of child welfare and child protection in the Middle East, this chapter addresses the circumscription of children's rights and needs, compounded by cultural meanings, and related religious imperatives. It also explores the implications for community awareness, social action, social policy and social development in a post-Western context of interpreting human rights, where Arab commentators, activists and leaders are creating pathways to change cultural meanings, religious imperatives, political will and social action. While acknowledging universal issues of child maltreatment, child abuse, child exploitation and preventable compromised development, this chapter focuses on diverse contextualized Middle Eastern expressions of problems, risks, needs and harm, as well as opportunities for child-centred solutions.

The Arab world

The Arab world is officially composed of 21 states and inhabited by a mostly young population. Views emphasizing the mosaic nature of Arab society have been reinforced over time by the transitions experienced by Arab society following the collapse of the Ottoman Empire, which initiated a desperate search for a new order. The emerging Arab society has been in flux, pulled constantly between conflicting poles: past versus future, East versus West, tradition versus modernity, sacred versus secular, ethnicity versus class solidarity and unity versus fragmentation. The greater Arab community appears to be in conflict with itself and with other societies. The inhabitants of Arab countries, deriving their overarching identity from shared social patterns and culture, rather than from an artificially imposed polity or religion, overwhelmingly perceive themselves, and are perceived by others, as Arab. This basic identity, rooted in territory and civilization, is reconstituted in individuals and in the collective memory (Barakat 1993).

Examination of the Arab situation in depth reveals a clearly pyramidal social class structure. This means that the majority of the people are relatively poor; the middle class is relatively small; and wealth and power is concentrated in a few hands (Barakat 1993). The family is the basic socioeconomic unit in traditional and contemporary Arab society, but is now being increasingly challenged by the state and other social institutions. It remains a relatively cohesive institution. It is patriarchal and hierarchical, particularly with respect to gender and age.

Notwithstanding social change, a network of interdependent kinship relations continues to prevail. In this network, the father continues to wield authority, assuming responsibility for the family, and expecting respect and unquestioning compliance with his directions. The continued dominance of the family, as the basic unit of social organization and production, has contributed to the diffusion of patriarchal relations to other social institutions: specifically, at work, at school and in religious, political and social associations (Barakat 1993).

Children in the Arab Muslim world

Children in villages become quite independent because their parents, reassured by their familiar environment, allow their children to explore their surroundings freely (Barakat 1993). Sharabi (1975, 1987) has proposed that children in the feudal-bourgeois Arab family have been socialized into dependency and escapism. The principal technique of childrearing is shaming, while the learning process emphasizes physical punishment rather than persuasion and reward. The results are dependency, inequality and the downplaying of normative challenges and difficulties. Furthermore, children learn to link love with certain expectations, and they consequently experience guilt feelings whenever they annoy or fail to perform their duties toward their parents. Their main commitment in later life is usually to the family – sometimes at the expense of society, or of their own personal interests (Barakat 1993).

An area of concern for the children and adolescents of the Arab region is the breakdown of the customary traditional extended families because of urbanization. New nuclear families suffer from two major shortcomings. First, the family's emotional support for children may be compromised by the demands of living both in a city and in poverty, in the absence of community safety nets, which can make psychosocial distress worse. Second, the median age of the population in many of the Arab countries in the Middle East is less than 20 years. Psychosocial problems and mental health-related morbidity are among the results of this demographic scenario.

In general, the hierarchical structure of the Arab family, based on gender and age, traditionally requires the young to obey the old and to adhere to their expectations. This hierarchy creates vertical rather than horizontal relationships between the young and the old. In such relationships, downward communication often takes the form of orders, instructions, warnings, threats, shaming and other control-oriented social expectations. Furthermore, while downward communication may be accompanied by anger and punishment, upward communication may be accompanied by crying, self-censorship, obfuscation and deception (Barakat 1993).

If a child's dominant first experiences in a society are violent actions, then it could be argued that their first experiences are abuses that compromise their development. If child abuse is to be reduced, then a variety of approaches are required to influence social change in the direction of valuing others and the acceptance of a non-violent lifestyle (Copeland 1995).

Palestinian society, for example, is heavily rooted in traditional, Arab-Islamic and tribal culture. Hence the social-cultural legacy of Palestinian children and youth not only influences, but also under some circumstances dictates, their responses to trauma and stress. Traditional Palestinian culture views children as personal and collective possessions. Child abuse has not been fully recognized in the Arab world for a long time; however, child maltreatment is a fact that can no longer be a hidden mystery (Baker and Shalhoub-Kevorkian 1999).

Circumscription of children's rights

The 1989 UN Convention on the Rights of the Child

Children in a Middle Eastern world may be perceived to have the same universal rights as other children: to be protected from preventable risk, trauma, exploitation, maltreatment, abuse and preventable compromises to normative child development (such as child marriage). Increased preventable risks and harm may be the result of direct or indirect actions (such as through becoming child soldiers); or through incidental exposure of children to political violence and military conflict (see Al-Eissa 1995); as well as by acts of omission (such as failing to act on cross-border human trafficking) as child-centred social responsibilities are undertaken (or not) by families, communities, regional governments and the global village. State controls (as espoused or as implemented) and international agreements may form the broad framework for intended social intervention and social care for children; but opportunities to make a difference to the lives of children may not be supported in practice, or may not be implemented with much effectiveness. Examples of such opportunities are the optional clauses of the 1989 *UN Convention on the Rights of the Child* (UNCRC) (UNICEF 2012) associated with involving children in armed conflict, sale of children, child prostitution and child pornography. Advocates and professionals responsible for state or non-governmental policies, programmes and practices guiding social intervention and social care in the Middle East are faced with meeting the needs of the most vulnerable and powerless: the task comprises child welfare promotion, maltreatment prevention, child-youth protection and the amelioration of problems, risks and harm associated with sex abuse, physical abuse, emotional abuse, exploitation[1] and compromised development.

Community and child welfare leaders and scholars have an interest in child protection and in the promotion of normative child-youth development, as well as in supporting the optimization of age-stage expected human potential. Child welfare and protection concerns, and compromised child development issues, are manifest, with relatively common sequelae, such as post-traumatic effects and dissociation (as described by Steele and Malchiodi 2012); with diverse expression (affected by the availability of contextually effective primary attachments, as described by Davies 2010); and as relatively unique experiences (such as children trafficked for use as camel jockeys) (Anti-Slavery International 2006; UNICEF 2006). Many such concerns signal a need for child-centred community and state interventions (see, for example, Chesler 2010).

While the UNCRC continues to give direction to child-youth centredness, neoliberal as well as relatively closed states (both infused with conservative sectarian interests) have not actively embraced their child-youth rights and children's needs commitments under the Convention, with a notable lack of support for the 'optional' clauses. State action (or inaction) may be consistent with religious conservatism, often interacting with

---

1   Exploitation is a broad term often used as a euphemism for the morally questionable market use of persons, including children, as products valued according to the individualized self-interest of those who use and abuse the children, and the interests of collective economic powers, often subsumed within a neoliberal economic, political and religious context. Neoliberal models often translate the 'common good' into the best interests of the political, economic, religious and military elites, as well as tribal elites. Use of children as marketable products, services or otherwise valued economic commodities seldom reflect the best interests of the child.

varying degrees of neoliberal economic thought, and a morality defined by the individual interests of the adults who contribute to family stability and success, and other economically contributing adults. Economic imperatives are supporting, sometimes going as far as tolerating, lucrative child slavery and sex tourism (End Slavery Now 2012).

While acknowledging common shared forms of child vulnerabilities and maltreatment, the emphases here are on some child welfare concerns that are more reflective of regional, cultural, religious and political contexts in the Middle Eastern Arab world. These include, for instance, the dynamic interplay between advocacy for freedom and equality, juxtaposed with religious conflicts and the imperative of Islamification. Progressive protection and welfare approaches will probably necessitate complex efforts at finding pathways to child-youth centred awareness, visions, policies and programmes, framed in ways which enable navigating the varied and diverse paths through the regional expressions of culture (such as the murder of women and children to uphold family honour), local politics (such as societal conflicts and violence) and religion (such as lack of active prohibitions on child brides). These political-religious interfaces are the contextual considerations facing Arab and external activists, professionals and governments, as they attempt to create, or expand, social action and social responsibilities in child protection and social care, locally and through multilateral action.

Among the situationally relevant child welfare concerns, the ones focused upon here are those related to particular Middle Eastern cultural phenomena that give rise to risk, harm, trauma and compromised child-youth development: female genital mutilation; murders and suicide imperatives supporting family honour; plural marriage family contexts and child development; exposure to violence including family, tribal, political, military incarceration and torture of children; and human trafficking, child prostitution and child pornography.

Contextualized cultural and religious imperatives

Current global directions in child welfare in the Middle East are being expressed as efforts to increase public awareness and to create respectful and feasible paths towards child-youth-centred social care. This is happening through a maze of cultural and religious dilemmas and imperatives, challenged by current political realities, such as the Arab Spring and the Palestinian–Israeli conflict. Collective and transcultural regional efforts to improve child-youth welfare are guided, in part, by working towards a more informed public, and the promotion of visions, policies and practices with respect to child welfare, child maltreatment, child abuse trauma, child exploitation and exposure to experiences of risk and harm, all of which are likely to compromise development. The challenge for child advocates is to promote more progressive thought and to transcend religious orthodoxies that contribute to unjust practices, sometimes expressed as holy imperatives, which fly in the face of the child-centred intents of the UNCRC and best-known evidence on child development. Relevant areas of knowledge about child development include attachment and bonding; neurological development; child trauma; common human needs; social care, protection and developmental support; and psychosocial development (Davies 2010).

Children and youth as political capital

Societal leaders, social care professionals, non-governmental organizations (NGOs) and social activists who wish to rise above regional, cultural and sectarian politics attempt to promote the progressive views of children's rights and needs that transcend neoliberal and conservative ideologies. Neoliberal attitudes may promote the use of children and youth as under-age workers (Anti-Slavery International 2006), or as sexual market commodities (Anti-Slavery International 2006), or as political commodities, such as child soldiers or human bombs (Defence for Children International 2012). Within the contexts outlined, a progressive position would support the rights of the child based on age-stage developmental needs, preventable risks, developmental harm reduction and amelioration, and availability of child-centred interventions in order to reduce risks and impacts and to provide social care with due respect to social context.

Progressive directions, rights, social justice, social support and social care

Contextually, societies vary in the cultural expressions of abuse, maltreatment, preventable trauma and exploitation. These patterns pose problems that require child-youth-centred solutions, including developing culturally variegated social development. This analysis explores some risks as they are expressed nationally and regionally in Middle Eastern societies, with special attention to the dynamic interaction of Arab-Middle Eastern cultural, religious and political communities.

Culturally involved expressions of child-youth maltreatment

This section reflects on current societal and cultural issues related to child welfare and protection that transcend the more common focuses on sex abuse, physical abuse, emotional abuse and developmental compromise, or lack of supports for optimizing personal potential. Consistent with the

UNCRC, the position taken is that improvements in child-centred societal and cultural development begin with:

- the best interest of the child, within a cultural context and physical environment

- the support and protection provided offering least harm to the child with the likelihood of most benefit

- the promotion of developmental needs and the reduction of controllable risks for the child

- the enabling of child-youth-centred family preservation[2] with respect to parent–child relationships, or to collective and extended family relationships

- the co-creation of coherent, child-centred, justified plans for protection and care, supported by best-known evidence.

Notwithstanding normative expressions of individual and collective resilience, as social workers our concerns of importance are related to risks and impacts, including trauma, and long-term developmental compromises of social justice significance and clinical significance, as well as to the tapping into of individual and collective strengths, and to the building of capacity in individuals and collectives.

FEMALE GENITAL MUTILATION AND CUTTING

Genital mutilation has been a very sensitive issue to confront. Besides the initial pain and suffering associated with the various forms of female genital cutting, there are risks of sepsis, post-traumatic effects (Behrendt and Moritz 2005), compromised psychosexual development (Catania *et al.* 2007; Lightfoot-Klein 1989) and other bio-psychosocial interactions (Al-Krenawi and Wiesel-Lev 1999). The moral suasion of the international community, and Arab countries that have tried to control female genital mutilation and cutting, have not been sufficient to stop, or otherwise control, this practice (Hassanin *et al.* 2008), but some localized reduction has been identified (Halila *et al.* 2009). Part of the systemic problem is that this form of trauma-inducing child abuse is mostly undertaken by

---

2   The reason for the use of the term 'family preservation' is that the best interests of the child, emotionally, relationally and developmentally, under conditions of risk and harm, may be served through supporting parents, or the extended family, in becoming sufficiently child-centred, based on the individualized needs of the child, so as to influence recovery, healing and strengths-optimizing impacts. The need in the Middle Eastern context is to promote, create and utilize support external to the extended family when its knowledge, skills or motivations are insufficient.

women who have, themselves, experienced female genital mutilation and cutting, many of whom are emotionally committed to this practice (Asali *et al.* 1995). It continues in sub-Saharan Africa as well as in the Middle East, from where it has spread to non-Islamic states with significant Muslim minorities. Future solutions may have to rely on an alliance of progressive social activists, progressive Islamic leaders and politicians with the political will to challenge this practice.

More reliable clinical information is needed on the immediate, post-trauma and developmental impacts of female genital mutilation and cutting. Some genital cutting is more consistent with mutilation, and is associated with post-traumatic stress disorder (PTSD), while some is more symbolic, less intrusive and more acceptable to, and even valued by, some women (Al-Krenawi and Wiesel-Lev 1999; Applebaum *et al.* 2008; Behrendt and Moritz 2005). The presenting needs of the children may be masked by family and cultural meanings that define female genital mutilation and cutting as a special *rite de passage* (Asali *et al.* 1995), or as something that a female puts behind her and then gets on with her life, within the context of a belief system under which children do as they are told, and female children are most at risk if they do not live up to family, extended family and community expectations. A narrow interpretation of female child 'resilience' would probably not support the association of female genital mutilation and cutting with long-term trauma, mental health problems or other personally significant psychosexual development challenges.

FAMILY HONOUR AND FAMILY VIOLENCE

Kifaya Husayn, a 16-year-old Jordanian girl, was lashed to a chair by her 32-year-old brother, then given a drink of water and told to recite an Islamic prayer, before he slashed her throat. Immediately afterwards, he ran out into the street, waving the bloody knife, crying, 'I have killed my sister to cleanse my honour.' Kifaya's 'crime' was that her 21-year-old younger brother raped her. Her uncles convinced her eldest brother that Kifaya was too much of a disgrace to the family honour to be allowed to live.

Today, honour killings are prevalent mostly among Muslim populations (Feldner 2000). An honour killing is one of the greatest violations against women because it denies women the right to life (Hashayka 2012). Families that kill for honour will threaten girls and women if they refuse to cover their hair, faces or bodies, to act as their family's domestic servant or to accept an arranged marriage; if they wear makeup or Western clothing, choose friends from another religion, date, seek to obtain an advanced education, seek a divorce from a violent husband or marry against their parents' wishes; or behave in ways that are considered too independent, which might mean anything from driving a car to spending time, or living, away from home or family (Chesler 2009).

There are very few studies of honour killing, as the motivation for such killings is cleansing alleged dishonour and the families do not wish to bring further attention to their shame, so do not cooperate with researchers. Often, they deny honour crimes completely and say the victim simply went missing or committed suicide. Nevertheless, honour crimes are increasingly visible in the media. Police, politicians and social and feminist activists in Europe, and in some Muslim countries, are beginning to treat them as a serious social problem (Chesler 2009).

The number of women killed in Palestine as the result of honour killings has been growing because of the absence of a deterrent law. In 1967, before the Israeli occupation, Jordan ruled the West Bank and Egypt ruled the Gaza Strip. As a result, the West Bank applies Jordanian law and the Gaza Strip applies Egyptian law. The legislative policy in the Jordanian 1960 Penal Code is to protect people from any crime and to impose sanctions on perpetrators. Although the legislature has criminalized the act of killing, it has also provided honour killers with leniency. In the circumstances of an honour killing, the male assailant either goes free without punishment in the case of 'extenuating circumstances', or he may be imprisoned for a period of one to six months. The current Palestinian Penal Code, which is still in draft form, treats honour killing differently. This law gives both women and men equal coverage under 'extenuating circumstances' when they are surprised to find their spouse in an adulterous relationship. However, Article 235 states that women can only benefit from extenuating circumstances if they catch their husband committing adultery in their house and in their marital bed. The husband benefits from extenuating circumstances wherever he discovers his wife's infidelity.

In May 2011, Aya Barde'a's dead body was found in Hebron City in the West Bank. She was a 21-year-old university student when her uncle killed her and threw her into a well, where she remained for a year until her body was discovered. Her uncle killed her because a young man kept asking Aya's family to allow him to marry her. His persistence led the uncle to believe that there was a sexual relationship, and for this belief, and without any supporting evidence, he killed his niece. The case sparked a wave of anger in Palestine, especially in the feminist movement. Honour killings became a significant public opinion issue and, on 15 May 2011, the President of the Palestinian National Authority, Mahmoud Abbas, issued a presidential decree to annul Article 340 of the Jordanian Penal Code in the West Bank so that honour killers would not benefit from extenuating circumstances. Despite the illegality of the manner in which Abbas attempted to amend this law, as such amendments require a two-thirds approval vote from the legislative council, it was nevertheless considered a positive step towards changing unjust laws against women (Hashayka 2012). It would appear that public education alone would not be sufficient to achieve significant social change. Media exposure, social action and strong sustained advocacy are required, particularly from regional governments and the international community.

PLURAL MARRIAGE FAMILY CONTEXTS

Polygamy refers to marriages with multiple partners, typically where the male has multiple wives. Polygamous marriage is common in the Middle East, Africa, Asia and Oceania, but it also occurs in Europe, North America and other Western countries (Al-Krenawi and Slonim-Nevo 2008; Broude 1994). The family dynamics of polygamous marriages are diverse, with some presenting clinically significant issues, especially for women and children.

In Islam, diverse patterns are found in polygamous families. Polygamous wives may live together in the same house or in separate households. The 'senior wife' is defined as any married woman who is followed by another wife in the marriage; a 'junior wife' is the most recent wife joining the marriage (Chaleby 1985). Ideally, the family unit can make decisions that benefit all its members equally, but the reality is that family members differ in their access to resources, and decisions may favour certain members over others. This family structure expects cooperation among the wives, although there is constant competition for their husband's attention, love and resources, all of whom are subject to his authority. The husband's pattern of relationships with his multiple wives and their children influences family dynamics and functioning. The father's style may be to 'divide and conquer', or he may be attentive and even-handed in his attention and provision (Al-Krenawi and Slonim-Nevo 2008). The social position of one wife relative to another, or of one child or a consanguine group of children relative to a group with another mother, can have an impact on both mental health and development. In Muslim society, the first wife often has lower status than the second wife (Al-Krenawi 2001), and her husband could even surprise her by marrying an additional wife without informing her in advance (Topouzis 1985). Marriage to a second wife is often the result of free choice, and the couple unites out of love or as an expression of independence. Junior wives may enjoy preferential status, as compared with first wives, with respect to attention, support and resources (Al-Krenawi 1998; Al-Krenawi, Graham and Al-Krenawi 1997).

Studies carried out in the Middle East and Africa indicate that children and adolescents of polygamous families may suffer more emotional, behavioural and physical problems (including lower self-esteem, lower school achievement and greater difficulties in social adjustment) than do children and adolescents in monogamous marriages. They report more behavioural difficulties in school compared with those from monogamous unions (Al-Krenawi and Lightman 2000; Al-Krenawi and Slonim-Nevo 2008; Cherian 1990, 1993; Eapen *et al.* 1998; Owuamanam 1984; Oyefoso and Adegoke 1992). Some studies indicate that children of polygamous families are exposed to a higher incidence of marital conflict, family violence and family disruption than children of monogamous families (Al-Krenawi 1998; Elbedour, Bart and Hektner 2000). In these circumstances, the psychosocial development of children and adolescents of polygamous families faces multiple clinically significant compromises (Elbedour *et al.* 2002).

Marital difficulties, discord and distress in a marriage, particularly a plural marriage, have a direct effect on the mental health status of children. In a study of children and youth between 8 and 18 years of age, Buehler and Gerard (2002) reported that marital conflict and ineffective parenting might account for 11 per cent of the variance in children's maladjustment. Developmental outcomes of children predicted by marital problems include poor social competence and a poorly developed sense of security (Davies, Myers and Cummings 1996). Furthermore, children of plural marriages who experience intense marital conflict often use aggressive behaviours as a means of problem solving (Cummings, Zahn-Waxler and Radke-Yarrow 1984), show hostile patterns of interaction (Katz and Gottman 1993) and may ally with one parent against the other (Grych and Fincham 1990, 1992). A negative appraisal of the marital relationship by a child's mother is linked to negative interactions among older siblings as well as between mother and children. Fifty per cent of parents reported that they experience tense interactions with their children associated with marital tension (Krishnakumar and Buehler 2000). Increased rates of negative behaviour by husbands toward their wives were associated with increased rates of negative behaviour by wives toward their five-month-old children (Pederson, Anderson and Cain 1977). Adolescents are often less accepting of polygamy than are adults (D'Hondt and Vandewiele 1980; Dorjahn 1988), objecting mainly to the economic difficulties and communication problems among children of multiple wives.

Studies across cultures suggest that women's attitudes towards polygamy may vary within and across societies (Adams and Mburugu 1994; Dorjahn 1988; Kilbride and Kilbride 1990; White and Burton 1988), and that their experiences and perspectives are best understood within their particular sociocultural, religious and personal contexts (Madhavan 2002). Polygamy has been associated with poor mental health among women, particularly somatization, depression and anxiety (Al-Krenawi 2001; Makanjuola 1987). A recent Turkish study of 42 senior wives and 46 junior wives found that senior wives reported more psychological distress than junior or monogamous wives (Ozkan *et al.* 2006). Further, compromised family functioning and lower marital satisfaction have been linked to poor mental health in polygamous women when compared with monogamous women (Al-Krenawi, Graham and Ben Shimol-Jacobson 2006). Al-Sherbiny (2005) documented a culture-specific condition in Egypt, which he termed the 'first-wife syndrome', which involves a range of compounding psychological and physical symptoms. Cross-cultural child development scholarship is clear that those exposed to parental mental health problems are more likely to express problems associated with affect, behaviour, interpersonal relationships and somatic complaints and mental health problems in adolescence or adulthood.

It is important to recognize that parental conflict, family violence and exposure to parental mental health problems all pose significant risks for child development and for the child's personal and social functioning. Research indicates that children of polygamous marriages may experience more harm and may be more at risk than children of non-polygamous marriages.

Family violence, political violence and exposure to military violence

There is much written about the developmental impact on children's emotional wellbeing and mental health as a result of exposure to violence and threat, including PTSD, modelling and bullying (see, for example, Crosson-Tower 2010). In the Arab-Muslin world, some patterns of family threat and violence have other forms of cultural expression, such as extended family conflicts, internal tribal conflicts and honour killing. Beyond these sources of exposure to violence, humiliation and threat, children and youth in the Middle East have for many decades been at high risk for, and experienced significant harm and trauma from (Dinshtein, Dekel and Polliack 2011):

- exposure to political violence and military action (such as the Gulf War, Arab Spring revolts and Arab–Israeli conflict)

- direct involvement in armed conflict as child soldiers, human bombs and as political prisoners

- personal humiliation, threat and violence, or vicarious trauma within the context of premature marriage, sexual exploitation, forced labour and human trafficking

- secondary and trans-generational family and community trauma.

Violence may be defined as any act or situation in which one person injures another, including direct attacks on a person's physical or psychological integrity, and destructive actions that do not involve a direct relationship between the victim and perpetrator(s) (Van Soest and Bryant 1995). This definition significantly expands traditional behavioural perspectives on violence in four ways:

- It emphasizes the consequences of violence from the victim's perspective.

- It treats all types of violence relatively equally, regardless of whether the aggressors are individuals, groups, institutions or society.

- It permits examination of the manifestation of violence without excluding socially sanctioned violence, and violence with long-term consequences.

- It includes any avoidable action that violates human rights, in the broadest sense, as well as personal boundaries, and actions that prevent the fulfilment of a basic human need.

Violence may take many forms, and voice given to victims and survivors who evidence vulnerabilities and scars. These are often unrecognized, disregarded or minimized, sometimes through exaggerating the clinical significance of resilience.

Conflicts are the cause of much preventable damage to populations in general; however, children often suffer the most (Corbin 2012; Werner 2012). Many researchers from the Arab world have investigated the impacts of war on the mental health status of children, and found it to be personally and clinically significant, including for PTSD symptoms and compromised development (Macksoud and Aber 1996), and psychosomatic symptoms (Ryhida, Shaya and Armenian 1986). Punamaki (1987) found that psychological disorders among Palestinian children in the occupied West Bank and Gaza were consistent with the number and levels of traumatic events to which they were exposed. Some studies, however, emphasize children's better ability to reconcile the impacts of war, as compared with adults, and to adapt quickly after a conflict trauma (Carballo et al. 2004). Children may have some advantage, because they have not evidenced the levels of psychological impairment that might have been expected (Gibson

1989). Additionally, children may be more affected by the response and emotions expressed by their parents after the conflict (Garmezy and Rutter 1985).

Armed conflict affects the wellbeing and behavioural outcomes of children. Al-Eissa (1995) discovered that Kuwaiti children exposed to aggression from the Gulf War expressed more symptoms of hostility, unhappiness, withdrawal, difficulties sleeping and suspicious attitudes. Children so exposed may evidence a decreased capacity for enjoyment, sense of wellbeing and trust in others (Baker and Kanan 2003). Children who grow up in a conflict zone struggle to react to social contexts and social situations in a manner congruent with cultural norms (Onyango 1998).

Children and youth who are exposed to violence and war believe that many problems may be solved through violent action or threat, as these are the norms in their lives as lived. Bachar *et al.* (1997) describe how violent situations may have positive outcomes when they are associated with changes that lead towards life becoming more normal, at least from a social perspective. The quick recovery of some children from social violence and armed conflict gives them an advantage, and some may present as not suffering psychologically and emotionally (Cairns and Dawes 1996).

Within the context of the political violence of the Arab Spring, war and related threats, thousands of children have been exposed not only to compromised safety, security, stability, continuity and structure in their lives, and to the modelling of violence as a coping pattern, but also to traumatic events. These carry an associated personal and collective developmental impact. Some children and young people have acted as soldiers; others know that friends have acted as human bombs; and some have become prisoners of political violence in undeclared wars (Defence for Children International 2012). At one level, some children may present as resilient and resourceful in terms of personal and social functioning. Too often, however, their resilience runs thin and is superficial, and they are seen, in reality, to be vulnerable, with a multitude of converging personal and relational problems and risks. This may be made manifest throughout their adult lives, and, where it is based on collective social trauma, it may include trans-generational family and community impacts (Hunt, Marshall and Rawlings 1997; Kellerman 2007; Kellerman and Hudgins 2000; Virag 2000).

Regarding treatment in the age of political violence, supportive counselling and therapy, and the treatment of widowed mothers jointly with their young children, hold promise (Beebe *et al.* 2012). There may be clinically significant interactions between a person's attachment style and their pattern of processing war trauma (Mikulincer, Florian and Weller 1993). Exposure to, and active involvement in, family, extended family, political and military violence, threat, abuse and trauma appear to have concurrent and long-term impacts on a high proportion of children's mental health and their developmental progress in a way that is summative. Children who present as adaptive and resilient may still evidence in therapy clinically significant developmental damage as adults, including damage that compromises their personal and social functioning (Dinshtein *et al.* 2011).

Interventions in the interest of social change

Politically and culturally significant social progress is evident in some of the areas of concern identified above, but much more is needed. Given the autocratic political context, and the active presence of unjustified controls on personal and collective freedoms, supported by closed family norms, it is difficult to obtain reliable information about child maltreatment. The limited information available about preventative measures and services available may not reach the public through government or religious channels. This leaves internal and external news services – those with reliable investigative journalists – and political activists as important sources of information to increase public awareness. For more in-depth understanding of children's risks and needs, often with narrower exposure, there are consultations and briefings by NGO representatives and professional sources. These sources are not bound by law, governmental or political restrictions, and can freely provide much-needed information and offer informed social advocacy. Within the context of the Arab Spring, more moral suasion may be possible (such as the support of public education on the rights and safety of female children).

While there is little opportunity to develop systematic inquiries at epidemiological or clinical levels, more *post hoc* studies could, through primary healthcare contacts, explore the self-presentation of some of the affected girls as teenagers or young adults. Large groups with significant organizational influence may be permitted to co-gather data, co-analyse data, create best-known evidence statements and make recommendations for societal change in the interests of social justice, including increased support for communities, families and individuals. This should include help with the clinically significant impacts of trauma and maltreatment.

In the age of the World Wide Web, social networking and the global village, the culturally aware therapist offering treatment must learn to address multiple identities within individuals' dominant culture, minority culture and hybrid identity contexts (see for example Gallardo and McNeil 2009). The creation of laws with the power to be acted upon is also presumed to be necessary for lasting and meaningful change. Moral suasion may be enhanced as more personal freedoms are achieved and acted upon, supported in part by open communications on the Internet, which is a challenge to any government wishing to control access to publicly needed, required or desired information. Even so-called 'free and democratic' political jurisdictions need protections for whistle blowers, who are often persecuted, and they need free and direct access to information sought, otherwise moral suasion and its impacts may depend on the interventions of the international community.

Conclusion

In policy and law, the UNCRC must be given prominence and strength in the Middle East, where child protection problems, risks and harm are mounting, and failures to protect children at risk are exacerbated (Hodgson 2009). While community capacity building based on existing strengths is important, it must be recognized that political and emotive resistance to change requires a multi-pronged approach to advocacy, political challenge, moral suasion and development of legal imperatives that have more power than presumed religious imperatives. In small groups, consciousness-raising about the rights of women and female children, and the unacceptability of honour murders, may help motivate and support change from the grass roots. However, one concern is that engaging women in self-advocacy, individually or as a group, could place them at added risk. Obtaining the support of progressive males and religious leaders would help in achieving meaningful and sustained protection of women and children.

References

Adams, B.N. and Mburugu, E. (1994) 'Kikuyu bridewealth and polygyny today.' *Journal of Comparative Family Studies 25*, 2, 159–166.

Al-Eissa, Y.A. (1995) 'The impact of the Gulf armed conflict on the health and behavior of Kuwaiti children.' *Social Science and Medicine 41*, 1033–1037.

Al-Krenawi, A. (1998) 'Family therapy with a multiparental/multispousal family.' *Family Process 37*, 65–81.

Al-Krenawi, A. (2001) 'Women from polygamous and monogamous marriages in an outpatient psychiatric clinic.' *Transcultural Psychiatry 38*, 2, 187–219.

Al-Krenawi, A. and Lightman, E. (2000) 'Learning achievements, social adjustment and family conflicts among Bedouin-Arab children from polygamous and monogamous families.' *Journal of Social Psychology 140*, 345–355.

Al-Krenawi, A. and Slonim-Nevo, V. (2008) 'Psychosocial and familial functioning of children from polygynous and monogamous families.' *Journal of Social Psychology 148*, 6, 745–764.

Al-Krenawi, A. and Wiesel-Lev, R. (1999) 'Attitudes toward and perceived social impact of female circumcision as practices among Bedouin Arabs of the Negev.' *Family Process 38*, 431–443.

Al-Krenawi, A., Graham, J.R. and Al-Krenawi, S. (1997) 'Social work practice with polygamous families.' *Child and Adolescent Social Work Journal 25*, 6, 445–458.

Al-Krenawi, A., Graham, J.R. and Ben Shimol-Jacobson, S. (2006) 'Attitude toward and reasons for polygamy differentiated by gender and age among the Bedouin-Arabs of the Negev.' *International Journal of Mental Health 35*, 1, 45–60.

Al-Sherbiny, L.A.M. (2005) 'The case of first wife in polygamy: Description of an Arab culture-specific tradition.' *Arabpsynet 8*, 9–26.

Anti-Slavery International (2006) *Information on the United Arab Emirates (UAE): Compliance with ILO Convention No.182 on the Worst Forms of Child Labour (Ratified in 2001). Trafficking of Children for Use as Camel Jockeys.* Available at: www.antislavery.org/includes/documents/cm_docs/2009/2/2006uae_cameljockeys.pdf.

Applebaum, J., Cohen, H., Matar, M., Abu Rabia, Y. and Kaplan, Z. (2008) 'Symptoms of posttraumatic stress disorder after ritual female genital surgery among Bedouin in Israel: Myth or reality?' *Journal of Clinical Psychiatry 10*, 6, 453–456.

Asali, A., Khamaysi, N., Aburabia, Y., Letzer, S. *et al.* (1995) 'Ritual female genital surgery among Bedouin in Israel.' *Archives of Sexual Behavior 24*, 571–575.

Bachar, E., Canetti, L., Bonne, O., Denour, A.K. and Shalev, A.Y. (1997) 'Psychological well-being and ratings of psychiatric symptoms in bereaved Israeli adolescents: Differential effect of war versus accident-related bereavement.' *Journal of Nervous and Mental Disease 185*, 6, 402–406.

Baker, A. and Shalhoub-Kevorkian, N. (1999) 'Effects of political and military traumas on children: The Palestinian case.' *Clinical Psychology Review 19*, 8, 935–950.

Baker, A.M. and Kanan, H.M. (2003) 'Psychological impact of military violence on children as a function of distance from traumatic event: The Palestinian case.' *Intervention 1*, 3, 13–21.

Barakat, H. (1993) *The Arab World: Society, Culture, and State.* Los Angeles, CA: University of California Press.

Beebe, B., Cohen, P., Sossin, K.M. and Markese, S. (2012) *Mothers, Infants and Young Children of September 11, 2001.* London: Routledge.

Behrendt, A. and Moritz, S. (2005) 'Posttraumatic stress disorder and memory problems after female genital mutilation.' *American Journal of Psychiatry 162*, 1000–1002.

Broude, G.J. (1994) *Marriage, Family and Relationships: A Cross-Cultural Encyclopedia.* Denver, CO: ABC-CLIO.

Buehler, C. and Gerard, J.M. (2002) 'Marital conflict, ineffective parenting, and children's and adolescents' maladjustment.' *Journal of Marriage and the Family 64*, 78–92.

Cairns, E. and Dawes, A. (1996) 'Children: Ethnic and political violence – a commentary.' *Child Development 67*, 1, 129–139.

Carballo, M., Arif, S., Damir, Z., Monika, D., Joy, G. and Joost, V.H. (2004) 'Mental health and coping in a war situation: The case of Bosnia and Herzegovina.' *Journal of Biosocial Science 2*, 1–15.

Catania, L., Puppo, V., Bladaro Verde, J., Abdulcadir, J. and Abdulcadir, D. (2007) 'Pleasure and orgasm in women with female genital mutilation/cutting (FGM/C).' *Journal of Sex Medicine 4*, 1666–1678.

Chaleby, K. (1985) 'Women of polygamous marriage in inpatient psychiatric services in Kuwait.' *Journal of Nervous and Mental Disease 173*, 1, 56–58.

Cherian, V.I. (1990) 'Academic achievement of children from monogamous and polygamous families.' *Journal of Social Psychology 130*, 117–119.

Cherian, V.I. (1993) 'The relationship between parental interest and academic achievement of Xhosa children from monogamous and polygynous families.' *Journal of Social Psychology 133*, 5, 733–736.

Chesler, P. (2009) 'Are honor killings simply domestic violence?' *Middle East Quarterly 16*, 2, 61–69.

Chesler, P. (2010) 'Worldwide trends in honor killings.' *Middle East Quarterly 17*, 2, 3–11.

Copeland, S.J. (1995) 'School intervention programs: An approach to preventing child abuse.' *New Jersey Medicine 92*, 104–106.

Corbin, J. (2012) *Children and Families Affected by Armed Conflicts in Africa: Implications and Strategies for Helping Professionals in the United States.* Washington, DC: NASW Press.

Crosson-Tower, C. (2010) *Understanding Child Abuse and Neglect* (3rd ed.). Boston, MA: Allyn and Bacon, Pearson Education.

Cummings, E.M., Zahn-Waxler, C. and Radke-Yarrow, M. (1984) 'Developmental changes in children's reactions to anger in the home.' *Journal of Child Psychology and Psychiatry and Allied Disciplines 25*, 63–74.

D'Hondt, W. and Vandewiele, M. (1980) 'Attitudes of Senegalese secondary school students towards traditional African way of life and western way of life.' *Psychological Reports 47*, 235–242.

Davies, D. (2010) *Child Development: A Practitioner's Guide* (3rd ed.). New York: Guilford Press.

Davies, P.T., Myers, R.L. and Cummings, M.E. (1996) 'Responses of children and adolescents to marital conflict scenarios as a function of the emotionality of conflict endings.' *Merrill-Palmer Quarterly 42*, 1–21.

Defence for Children International (2012) *Resources.* Available at: www.defenceforchildren. org/resources.html.

Dinshtein, Y., Dekel, R. and Polliack, M. (2011) 'Secondary traumatization among adult children of PTSD veterans: The role of mother–child relationships.' *Journal of Family Social Work 14*, 2, 109–124.

Dorjahn, V.R. (1988) 'Changes in Temne polygamy.' *Ethnology 27*, 367–390.

Eapen, V., Al-Gazali, L., Bin-Othman, S. and Abou-Saleh, M.T. (1998) 'Mental health problems in school going children in Al Ain, UAE: Prevalence and risk factors.' *Journal of the Academy of Child and Adolescent Psychiatry 37*, 8, 880–886.

Elbedour, S., Bart, W.M. and Hektner, J.M. (2000) 'Scholastic achievement and family marital structure: Bedouin Arab adolescents from monogamous and polygamous families in Israel.' *Journal of Social Psychology 140*, 503–515.

Elbedour, S., Onwuegbuzie, A.J., Caridine, C. and Abu-Saad, H. (2002) 'The effect of polygamous marital structure on behavioral, emotional, and academic adjustment in children: A comprehensive review of the literature.' *Clinical Child and Family Psychology Review 5*, 4, 255–271.

End Slavery Now (2012) *Resources.* Available at: www.endslaverynow.com/?goto=main& section=resources&gclid=CN_Hq_2ey7ICFUEa6wodpB8ARg.

Feldner, Y. (2000) 'Honor murders – why the perps get off easy.' *Middle East Quarterly 7*, 4, 41–50.

Gallardo, M.E. and McNeil, B.W. (eds) (2009) *Intersections of Multiple Identities: A Case Book of Evidence-Based Practices with Diverse Populations.* London: Routledge.

Garmezy, N. and Rutter, M. (1985) 'Acute Reactions to Stress.' In M. Rutter and L. Hersov (eds) *Child and Adolescent Psychiatry: Modern Approaches.* Oxford: Blackwell.

Gibson, K. (1989) 'Children in political violence.' *Journal of Social Science and Medicine 28,* 7, 659–667.

Grych, J.H. and Fincham, F.D. (1990) 'Marital conflict and children's adjustment: A cognitive–contextual framework.' *Psychological Bulletin 108,* 2, 267–290.

Grych, J.H. and Fincham, F.D. (1992) 'Marital Dissolution and Family Adjustment: An Attributional Analysis.' In T.L. Orbuch (ed.) *Close Relationship Loss: Theoretical Perspectives.* New York: Springer.

Halila, S., Belmaker, R.H., Abu Rabia, Y., Froimovici, M. and Applebaum, J. (2009) 'Disappearance of female genital mutilation from the Bedouin population of Southern Israel.' *Journal of Sexual Medicine 6,* 1, 70–73.

Hashayka, A. (2012) 'Amending Palestine's laws for honor killings.' *Jurist,* 25 June. Available at: http://jurist.org/dateline/2012/06/abeer-hashayka-honor-killings.php

Hassanin, I.M., Saleh, R., Bedaiwy, A.A., Peterson, R.S. and Bedaiwy, M.A. (2008) 'Prevalence of female genital cutting in upper Egypt: 6 years after enforcement of prohibition law.' *Reproductive BioMedicine Online 16,* 17–31.

Hodgson, D. (2009) *The Rise and Demise of Children's International Human Rights.* Available at: www.forumonpublicpolicy.com/spring09papers/archivespr09/hodgson.pdf.

Hunt, L., Marshall, M. and Rawlings, C. (1997) *Past Trauma in Late Life: European Perspectives on Therapeutic Work with Older People.* London: Jessica Kingsley Publishers.

Katz, L.F. and Gottman, J.M. (1993) 'Patterns of marital conflict predict children's internalizing and externalizing behaviors.' *Developmental Psychology 29,* 940–950.

Kellerman, P.F. (2007) *Sociodrama and Collective Trauma.* London: Jessica Kingsley Publishers.

Kellerman, P.F. and Hudgins, M.K. (eds) (2000) *Psychodrama with Trauma Survivors: Acting Out Your Pain.* London: Jessica Kingsley Publishers.

Kilbride, P. and Kilbride, J. (1990) *Changing Family Life in East Kenya: Women and Children at Risk.* Philadelphia, PA: University Park Press.

Krishnakumar, A. and Buehler, C. (2000) 'Interpersonal conflict and parenting behaviors: A meta-analytic review.' *Family Relations 49,* 29–40.

Lightfoot-Klein, H. (1989) 'The sexual experience and marital adjustment of genitally circumcised and infibulated females in Sudan.' *Journal of Sex Research 26,* 375–392.

Macksoud, M.S. and Aber, J.L. (1996) 'The war experience and psychosocial development of children in Lebanon.' *Child Development, 67,* 70–88.

Madhavan, S. (2002) 'Best of friends and worst of enemies: Competition and collaboration in polygyny.' *Ethnology 41,* 1, 69–84.

Makanjuola, R.O.A. (1987) 'The Nigerian psychiatric patient and his family.' *International Journal of Family Psychiatry 8,* 4, 363–373.

Mikulincer, M., Florian, V. and Weller, A. (1993) 'Attachment styles, coping strategies, and posttraumatic psychological distress: The impact of the Gulf War in Israel.' *Journal of Personality and Social Psychology 64,* 5, 817–826.

Onyango, P. (1998) 'The impact of armed conflict on children.' *Child Abuse Review 7,* 219–229.

Owuamanam, D.O. (1984) 'Adolescents' perception of polygamous family and its relationship to self-concept.' *International Journal of Psychology 19,* 6, 593–598.

Oyefoso, A.O. and Adegoke, A.R. (1992) 'Psychological adjustment of Yoruba adolescents as influenced by family type: A research note.' *Journal of Child Psychology and Psychiatry 33,* 4, 785–788.

Ozkan, M., Altindag, A., Oto, R. and Sentuneli, E. (2006) 'Mental health aspects of Turkish women from polygamous versus monogamous families.' *International Journal of Social Psychiatry 52*, 3, 214–220.

Pederson, F., Anderson, B. and Cain, R. (1977) 'An approach to understanding linkages between parent–infant and spouse relationships.' Paper presented at the biennial meeting of the Society for Research in Child Development, May, New Orleans.

Punamaki, R. (1987) *Childhood Under Conflict: The Attitudes and Emotional Life of Israeli and Palestinian Children* (Research Report). Tampere, FI: University of Tampere, Tampere Peace Research Institute.

Ryhida, J., Shaya, M. and Armenian, H. (1986) 'Child Health in a City at War.' In J. Bryce and H. Armenian (eds) *War Time: The State of Children in Lebanon*. Beirut, LB: American University Press.

Sharabi, H. (1975, 1987) *Muqaddimat li Dirasat al-Mujtama al-Arabi* [*Introduction to the Study of Arab Society*]. Acre, IS: MA Polyflex.

Steele, W. and Malchiodi, C. (2012) *Trauma-Informed Practices with Children and Adolescents*. London: Routledge.

Topouzis, D. (1985) 'The man with many wives.' *New Society 74*, 13–15.

UNICEF (2006) *Trafficking of Children for Use as Camel Jockeys* (May). Available at: www.unicef.org/media/media_26692.html.

UNICEF (2012) *United Nations Convention on the Rights of the Child*. Available at: www.unicef.org/crc/index_30229.html.

Van Soest, D. and Bryant, S. (1995) 'Violence reconceptualized for social work: The urban dilemma.' *Social Work 40*, 4, 549–557.

Virag, T. (2000) *Children of Social Trauma: Hungarian Psychoanalytic Case Studies*. London: Jessica Kingsley Publishers.

Werner, E.E. (2012) 'Children and war: Risk, resilience, and recovery.' *Development and Psychopathology 24*, 2, 553–558.

White, D.R. and Burton, M.L. (1988) 'Causes of polygyny: Ecology, economy, kinship, and warfare.' *American Anthropologist 90*, 4, 871–887.

11

Ghana

Marie-Antoinette Sossou

Introduction: The social, political, religious and cultural context

The Republic of Ghana (henceforth, Ghana) covers 238,537 square kilometres, and lies along the West Coast of Africa. It is divided into ten administrative regions: Ashanti, Brong Ahafo, Central, Eastern, Greater Accra, Northern, Western, Upper East, Upper West and Volta. The political head of each region is a regional minister, who is responsible for the administration and coordination of the various activities of the districts forming the region. Each region is divided into districts or counties and these districts constitute the focal points in the decentralized administration of the country. Presently, there are 110 districts, and three of these districts, Accra-Tema, Kumasi and Sekondi-Takoradi, have been designated as metropolitan areas. A district chief executive responsible for the daily administrative activities heads each district.

Ghana's population increased from 18.9 million in 2000 to 24.2 million in 2010. a rise of 28 per cent. Present-day Ghana is ethnically very diverse, with more than 100 identifiable ethnic groups speaking more than 50 languages and dialects, contributing in various ways to its diversity (Roe, Schneider and Pyatt 1992). The largest ethnic group, the Akans, constitutes 49 per cent of the population and is found in the Ashanti, Brong Ahafo, Central, Western and Eastern regions of the country. At the beginning of the decade the Ewes, found mainly in the Volta region, formed 13 per cent of the population, with the Ga-Adangbe, concentrated in the Greater Accra and Eastern regions, accounting for 8 per cent of the total population. In the Northern and the Upper regions of the country, the Mole-Dagbani form 17 per cent; the Guam, 4 per cent; and the Mamprussi, 2 per cent. Non-Ghanaians made up just 4 per cent (Ghana, GSS 2000). Intergroup relations are usually cordial, and Ghana has avoided major ethnic hostilities and pressure for regional secession. However, there is a major cultural divide between the northern and southern parts of the country. The north is poorer and has received less educational and infrastructure investment compared to the south.

In terms of religion, Christians make up 69 per cent of the population, followed by Muslims (16%) and traditionalists (9%) (Ghana, GSS 2000). Traditional supernatural belief differs according to each ethnic group, including ancestor worship through the intercession of fetish priests and chiefs.

Economically, Ghana relies largely on the exportation of cocoa, timber, industrial diamonds, bauxite, manganese, gold and coffee, which accounts for 36 per cent of Gross Domestic Product (GDP) and employs 60 per cent of the workforce. The three major commodities – gold, cocoa and timber – contribute over 70 per cent of Ghana's foreign exchange earnings. Both GDP and per capita incomes declined early this century due primarily to external shocks that began in late 1999 and worsened the following year. Despite several years of economic reform, aimed at reducing government involvement in the economy and encouraging private-sector development, Ghana still remains vulnerable to trade shocks. This is partly because it is one of the most open market economies in the sub-region, partly because of the relatively low price of cocoa on the world market and partly because of increases in the price of crude oil. Since mid-2009 the economy has shown strong signs of stabilization as a result of significant fiscal stabilization efforts and the impact of positive exogenous factors, such as high hydroelectric reserves with good rains, lower oil prices, higher cocoa and gold prices, and good cocoa harvests (World Bank 2011). The World Bank estimated Ghana's GDP at 14.4 per cent for 2011 and it is expected to be around 7 per cent for 2012, linked to strong cocoa production, increased gold output and the commercialization of oil, among other factors (World Bank 2013).

Occupationally, the majority of both men and women are farmers. According to the 2000 population census, the structure of the workforce was: agriculture and fishing (55%), industry (19%), clerical and sales (15%), transportation and communication (8%), and professional services (3%) (Ghana, GSS 2003).

Educationally, Ghana had one of the most highly developed educational systems in the West Africa region. Under the leadership of the first President of Ghana, the 1961 Education Act heralded the introduction of a massive programme of nation-wide compulsory and free primary education for all children in the country. Enrolment in primary schools rose from 641,700 to over one million, and secondary school enrolments expanded from less than 20,000 students to over 60,000 students between 1961 and 1973.

Primary education includes a child attending school from grades one to six, and junior secondary school is from grades seven to nine.

This programme of expansion of education was not, however, sustained. For example, in 1975 there were over 2.3 million children in primary school, but by the early 1980s this had fallen by over one million (World Bank 2004). The government embarked on an ambitious reform programme in 1986 to restructure pre-university education and to introduce greater cost recovery at the secondary and tertiary levels. In 1996, even though in principle there has always been free universal primary education in Ghana, free compulsory universal basic education was introduced to eliminate the kinds of fee regimes that existed in the school system. This reform led to a steady recovery in the number of children attending school.

Also, education services have been decentralized, including the introduction of school management committees and school performance assessment meetings, so as to increase community management and accountability (World Bank 2004). This strategy has been very successful so far. Gross enrolment for primary schools increased from 22 per cent to 97 per cent between the academic years 2002–2003 and 2009–2010, and net enrolment increased from 19 per cent to 54 per cent for the 2008–2009 academic year, and may be higher now. Gross enrolment at the junior secondary school level also increased from 64 per cent to 80 per cent and net enrolment from 30 per cent to 48 per cent during the same period (World Bank 2000). Currently Ghana has 12,130 primary schools, 5,450 junior high secondary schools and 503 senior secondary schools. There are also 21 teacher-training colleges, 18 technical and polytechnic institutions, 6 university colleges and 9 public and private universities serving the Ghanaian people. This compares with only one university and a few secondary schools at the time of independence.

Ghana is a low-income country, and children and youth represent a very large proportion of the total population. According to the World Bank (2011), about 40 per cent of the total population was less than 15 years old in 2005 and the median age among the general population was 19.8 years. Given the current population structure and growth patterns, it is estimated that the median age will reach 21.5 years by 2015. The young age profile of Ghana's population suggests that the future survival of the nation depends on the mental, moral, physical, emotional and psychological development of its children. The government recognizes that children are vulnerable and require special protection, appropriate to their age, level of maturity and individual needs, and has ratified the 1989 *UN Convention on the Rights of the Child* (UNCRC) (UNICEF 2012); indeed, it was the first country to do so in February 1990 after the Convention came into force in September 1989.

The UNCRC emerged as a response to concern about the grave injustices and crimes that have been, and continue to be, committed against children in all parts of the world. Article 19 directly stipulates that it is the right of the child to be protected from all forms of neglect, negligent treatment, abuse and exploitation which is detrimental to their health and wellbeing. It also stipulates the responsibilities of parents, guardians and governments regarding the prevention and management of child maltreatment.

The Organization of African Unity (OAU), now the African Union (AU), created the *African Charter on the Rights and Welfare of the Child* (ACRWC) (OAU 1990) in July 1990, which came into force in November 1999, ten years after the UNCRC was ratified. This was developed to complement the UNCRC, and informed by critical and precarious situations of most African children, due to the unique factors of their socioeconomic, cultural, traditional and developmental circumstances, natural disasters, armed conflicts, and exploitation, poverty, hunger and refugee plights. It did so by addressing and supporting the various African countries to develop their country-specific frameworks to address special safeguards, policies and culturally specific solutions and programmes to meet the physical, social, psychological, economical, emotional and mental needs and development of all African children. Ghana, by ratifying the ACRWC, has accepted that the government has the primary obligation and responsibility to promote and protect the rights and welfare of its children.

Although Africa is the only continent that has its own charter of children's rights, it is still a developing region with multiple challenges that are unique in terms of multi-ethnicity, and the diversity of religious and cultural practices. Additionally, high child mortality rates, childhood diseases, child marriages, child soldiers and refugee children are still major challenges facing many African countries, and Ghana is no exception.

The evolution of child welfare services

In Ghana, child welfare policies operate within a constitutional framework and are informed by international and regional conventions, with administrative structures impacting the manner in which these policies are implemented. The overall goals of child welfare policies include the promotion of child safety and the ultimate goal of the general wellbeing of children in Ghana.

The development of a formal child protective system in Ghana has its roots in the 1989 UNCRC, the 1997 ACRWC and the 1992 Constitution of Ghana. Article 28(5) of the Constitution defines a child as a person less than 18 years of age. A child may be the natural offspring of a couple, or may be their child by reason of adoption under the Adoption Act, or be a foster child under customary law. The Children's Act (Act 560 of 1998) conforms to the principles expressed in Article 12 of the UNCRC. The 1998 Children's Act protects the rights of all children and regulates various aspects of their development. It has six parts which include the rights of the child; quasi-judicial and judicial child adjudication; parentage, custody, access and maintenance; fostering and adoption; employment of children; and institutionalized care and miscellaneous matters. It is a comprehensive law, which covers the involvement of the various institutions that are mandated to play effective roles in the general welfare and protection of children in Ghana.

There is a wide range of institutions in Ghana that have important roles to play in promoting the rights and welfare of children. These include the family tribunals, which are responsible for dealing with legal issues involving child support and maintenance, child custody and paternity disputes. The Ministry of Women and Children's Affairs (MWCA), which replaced the former National Commission on Children, is the umbrella governmental organization that is responsible for policy development and formulation concerning the welfare of children and women. This Ministry was established in 2001 to promote the welfare of women and children in Ghana. Its main responsibilities and objectives are to formulate gender- and child-specific development policies, guidelines, advocacy tools, strategies and plans for their implementation by district assemblies, private sector agencies, non-governmental organizations (NGOs), civil society groups and other development partners. The Ministry is also responsible for preparing national development plans and programmes for women and children across the country. In addition, it is responsible for ensuring that its development programmes are effectively implemented, through continuous monitoring and evaluation of the implementation process and the fulfilment of stipulated objectives (MOWAC 2010). Child panels are non-judicial boards charged under the Children's Act to mediate in matters concerning children and to permit children to express their opinions and participate in any decision that affects their wellbeing.

Another institution responsible for child welfare is the Department of Social Welfare, which has the official governmental responsibilities for the day-to-day protection and promotion of the welfare of all children in Ghana. The Department's core function of child rights and protection covers child survival and development, probation services, institutional care, foster care and adoption, maintenance, and the custody and paternity of children. This Department is also responsible for the registration, inspection and maintenance of standards in all crèches and daycare centres for children aged two years or younger in Ghana, while the Ghana Education Service has the responsibility of implementing education policies and curriculum development for children aged between three and five years.

The juvenile justice system

The arrangements made by the state when children and young people break the law, or are thought to have broken the law, are an important aspect of its response to children and young people's need for recognition of their special status and need for protection, even when they are offenders. There is specific legal protection for the situation of children and young people under 18 years of age who become involved in the justice system as offenders. The Juvenile Justice Act (Law 653 of 2003) protects the rights of all children less than 18 years of age who are juvenile offenders. The main object of this Act is to provide a juvenile justice system that is in accordance with international standards in the UNCRC and the UN Standard Minimum Rules for the Administration of Juvenile Justice. It became necessary when the Criminal Procedure Code (Act 30 of 1960), which hitherto provided for a juvenile or young offender to be dealt with in a manner different from an adult, was found to be inadequate in many respects. The best interests of the young person are now taken into consideration, both in the way the case is conducted, and at disposal if they are found guilty.

Since the 2003 Juvenile Justice Act, a juvenile court consisting of three panel members, comprising a magistrate as the chairperson, a social worker and a member of the community, is responsible for the adjudication of cases. A juvenile court should sit in a different building or room from that in which sittings of other courts are held, or on different days from those on which sittings of other courts are held. Children and young people have a right to anonymity in this court, and court hearings are adapted to make them more suitable for hearing children's cases. No person shall be present at any sitting of a juvenile court except the members and officers of the court, parties to the case, their lawyers and witnesses, and other persons directly concerned in the case. Prosecuting police officers are not allowed to appear in their uniforms, and press reports are not permitted. Section 23 of the Act provides a maximum period of a seven-day remand warrant, the total period not to exceed three months, or six months in the case of a capital offence. The Act also makes provision for a social enquiry report to be prepared by probation officers from the Department of Social Welfare, which must include particulars on the background of the juvenile, their present circumstances, the conditions under which the offence was committed, and recommendations for sentence. This report is taken into account by the court before a court order is made for the disposal of the case. The purpose of the report is to ensure that whatever court order is made is in the best interest of the juvenile.

Human trafficking and exploitation: The response of the Ghanaian government

Exploitation of children and young people includes, at the minimum, induced prostitution and other forms of sexual exploitation, forced labour or services, salary or practices similar to slavery, and servitude. Human trafficking refers to the recruitment, transportation, transfer, harbouring, trading or receipt of persons within and across national borders. This can involve the use of threats, force or other forms of coercion, abduction, fraud or deception; the abuse of power or exploitation of vulnerability; or the giving or receiving of payments and benefits to achieve consent for the trafficking of a child. In addition, human trafficking also includes the placement for sale, bonded placement, temporary placement and placement in service where exploitation by someone else is the motivating factor. The Ghanaian government has made specific provisions to address these problems. The Human Trafficking Act (Law 694 of 2005) was instituted to protect children from exploitation and to provide for the rehabilitation and integration of child victims of human trafficking. Children are protected even when their parents or guardians are complicit, or it is claimed they are complicit, in the trafficking of a child. The law on human trafficking specifically states that, where children are trafficked, the consent of the child, parents or guardian of the child cannot be used as a defence against prosecution under this Act.

A legally mandated management board is responsible, under the 2005 Human Trafficking Act, for making recommendations on strategies to prevent and combat human trafficking for inclusion in a national plan of action, for monitoring and reporting on the progress of the national plan, and for providing assistance in the investigation and prosecution of trafficking cases. This management board consists of various government and private officials from various sectors of society. It is also responsible for liaising with government agencies and organizations in order to promote the rehabilitation and reintegration of victims of trafficking, and to conduct research on international and regional developments and standards on human trafficking.

Domestic violence, forced labour and the protection of Ghanaian children

In 2006, after much lobbying and persuasion by civil societies in Ghana, the Domestic Violence Act (Law 732 of 2008) provided a platform for resolving cases of domestic violence affecting women and children. The scope of this Act extends to protecting children from some of the most long-lasting negative effects of violence within the family on their development. Violence is defined as the deprivation of a person of his or her basic needs such as food, shelter, clothing, love and, in the case of children, the right to education. It also seeks to ensure that children are not physically, financially or emotionally abused. One intention of this Act is to eliminate the worst forms of child labour that persists in Ghana, namely those related to abusive domestic life. Child labour refers to work that is mentally, physically, socially or morally dangerous and harmful to children; that interferes with their education by depriving them of the opportunity to attend school or by obliging them to leave school prematurely; or by requiring them to attempt to combine school attendance with excessively long and heavy work. This definition is derived from the UNCRC, International Labour Organization Conventions 138 (on the minimum age for admission to employment and work) and 182 (on the prohibition and immediate action for the elimination of the worst forms of child labour), and the 1998 Children's Act. This definition refers to all work that is harmful and hazardous to a child's health, safety and development, taking into account the age of the child, the conditions under which the work takes place and the time at which the work is done (Ghana, MMYE 2003). Children who go with their parents to their farm to perform menial activities not only fail to attend school, but they also run the risk of being injured if they undertake activities that may be too difficult and even hazardous. Even though this law is relatively new, its existence is proof of the willingness of the government to tackle any cases of domestic violence that emerge in the context of child labour.

Family policy and family values: The Ghanaian child's two families

A Ghanaian child belongs to two families: their nuclear family (mother and father and other siblings), and their extended family (also including grandparents, cousins, uncles and aunts living together). The family system does depend on family system to which the child belongs can be a patrilineal or matrilineal family system. The *patrilineal* family system consists of two or more brothers with their wives and children, who usually occupy a single household with separate rooms for each wife and her children. This family could also include some or all of the sons and grandsons of one male ancestor together with their wives, children and unmarried sisters. In the patrilineal family, children belong to their father's family and also inherit property and traditional office according to the male line (Mensa-Bonsu 1996). The *matrilineal* family system includes the father's mother, his maternal uncles and aunts, his sisters and their children, and his brothers. In a matrilineal system, a man's children, and those of his brothers, belong to the families of their respective mothers. Family members may occupy one or several houses in the same village. A man's children, and those of his brothers, belong to the families of their respective mothers (Ollennu 1960). In this type of family system, children belong to their mother's family and inherit property as well as traditional offices within the matrilineal family. That is to say, a father and his children do not belong to the same family and the children cannot inherit their father's properties (Mensa-Bonsu 1996).

Marriage is a very important social institution in Ghana and continues to be the main family unit for the purpose of reproduction. Children are regarded as the reason for the existence of the family and essential to the proper functioning of society: no Ghanaian family is considered to be complete without children (Nukunya 1992). Children are important in every Ghanaian family because the status of a family depends upon the presence of children in the lives of the couple. Children in Ghana serve many purposes in the family. For example, their presence adds to parental prestige by strengthening the marital bonds between couples. They actually validate the parents' marriage. Also, they provide security for parents in old age and during illness. Parental responsibilities and duties toward their children include assisting in the successful integration of children into society through nurturing and education. Parents perform these primary roles by providing care, maintenance and protection for their children. Certain parental duties are imposed on parents by Ghanaian law. These include ensuring their physical protection, moral protection and maintenance, and securing their education and training (Mensa-Bonsu 1996). The law under the 1998 Children's Act recognizes the liability of parents, who must pay any fines imposed on juveniles for crime committed, and who are legally obliged to provide child support and maintenance for their children until they reach 18 years of age (Mensa-Bonsu 1996).

Children in Ghana also have certain rights, duties and responsibilities as members of their families. For example, every child has a right to a name, and the child's father gives this name on the eighth day after his or her birth. The child's name establishes his or her paternity (Yeboa 1994). Every child has the right to residence in his or her father's household, and every child has a right under both the customary law and common law to be maintained by the father. This obligation legally covers both parents. In addition, every child has the right to physical and moral protection and this includes the need to have food, shelter and clothing. Physical protection involves protection from moral danger or exposure to moral hazards due to parental neglect. Traditionally, a child also has the duty of providing household services to his or her parents, and such services are not considered to be child labour, but a necessary part of the socialization process. A child may contribute to the acquisition of property by the father by rendering services towards such acquisition, but the child is not a joint owner of the property (Mensa-Bonsu and Dowuona-Hammond 1996). A child also has a moral obligation to care for his or her aged parents in times of sickness and in death.

As a result of rapid demographic and socioeconomic changes, due to urbanization and modernization, patterns of family formation and family life have undergone considerable changes, altering the composition, structure and responsibilities of families. The extended traditional family structure, which used to provide a safety net for its members, has undergone rapid erosion due to social and economic changes. As a result, it is no longer fully capable of meeting its primary roles of socialization, production and social control of its members. The extended family system has been increasingly replaced by the nuclear family, as individuals move from their traditional homes to the urban areas for education and paid employment. Urbanization and modernization have placed heavy burdens on nuclear families as they battle with full-time employment and childcare in the cities as well as with meeting their responsibility to care for elderly members of the extended family. It is very difficult for these families to provide their children with the same amount of care and attention they previously received, automatically, from their extended families. It is evident that urbanization and modernization have contributed to changes in the traditional residential patterns of families, and a decrease in the mutual social, spiritual and economic cooperation of its members.

The inherent tensions in, and the uncertainties of, the new social structure have their implications for the physical, social, psychological and mental wellbeing of various members of families, and especially for children. For example, an effect of changes in residential patterns, and in both formal and informal employment, has been that parents have been required to live with unrelated tenants and people from different backgrounds in the same households. They have also had to employ unrelated individuals as childcare providers for their young children while they work outside the home to earn money to supplement the household income. As a result, many parents find it increasingly difficult to carry out concurrently all their work and family responsibilities, and children often have to help their families by engaging in income-generating activities to supplement parental incomes. This situation can, if it gets out of control, contribute to child labour, child physical abuse and increases in school dropout rates. This is especially the case for female children. For example, the Ghana Statistical Service (Ghana, GSS 2005) reported that at least 10 per cent of children less than 15 years of age have worked, and 34 per cent of girls between 5 and 14 years of age have been engaged in child labour activities. The worst forms of child labour include child domestic work, fishing, child porters, commercial sexual exploitation, customary or ritual servitude, small-scale mining and quarrying, and commercial agriculture. Even though Ghana has made some good progress towards increasing access to education and narrowing gender gaps among school-age children, negative social and cultural perceptions about formal education, especially for girls, are still persistent, especially in the northern part of Ghana. Additionally, the inability of parents or guardians to bear related costs of education, including uniforms, stationery and food, as well as the opportunity costs of sending girls to school, are still barriers to girls' education (UNICEF 2004).

Other significant factors that affect the psychosocial wellbeing of children in Ghana include poverty, malnutrition, lack of healthcare and HIV/AIDS. Ghanaian Demographic and Health Surveys over the past two decades indicate that the health and nutritional status of the average Ghanaian child is poor.

The United Nations Population Fund (UNFPA 2003) defines poverty as unacceptable physiological and social deprivation that is caused or aggravated by a wide range of factors, including the lack of capacity of the poor to influence social processes through lack of education, vocational skills, entrepreneurial abilities, poor health and myths about poverty giving rise to anti-social behaviour. The effects of poverty among children contribute to their experiencing a lack of formal education and incidence of school dropout, child labour migration and child trafficking. About 20–25 per cent of school-age children are not attending school. To illustrate the difficulty of this situation, 25–27 per cent of children under five years of age are underweight and stunted due to malnutrition, and young children from poor families are the most vulnerable, especially girl children. The percentage of girls under five years of age who are underweight is 55 per cent compared to 45 per cent of boys. Additionally, 50 per cent of households have underweight children aged four years or younger (UNICEF 2009).

It is evident that while every member of a poor household is adversely affected, it is the children who suffer most. In the absence of the traditional family role in upholding moral and social responsibilities, the social stability of the family and its members is under threat. It is imperative that the government of Ghana protects and invests in children as part of its fulfilment of its strategic economic, social, legal and moral obligation toward its young citizens.

The state as parent: A diversity of policies to promote child and family wellbeing

A significant number of policies and laws have been passed and implemented by the government in the last decade to promote the welfare and wellbeing of children. Some have been mentioned already, such as the Law against Domestic Violence. The Domestic Violence and Victims Support Unit of the Ghana Police Service was set up in October 1998 to protect victims of domestic violence and sexual abuse, especially children and women and other vulnerable victims. The government ratified the Convention on the Elimination of All Forms of Discrimination against Women. It also committed itself to working and attaining the United Nations Millennium Development Goals (MDGs), especially by promoting education for all children and working to promote gender equality and empowerment of women in the country.

In 1987 a law was enacted to criminalize injurious sociocultural practices such as female genital mutilation and *trokosi* practice in the southern Volta region of the country. *Trokosi* is a traditional fetish practice in which young virgin girls, as young as ten years old, are sent to fetish shrines as slaves to atone for the sins and crimes committed by their relatives, who usually were already dead. The crimes committed by the dead ancestors ranged from murder to petty crime, such as stealing and committing adultery with other people's wives. This practice, which is based on traditional religious beliefs, is discriminatory against women and children. The young girls are mostly denied any chance of formal education or healthcare, and, very often, they are sexually abused by the custodial fetish priests in the shrines (Brooker 1996; Gadzekpo 1993; Laird 2002).

Another policy implemented in the last decade is the 1985 Law on Intestate Succession.[1] This covers inheritance rights and provides a uniform system for the distribution of common property, irrespective of the class of intestate person and type of marriage contract. It provides that the matrimonial home and related belongings shall go to the spouse and children, in equal shares. That law does not address polygamy and, thus, has no mechanism to ensure equity in relation to distributing property upon

---

1   A person who dies without leaving a valid will is intestate (editors' note).

the death of a man with multiple wives. Judges are encouraged to use their discretion in such cases.

Since its creation, the Ministry for Women and Children has been credited for achieving a number of progressive programmes, including ones that promote and encourage women into seeking political decision-making positions. It has also acquired and distributed 200 *Garri* processing machines to provide to women in rural communities to promote small income-generating programmes among poor rural women.[2] It was also instrumental in providing advice on domestic violence and in lobbying for the domestic violence legislation that was passed in 2007 to protect women and children from various forms of abuse.

All child welfare policies are guided by the fact that parents have a fundamental liberty and interest, protected by the Constitution, to raise their children as they choose (Goldman and Salus 2003). However, government intervention seeks to achieve a balance between the rights and responsibilities of parents, and the legal right mandated by laws for intervention in the protection and best interests of children, particularly when parents are incapable or unwilling or have failed to assume their parental responsibilities toward their children. Additionally, the government has implemented the enforcement of certain policies and laws to supplement parental control in areas of child survival, child labour and education of children, maintenance and support of children, juvenile delinquency and prevention of other harmful acts toward children. Some of the policy directives and legal frameworks that have been put in place to support child survival include the national early childhood care and development policy, the 1994 revised national population policy, the 1987 free compulsory universal basic education programme, the education strategy plan (ESP) for 2003–2015, the 2004 Juvenile Justice Act and the 2006–2009 growth and poverty reduction strategy (GPRS II) (Ghana, MFEP 2006). These national policies were conceived to impact on communities, households and maternal variables that influence child poverty.

Education

The government is committed to providing free and compulsory basic education to all children in the country. Basic education is a constitutional right of every child as mandated in Article 25, Section 1(a), of the Constitution. Additionally, the government is committed to achieving MDG 2, which seeks to achieve universal primary education by 2015. Other

---

2   *Garri* processing machines are used to turn cassava into a starchy powder, which is widely used in Ghanaian cooking (editors' note).

international commitments include the 'Education for All' goals adopted in Dakar in 2000, and the 'Fast Track Initiative', which was established to expedite the 'Education for All' agenda. These commitments are being implemented through an education strategic plan, which is responsible for guiding the management and improvement of education for all children in the country by the year 2015 (ISODEC 2009).

The education strategic plan is integrated into the growth and poverty reduction strategy (GPRS) II outlined by the government. The GPRS is a macro-economic development and poverty reduction strategy created to accelerate the growth of the economy so that Ghana can achieve middle-income status within a measurable planning period. The GPRS II policy objectives for education include increasing access to, and participation in, education and training; bridging the gender gap in access to education; and improving quality of teaching and learning, and quality and efficiency in the delivery of education services. This last objective includes promoting and extending the teaching of science, mathematics, technology and ICT, and addressing issues of population, gender, health, HIV/AIDS and sexually transmitted infections, fire safety, road safety and the environment in the curricula of schools and institutions of higher learning.

Other GPRS II objectives are focused on poverty reduction, through creating educational standards to improve and equalize access to a six-year basic education for all children up to 12 years of age. This involves plans to make school attendance compulsory for all children for 11 years, from 4 to 15 years of age, including two years of kindergarten, and three years of junior high school with genuine secondary school content. The policy also includes improving the physical environment of schools and assuring quality standards, especially in basic numeracy and literacy (Ghana, MFEP 2005).

The government believes that the most crucial key to the attainment of economic success of the country is the educational quality of the nation's human resource, hence the commitment to the provision of universal basic education for all children. The 2008 budget earmarked 3.8 million Ghana Cedis[3] to subsidize the 2008 basic education certificate examination fees for poor children. Another initiative implemented in most basic schools was the introduction of the school feeding programme. This programme increased the enrolment and retention of about 560,000 pupils in 1,556 schools nation-wide. Other child-friendly policies in the budget were the proposed distribution of school uniforms to basic school pupils and the payment of an additional 20 per cent of the basic salary to teachers who accepted being posted to deprived areas in the country. Other initiatives

---

3 A Ghanaian Cedi is worth approximately US$0.50 at the time of writing (editors' note).

included the one laptop per child programme, developed primarily for basic school education (ISODEC 2009). However, these initiatives have had mixed results.

Child labour

One-half of rural children and one-fifth of urban children were economically active, and 88 per cent of working children were unpaid family workers and apprentices. Additionally, as many as 1.6 million children were working while attending school and nearly 20 per cent of children (about 1.3 million) were engaged in activities classified as child labour. This phenomenon is prevalent in all regions of the country (Ghana, MMYE 2006).[4] Some particularly severe forms of child labour prevalent in Ghana are *kayaye* (female porters carrying burdens on their heads), child domestic servants, the *trokosi* system (ritual servitude of female children), the commercial sexual exploitation of children, and children working in stone quarries and *galamsey* (workers in illegal small-scale mining). Others include children working in fishing and cash-crop agriculture (Ghana, MMYE 2006).

Child labour is regarded as an age-old global problem: poverty and sociocultural practices have been named as its main causes. The situation in Ghana became a national socioeconomic problem when American and European consumers of chocolate products from the cocoa produced in Ghana threatened to boycott Ghana's cocoa export if the practice of child labour on cocoa farms across the country was not stopped (Ghana, MMYE 2003). The government implemented a number of programmes to tackle the issue of child labour, especially children working under hazardous conditions and in agriculture, with particular efforts focused on removing children from working in cocoa farms.

In 2006 the Ministry of Manpower, Youth and Employment created the national programme for the elimination of the worst forms of child labour in cocoa. This programme was to serve as a framework and direction for all partners implementing interventions toward the elimination of this worst form of child labour (Ghana, MMYE 2008). In 2007, the programme conducted a number of pilot surveys in various cocoa-growing areas in the country to determine the actual situation of the children engaged in child labour. This brought about a number of actions to ameliorate the problem, with implementation funded by UNICEF and the Danish Embassy in Ghana. Among the programmes implemented were sensitization and mobilization workshops in cocoa-growing districts throughout the country,

---

4   Cocoa production contributed over US$1 billion in foreign exchange earnings in 2004 (about 72 per cent of agricultural foreign exchange earnings).

and the formation of district child protection committees and community child protection committees.

These committees were made responsible for continuous sensitization activities and community surveillance toward eliminating the worst forms of child labour in the cocoa farms (Ghana, MMYE 2008). Other activities included enrolment of children in school and provision of support to children in cocoa-growing communities to access formal education and employment skills. In order to sustain this programme and increase community participation, the community-based Child Labour Monitoring Programme was created to ensure annual data collection, analysis and reporting on the prevalence of the worst forms of child labour (Ghana, MMYE 2008). Additionally, the government signed a memorandum of understanding with the International Labour Organization for the provision of technical support in building national capacity to eliminate the worst forms of child labour in Ghana. The resulting Child Labour Unit became the focal point for the governmental national child labour elimination programme in Ghana. This unit has collaborated with state ministries, governmental departments and agencies, employers' and workers' organizations, and local and international NGOs and international agencies such as the ILO, UNICEF and the International Organization for Migration (IOM) in the development of policy and legislation in respect to the elimination of the worst forms of child labour (Ghana, MMYE 2008).

Conclusion

Ghana was one of the first countries to ratify the *United Nations Convention on the Rights of the Child* and the *African Charter on the Rights and Welfare of the Child*. In addition, the Ghanaian legislature has passed a number of national child welfare policies and laws to promote and protect the children of Ghana. Some of these policies and laws have seen direct implementation through the provision of services and programmes to children, increases in advocacy, awareness raising, and education about the human rights of children in Ghana.

The introduction of the school feeding programme and the capitation grant, which provided funds to cover children's cultural, sports and other school-user fees, have seen an improvement and expansion of public educational facilities at all levels across the country. Access to basic education for both girls and boys has increased due to government investment in education for children. School census data for 2008–2009 indicate that the primary school completion rate reached 87 per cent, an increase of nearly 10 per cent since the 2003–2004 school year (World Bank 2011). Additionally, the current educational policy supports the admission of more girls to schools to address their generally low enrolment. Through the Girls Educational Initiative Programe, efforts have been made to lower admission requirements for girls into educational institutions, which has led to an increase in the ratio of girls to boys in some coeducational senior high institutions. Also, students from the more deprived areas, such as in the northern regions of Ghana, continue to enjoy free education up to the tertiary level (CRIN 2008).

The government's introduction of the School Feeding Programme and the Capitation Grant Scheme put in place during the 2005–2006 academic year did not cover all the costs of education at the basic level and it is estimated that about 1.4 million children in Ghana were not in school as of December 2006 (CRIN 2008). As a result, there is still a high level of illiteracy among girls, especially in rural communities, and this disparity is attributed to various cultural and socioeconomic factors including parents' attitude to education, child labour, mother's educational level, the sexual harassment of girls, the unavailability of schools within easy reach, and parents' inability to bear the extra cost. According to UNESCO (2006), even though attendance rates are over 85 per cent, the chances of a poor child not attending school are at least eight times higher than those of a child from the wealthiest households.

Despite the commitment of the past and present Ghanaian governments to promote and protect the welfare and human rights of children through legislative initiatives and programmes, it is evident that millions of children in Ghana still continue to be victims of various abuses of their basic human rights, such as lack of basic education, poverty, child labour and exploitation, and physical and sexual abuse, as well as neglect in their homes, schools and within their local communities.

Child labour still remains a serious socioeconomic problem for many children in Ghana, despite the human trafficking and child labour legislation. The ILO Global Report (2006) indicated that there are about two million children still engaged in child labour in Ghana and children are still being trafficked as domestic servants and labourers, and for work in the fishing industry, as well as for sexual exploitation (CRIN 2008).

The persistence of various abuses against children indicates that the issues of child welfare and protection are complex and multifaceted, requiring concerted efforts by multiple shareholders to bring about sustainable changes in the general wellbeing of children in Ghana. The government has to distribute resources fairly to all regions and districts within the country, and especially target deprived rural and local communities. It also needs to strengthen its capacity to monitor policy implementation, to increase budgetary allocations and to promote the sustainability of successful programmes.

Children also deserve protection and humane treatment from their parents, guardians, teachers and society as a whole, as children are particularly sensitive to the conditions in which they live and are vulnerable to the effects of poverty and exposure to violence, abuse and maltreatment. Corporal punishment is still lawful in homes and schools in Ghana. The Ghana Education Code of Discipline for second cycle schools provides for caning up to six strokes by a head teacher or an authorized person, although Article 28(2) of the UNCRC states: 'State parties shall take all appropriate measures to ensure that school discipline is administered in a manner consistent with the child's human dignity and in conformity with the present convention.' Additionally, Article 13(2) of the 1998 Children's Act states:

> Correction of a child is not justifiable when it is unreasonable in kind or in degree according to the age, physical and mental condition of the child, and no correction is justifiable if the child by reason of tender age or otherwise is incapable of understanding the purpose of the correction.

Hence, efforts should be made to provide social educational programmes to parents, guardians and school personnel on the psychological effects and implications of corporal punishment on children. This would help strengthen and build relationships and understanding between parents, school personnel and children on the use of alternative forms of discipline to physical punishment.

Ghana's population has since independence increased from over five million in 1960 to over 24 million in 2010. It has a young population; children and young people constitute about 50 per cent, while those aged above 65 years make up only 5 per cent. This represents a very high dependency ratio. Since the 1990s, Ghana has implemented various policies and legislation to improve the general welfare and social protection of children. Additionally, there have been some improvements with national pro-poor policy formulations and programmes, such as 'Vision 2020' and the Ghana poverty reduction strategies I and II, all of which are geared towards the reduction of poverty and improving the livelihoods of the citizens.

Despite all these policies and associated legislation, children continue to face developmental challenges, such as stunting and wasting, physical and psychological abuse, trafficking and sexual exploitation, and youth unemployment. The situation indicates that policies and legislation alone are not enough to mitigate the various abuses and deprivations confronting children in Ghana. To become a just, free and prosperous society in which all citizens, including children, are able to pursue and enjoy decent lives and incomes, the incidence of poverty among families has to be radically reduced, in both urban and rural communities. Incidence of poverty among the citizens of Ghana is one of the obstacles impeding socioeconomic growth. For example, even though the level of material poverty nationally over the last 15 years has fallen from 52 per cent in 1991–1992, to about 40 per cent in 1998–1999, and then to 30 per cent by 2005–2006, a number of regions in the country have higher poverty levels compared with the national level (Ghana, GSS 2008). The Ghana Living Standards Survey Round Five (Ghana, GSS 2008) indicates that, in five out of the ten regions of Ghana, poverty rates are higher than the national rate: three in the northern part of the country have the highest incidence of poverty rates at 70 per cent, 88 per cent and 52 per cent respectively; two regions in the southern part of the country (Volta and Brong Ahafo) have poverty rates above the national average (Ghana, Parliament 2010). The incidence of poverty is much higher in the rural areas than in urban areas, even though the trends suggest this gap is narrowing from about 36 per cent in 1991–1992 to about 28 per cent in 2005–2006 (Ghana, Parliament 2010).

Eradication or reduction of extreme poverty among families in Ghana is the way forward. This demands aggressive economic and social developmental growth through accelerated job creation, integrated industrial development, agricultural modernization, and formal and informal educational programmes across the country. The *World Education Forum* (UNESCO 2000) and *World Summit for Social Development* (United Nations 1995) both agreed that extreme poverty is a severe injustice and an abuse of human rights, and that education is important in reducing poverty. It is also a key to wealth creation. The role of education in Ghana must become a priority, with more investment in achieving universal primary education for all children in rural and urban communities, and adult literacy and social educational programmes to educate the adult population. Investment in macro-economic programmes, such as the Millennium Development Goals, are critical to make sure all children in Ghana have improvement in their human rights with access to equal universal basic education, improved health and social services, the eradication of hunger through the modernization of agriculture and agro-based industries, and income-generating programmes for poor families.

In conclusion, children and young people constitute the true wealth and future of Ghana. Addressing their wellbeing, hopes and aspirations must be an essential component of all socioeconomic development programmes and initiatives undertaken in the country. All stakeholders, including the state, parents and guardians, and educational, cultural and religious institutions, should make efforts to engage young people in meaningful partnership to develop appropriate sustainable interventions and services for their full development. These interventions should include provision of the resources needed to enable children and young people to contribute to the economic, social and cultural advancement of themselves, their families and the nation as a whole.

References

Brooker, E. (1996) 'Slaves of the fetish.' *New England International and Comparative Law Annual 4*, 53–72.

Children's Rights Information Network (CRIN) (2008) *Ghana: Children's Rights References in the Universal Periodic Review*. Available at: www.crin.org/resources/infodetail. asp?id=17126.

Gadzekpo, A. (1993) 'Sexual bondage.' *Awo Magazine 5*, 5–7.

Ghana, Ghana Statistical Service (GSS) (2000) *Ghana Population and Housing Census*. Accra, GH: GSS.

Ghana, Ghana Statistical Service (GSS) (2003) *Living Standards Survey Round 3*. Accra, GH: GSS.

Ghana, Ghana Statistical Service (GSS) (2005) *Socio-Economic and Demographic Trends*. Accra, GH: GSS.

Ghana, Ghana Statistical Service (GSS) (2008) *Ghana Living Standards Survey Round Five*. Accra, GH: GSS.

Ghana, Ministry of Finance and Economic Planning (MFEP) (2005) *The Budget Statement and Economic Policy of the Government of Ghana for the 2005 Financial Year*. Accra, GH: MFEP.

Ghana, Ministry of Finance and Economic Planning (MFEP) (2006) *The Budget Statement and Economic Policy of the Government of Ghana for the 2006 Financial Year*. Accra, GH: MFEP.

Ghana, Ministry of Manpower, Youth and Employment (MMYE) (2003) *Combating the Worst Forms of Child Labour in Ghana*. Accra, GH: MMYE.

Ghana, Ministry of Manpower, Youth and Employment (MMYE) (2006) *Pilot Labour Survey in Cocoa Production in Ghana: National Program for the Elimination of Worst Forms of Child Labour (WFCL) in Cocoa*. Accra, GH: MMYE.

Ghana, Ministry of Manpower, Youth and Employment (MMYE) (2008) *Cocoa Labour Survey in Ghana: 2007/2008*. Accra, GH: MMYE.

Ghana, Ministry of Women and Children's Affairs (MOWAC) (2010) *Who are we?* Available at: www.mowacghana.net/who.

Ghana, Parliament (2010) 'The coordinated program of economic and social development policies, 2010–2016: An agenda for shared growth and accelerated development for a better Ghana.' Speech presented to the 5th Parliament by the President of Ghana. Available at: www.ghana.gov.gh/documents/coordinatedprogramme.pdf.

Goldman, J. and Salus, M.K. (2003) *A Coordinated Response to Child Abuse and Neglect: The Foundation for Practice*. Washington, DC: US Department of Health and Human Services.

Integrated Social Development Centre (ISODEC) (2009) *The 2009 Budget and Issues Relating to Women and Children Welfare*. Accra, GH: ISODEC.

International Labour Organization (ILO) (2006) *The End of Child Labour: Within Reach. Global Report under the Follow-up to the ILO Declaration on Fundamental Principles and Rights at Work.* Geneva: ILO.

Laird, S. (2002) 'The 1998 Children's Act: Problems of enforcement in Ghana.' *British Journal of Social Work 32,* 893–905.

Mensa-Bonsu, H. (1996) 'Family Law Policy and Research Agenda.' In A. Ardayfio-Schandorf (ed.) *The Changing Family in Ghana.* Accra, GH: Ghana Universities Press.

Mensa-Bonsu, H.J.A.N. and Dowuona-Hammond, C. (1996) 'The Child within the Ghanaian Family.' In Ardayfio-Schandorf, E. (ed.) *The Changing Family in Ghana.* Accra, GH: Ghana Universities Press.

Nukunya, G.K. (1992) *Tradition and Change in Ghana: An Introduction to Sociology.* Accra, GH: Ghana Universities Press.

Ollennu, N.A. (1960) *The Law of Succession in Ghana.* Accra, GH: Presbyterian Book Depot.

Organization of African Unity (OAU) (1990) *African Charter on the Rights and Welfare of the Child* (OAU Doc. CAB/LEG/24.9/49). Addis Ababa, ET: OAU.

Roe, A., Schneider, H. and Pyatt, G. (1992) *Adjustment and Equity in Ghana.* Washington, DC: Bernan Associates.

UNESCO (2000) *World Education Forum.* Paris: UNESCO.

UNESCO (2006) *Ghana: Early Childhood Care and Education (ECCE) Programs.* Geneva, HE: International Bureau of Education.

UNFPA (2003) *State of World Population 2003: Making 1 Billion Count: Investing in Adolescents' Health and Rights.* New York: UNFPA.

UNICEF (2004) *Changing Lives of Girls: Evaluation of the African Girls' Education Initiative.* New York: UNICEF.

UNICEF (2009) *Global Study on Child Poverty and Disparities* (Ghana National Report). Accra, GH: UNICEF.

UNICEF (2012) *United Nations Convention on the Rights of the Child.* Available at: www. unicef.org/crc/index_30229.html.

United Nations (1995) *World Summit for Social Development.* New York: United Nations Department of Economic and Social Affairs.

World Bank (2000) *World Bank Support to Basic Education in Ghana.* Washington, DC: World Bank.

World Bank (2004) *Books, Buildings and Learning Outcomes: An Impact Evaluation of World Bank Support to Basic Education in Ghana.* Washington, DC: World Bank.

World Bank (2011) *Republic of Ghana: Education in Ghana: Improving Equity, Efficiency and Accountability of Education Service Delivery* (Report No. 59755-GH). Available at: www-wds.worldbank.org/external/default/WDSContentServer/WDSP/IB/2012/02/10/000386194_20120210030644/Rendered/PDF/597550replacement0box35831 1B00PUBLIC0.pdf.

World Bank (2013) *Ghana Overview.* Available at: www.worldbank.org/en/country/ghana/overview.

Yeboa, K.Y. (1994) 'The Civil Rights and Obligations of the Child.' In H.J.A.N. Mensa-Bonsu and C. Dowuona-Hammond (eds) *The Rights of the Child in Ghana: Perspectives.* Accra, GH: Woeli Publishing Service.

12

Australia

Menka Tsantefski and Marie Connolly

Introduction: The cultural context

Australia is a colonized country, and in many ways the development of services to children and families has been shaped by the history of this vast land. Aboriginals and Torres Strait Islanders, collectively referred to as indigenous people, once outnumbering the early settlers, now comprise only approximately 2.5 per cent of the population. Aboriginal children are nevertheless overrepresented in child protection statistics, and generally face significant disadvantage across a range of wellbeing measures.

Modern Australia is a culturally, linguistically and ethnically diverse society. Since British settlement in the late eighteenth century, there have been successive waves of migration, predominantly from Europe. For many years the 'White Australia' policy restricted migration to white people who generally emigrated to Australia from the United Kingdom and Europe. This policy, however, was abolished in the mid-1970s, stimulating increased migration from other parts of the world, particularly from the Middle East and Asia. There is no official religion. Ethnically diverse Christian denominations comprise the largest religious grouping. Almost one-in-three people report no religious affiliation (Australia, Department of Foreign Affairs and Trade 2008). Freedom of religion and worship is protected but, with the exception of some concessions to indigenous communities, Australian society adheres to one set of secular laws, with considerable support amongst the broader community for the fundamental values of tolerance and freedom (Black 2010).

As in many developed countries, low fertility rates and high life expectancy in Australia has resulted in an ageing population, with disproportionately fewer children under 15 years of age. In the decade between 1990 and 2010, the proportion of children 14 years of age and younger fell by 3.1 percentage points from 22.0 per cent to 18.9 per cent, except among indigenous populations in which the number of children aged 15 years and under is approximately double the national average (Gordon 2006). Population growth has been largely sustained in recent decades by migration, which accounts for between 43 per cent and 65 per cent of annual growth. With the exception of indigenous people, two-thirds of whom live in regional (43%) or remote areas (25%), Australia is largely an urbanized population. Although only 12 per cent of indigenous people live in the Northern Territory, they comprise almost one-third of the population in that area (Australia, Australian Bureau of Statistics 2011).

Australia is one of the world's best-performing economies with sustained economic growth over the past two decades. A well-functioning regulatory environment, developments in information technology, low unemployment and investment growth have led to increased Gross Domestic Product. Consequently, the 2008 global recession impacted less on Australia than many other countries (OECD 2010). While incomes have risen, economic prosperity has not benefited all citizens or families equally (Qu 2011; Saunders 2008). Calls to eradicate child poverty have been made since the late 1980s, and over the past few decades child poverty rates have fallen to approximately the OECD average (Hayes and Gray 2008; Qu 2011) as a result of social security reform. Nevertheless, more than 750,000 Australian children continue to live in poverty, attributed, in part, to the growing gap between rich and poor (Simpson 2008). In the Australian policy context, poverty is more broadly defined than income to include indicators of social exclusion and inclusion (Huston 2011). Indigenous children experience higher prevalence and greater depth of poverty (Hunter 2009). Concern for children in sole-parent-headed households, who are at increased risk of living in poverty through parental unemployment, underemployment or low-paid employment, has led to social security reforms and changes in family tax benefits (Qu 2011; Simpson 2008). Nevertheless, social policy remains focused on an economic agenda centred on workforce participation (Spratt 2008). Family policy in Australia is designed to redistribute income between families and involves income-tested transfers to low-income families, rather than universal family payments as delivered in some countries (Kalb and Thoresen 2010).

The Australian Constitution, which underpins all jurisdictional limits and reforms, divides legislative power between the Commonwealth and State or Territory governments (Peel and Croucher 2011, p.21). The Commonwealth contributes to child welfare through social security payments for children and families, the provision of childcare services, and various family support schemes and parenting support programmes (Fogarty 2008).

The Commonwealth also has jurisdiction over custody, guardianship, access to children, and child maintenance. Responsibility for the administration and operation of child protection services rests with individual Australian States and Territories, each of which funds its own child protection, out-of-home care and family support programmes, delivered by government, the non-government sector, and a smaller number of for-profit providers. All Australian child protection systems have well-developed infrastructure supported by legislation and policy, programmes for children and families, professionally trained staff and public awareness campaigns (Svevo-Cianci, Hart and Rubinson 2010).

Child abuse and neglect is costly, not just for the individual child and family, but for society more broadly. Consequently, Australia aims to reduce the likelihood of abuse and neglect from occurring, and to intervene early to ameliorate the effects of child maltreatment (Holzer *et al.* 2006). Policy areas with relevance to child welfare include maternal and child health, parenting education and family support programmes, poverty alleviation and childcare assistance. Expenditure on child protection and out-of-home care has steadily increased over several years. In 2009–2010, A$2.5 billion was spent on child protection and out-of-home care services, an increase of 13.2 per cent from the previous annual reporting period. More than half of the funding is spent on providing out-of-home care to a comparatively small number of children.

In 2010–2011, Australia received 163,767 notifications of suspected child abuse and neglect: a rate of 31.9 per thousand children. This figure refers to the number of reports, not the number of individual children; some children can be notified more than once in a reporting period. Of these notifications, 76,552 were investigated, representing 14.9 per 1,000 children. In this reporting period 31,527 children were subject to a substantiated notification, or 6.1 per 1,000 children. These figures translate to 34.6 per 1,000 children subject to a substantiated notification among indigenous children compared with 4.5 for their non-indigenous peers. In the year ending June 2011, 39,058 Australian children were on care and protection orders (7.6 per 1,000 children). This figure has been steadily increasing since 2007 when 28,954 children were on orders (5.9 per 1,000 children). Indigenous children are vastly overrepresented on care and protection orders (51.4 compared with 5.4 per 1,000 among non-indigenous children). Rising use of care and protection orders has correlated with an increase in out-of-home care. In the same period, 37,648 children were in out-of-home care, a rate of 7.3 per 1,000 children in the population, an increase from 28,379 children, or 5.8 per 1,000, in out-of-home care at June 2007. Indigenous children are ten times more likely to be removed from parental care than other Australian children. At June 2011, 12,358 indigenous and 24,929 non-indigenous children were in out-of-home care (51.7 and 5.1 per 1,000 children respectively) (Australia, Productivity Commission 2012).

In 2009–2010, A$498 was spent on child protection services per Australian child; however, the amount spent varies considerably between jurisdictions. In the above period, Victoria spent A$362 per child, whereas the sum in the Northern Territory was A$938 (Australia, Productivity Commission 2011). It is worth noting that differences in demographics and in reporting requirements make comparisons across jurisdictions difficult (Scott 2009). The tertiary child protection and out-of-home care systems account for much of the spending. Investment in intensive family preservation programmes has, however, also increased each year from A$277 million in 2005–2006 to A$81.7 million in 2009–2010 (Australia, Productivity Commission 2011). Increasingly, traditionally adult-focused services – domestic violence, parental substance abuse and mental health – have been considered a worthy avenue for addressing risk factors associated with child abuse and neglect. As these latter services are not specifically provided to attend to children's needs, it is difficult to quantify expenditure on programmes designed to improve child outcomes. Overall, the estimated annual cost of child abuse and neglect in Australia is A$11 billion. Overall, the estimated annual cost of child abuse and neglect in Australia is A$11 billion. Expenditure on family support was $375.3 million in 2011–2012 (Bromfield, Holzer and Lamont 2011; Australian Government 2013).

The evolution of Australian child welfare services

Australian child protection and child welfare systems have continuously evolved to reflect changing definitions of child maltreatment and community expectations for government action. In recent decades, numerous factors have contributed to inflated notification rates and significant expansion of the statutory child protection system. These include: the broadening definitions of child maltreatment to include emotional abuse, exposure to domestic violence and the concept of cumulative harm; the growth in public interest and media reporting; the introduction of mandatory reporting laws across jurisdictions, particularly from the 1980s onwards; the professionalization of the child protection workforce; the response to alcohol and other drug use by parents or other carers; an increasingly risk-averse culture; and the government assuming responsibility for child protection matters that had previously been dealt with by the non-government sector (Fogarty 2008; Higgins 2011).

Chronologically, Australia has followed most English-speaking countries in terms of service development in child and family welfare. The 1960s tended to be concerned with severe physical punishment of children and matters relating to neglectful parenting. When children were abused or neglected, they were removed from their families and it was not unusual for them to be placed in residential settings, children's homes and other such institutions. In the 1970s and 1980s, focus on the needs of young people increased; permanency-planning principles were progressively incorporated into child protection practice, simultaneously with a move away from the institutional care of children towards home-based care. When Aboriginal children were removed from their parents, placements in alternative care would have seen them being disconnected from family and often placed outside their cultural network. Concern about this cultural dislocation rests at the heart of the Aboriginal Child Placement Principle, which requires that placements for Aboriginal children be sought within the child's cultural network. While child protection initially focused on child physical abuse and neglect, during the 1980s awareness of child sexual abuse grew.

While the States and Territories of Australia continued to develop individual responses to local needs, during the 1990s they all moved toward the professionalization of the child protection workforce (Lamont and Bromfield 2010). The ensuing practice response became much more legalistic, introducing risk-assessment instruments that transformed 'needs' into 'risks' (Walsh and Douglas 2009). At this time, funding to child protection and non-government family support programmes was reduced (Lamont and Bromfield 2010) and the available resources were directed towards the tertiary child protection service. This limited the availability of support for families that did not meet the threshold for mandated intervention through the statutory system. Increased reliance on the tertiary child protection system resulted in more and more families being reported to statutory services in order to be provided with services (Wise 2003). Thus the statutory system became increasingly the gateway for service delivery.

During the 1980s and 1990s child maltreatment was also more broadly defined to include exposure to domestic violence, resulting in an increase of reported children to child protection services. Exposure to family violence was acknowledged as a form of emotional abuse and became a trigger for mandatory reporting in the 2000s. By the end of the twentieth century, all Australian child protection systems were grappling with high notification rates and were exploring ways in which families could be provided with services that better suited their needs.

For more than a decade, questions about the effectiveness of child protection systems (Mathews 2008) has shaped public opinion and has largely driven developments in Australian legislation, policy and service provision (Ainsworth and Hansen 2006; Babington 2011). Australian child protection systems have undergone intense public scrutiny. Media attention to the deaths of individual children has created a context in which policy developments have become very reactive (Gilbert *et al.* 2011). A series of national, state and territory inquiries, particularly in the years between 1997 and 2005, highlighted the experiences of, and poor outcomes amongst, several groups of children removed from parental care; indigenous children placed in institutions or with White families; non-indigenous children placed in institutions; and unaccompanied British child migrants sent to Australia until well into the twentieth century (Babington 2011). Evidence of children being abused in care, in tandem with more recent research indicating worse outcomes for many children removed from parental care, has 'undermined confidence in removal of children from birth families as a successful protective intervention' (Higgins and Katz 2008, p.45). Government and public awareness of child maltreatment also grew in response to disclosures by adult survivors, particularly of child sexual assault, within the home, or committed within institutions often run by various religious orders. Some disclosures received significant media attention and led to additional parliamentary inquiries.

Mandatory reporting of suspected child abuse and neglect has been introduced in most jurisdictions. Australia continues to receive overwhelming numbers of notifications, approximately only 5 per cent of which are substantiated. A widening gap between the number of notifications received and those substantiated suggests that an increasing number of families that do not meet the threshold for mandated intervention continue to be referred to child protection services (Higgins and Katz 2008). Significantly, steadily rising notifications have doubled the number of children removed from parental care. The overall trend has seen a dramatic increase in children on care and protection orders, rising by 57 per cent in the years between 2005 and 2010. Indigenous children are eight times more likely to be placed on orders than other children (McCallum 2008). Concern regarding the over-representation of infants in annual child death reviews, and the introduction of infant-specific programmes in some jurisdictions, has increased the number of infants in out-of-home care. Infants tend to enter alternative care earlier and to remain longer. The net result is a 'bottle-neck' effect that places considerable strain on the out-of-home care system.

There has recently been a slight decline in notifications, a change attributed by some to improvements in family support and prevention of child maltreatment (Australia, Council of Australian Governments 2009), while others argue that the reduction in notifications may be an artifice of reporting systems in some jurisdictions whereby a number of families that may previously have come to the attention of child protection are diverted to family support agencies (McCallum 2008). Although gaps in data collection and reporting make it difficult to determine the extent to which child maltreatment has been reduced (Babington 2011; Price-Robertson, Bromfield and Vassallo 2010; Svevo-Cianci *et al.* 2010), by and large the financially costly response to child protection in Australia has failed to reduce the constellation of family and community factors known to increase the risk of child maltreatment: poverty, parental substance use, mental illness and family violence (O'Donnell, Scott and Stanley 2008). Recognition of the complexity of presenting concerns has resulted in a range of services for families, although collaboration between sectors tends to be problematic (McArthur and Thomson 2011), particularly at the interface between child-focused services and those that address adult needs. For example, while parental alcohol and other drug use, and family violence, largely characterize families involved with child protection services, the service sectors typically remain apart with minimal joint planning or decision making in regards to children's issues (Higgins and Katz 2008).

In 2009 a National Framework for Protecting Australia's Children (Australia, Council of Australian Governments 2009) was introduced, providing Australia's first shared agenda for child protection between the federal and the state and territory governments. The non-government sector is a major partner in policy development. Five key action areas are identified within the framework: the provision of universal support to families; early intervention programmes targeted to families with known risk factors in child maltreatment; a statutory response to investigate child abuse and neglect, with support to families and provision of out-of-home care; greater attention to the specific needs of indigenous children; and an improved response to child sexual abuse. Responsibility is to be assumed by all levels of government, with each state and territory retaining responsibility for statutory child protection (Babington 2011). A key factor in current reform is the notion that the child protection service should be regarded as an emergency service and should not be confused with programmes that address welfare concerns. A public health model is proposed, conceptualizing child abuse and neglect risk at a whole-of-population level. Voluntary support is provided to children and families at lower risk, whilst more coercive, interventionist responses are reserved for families that pose significant risk of harm to children (O'Donnell *et al.* 2008). Further resources have been allocated to both statutory systems and allied services, more frontline child protection positions have been created and children's commissioners have been established in some jurisdictions, with more to follow (Ainsworth and Hansen 2006; Babington 2011). The federal government has recently announced its intention to establish a national commissioner for children.

Family policy and family values

Social developments in the 1970s and 1980s resulted in changes to the structure of Australian families that also influenced the experience of Australia's most vulnerable children. A significant number of children now live in sole-parent-headed or blended families, which include non-biological parents and siblings (Lamont and Bromfield 2010). The prevalence of, and response to, parental factors including substance use, mental health issues and family violence has vastly increased the number of kinship carers, most of whom are grandparents. In the years between 1998 and 2004, kinship care grew by 50 per cent to become the most frequent form of out-of-home care for children. Consequently, there are a significant number of grandparent-headed households (Horner *et al.* 2007). The Australian Bureau of Statistics defines family as the 'nuclear' family comprising parents and children. By contrast, traditional indigenous cultures, particularly those less connected to the 'economic mainstream', adopt a wider view based on kinship and are more likely to live in larger and more compositionally complex households (Morphy 2006, p.24), with greater mobility amongst household members than the general population (Gray 2006). Responsibility for children's wellbeing is often shared by families and the community (Gordon 2006). Collectivist cultural practices conflict with the individualistic perspective of child welfare, and this has been significant in the overrepresentation of indigenous children in child protection. The Aboriginal Child Placement Principle has been enshrined in all state and territory legislations. At the outset, the Principle calls for placement with extended family, followed by placement within the child's community, or if this is not possible, with other indigenous people, and finally, placement with non-indigenous carers (Bamblett and Lewis 2007).

In common with other Anglophone countries, notably the United Kingdom, the US, and Canada, Australia has adopted a regulatory *child protection* orientation to the protection of children. This is in contrast to the *family service* orientation, characterized by the provision of greater access to services and assistance for families through voluntary engagement with parents (Lewig, Arney and Salveron 2010), most typically found in countries such as Denmark, Sweden and the Netherlands. While child welfare has long been premised on the value of universal, early intervention programmes to support parents in raising children, this has occurred in the context of a long-standing tension between the family support model and the child protection orientation where a child-rescue model results in resources being diverted to the statutory child protection and out-of-home care systems (Humphreys *et al.* 2009).

Policy initiatives and supporting guidelines promote the best interests of the child within the context of the family, unless the child's safety and wellbeing is compromised, in which case the child's right to protection and care by state authorities takes precedence. While there are differences in response across States and Territories, an overall philosophy of government intervention when parents are unable, or unwilling, to provide an adequate level of care and protection, and a commitment to early intervention and prevention, underpins all relevant legislation (Australia, Productivity Commission 2011). There is not only community acceptance, but also expectation, that government will intervene in the private sphere of the family to protect vulnerable or abused and neglected children (Higgins 2011).

The child welfare field is complex, with a raft of services provided by government at the local, state and territory, and federal levels, and by the non-government sector. A small number of services are provided by the for-profit private sector. Roles and responsibilities are varied and reflect mandate and auspice. Services for families in Australia are referred to as a continuum from early intervention and prevention, to a range of secondary services targeted to vulnerable children and families, through to tertiary child protection services mandated to intervene in family life when there is significant risk of abuse or neglect, or after children have been abused. In reality, families move across the continuum, and service delivery overlaps. To ensure a timely, appropriate response to child safety and wellbeing, some jurisdictions have moved towards greater integration between the statutory child protection service and community-based family support services (Lamont and Bromfield 2010, p.4). In general, however, Australia's child protection systems are skewed toward the tertiary end of the spectrum.

Child protection services aim to protect children up to 17 years of age from abuse and neglect from within the family, or when families are unable to provide an adequate level of care and/or protection. Child protection services receive notifications from professionals mandated to report more serious cases of child abuse, as well as community members. If an investigation substantiates abuse or neglect, child protection services are legally obligated to initiate care and protection orders through children's courts, and when deemed necessary, to place children in out-of-home care, temporarily or permanently, when their safety and wellbeing cannot be assured, or when the family is unable to care for the child for various reasons, such as parental death, disability, illness or serious family problems (Australia, Productivity Commission 2011). Child protection services work directly with families to resolve issues related to children's safety and wellbeing, as well as referring families to a range of service providers that aim to improve the circumstances in which children live, increase parenting capacity or ameliorate the effects of abuse and neglect. In some instances, families are able to accept monitoring, counselling and referral to parenting education and other family support programmes and negate the need for court action, although the 'voluntary' nature of such involvement is questioned (Ainsworth and Hansen 2006). Statutory child protection services also assist with the reunification of children to parental care after out-of-home placement, once protective concerns have been addressed, or ensure that children are placed in suitable permanent care when reunification is not considered viable. Young people transitioning from out-of-home care to independent living are also assisted to find suitable accommodation (Australia, Productivity Commission 2011). Involvement with child protection services, as distinct from voluntary engagement with family support services, is mandated for families when allegations of abuse and neglect have been made or children have been harmed, and the action taken is often coercive. Some jurisdictions allow early intervention with unborn infants, with the consent of the mother, to plan for the infant's care and protection in the postnatal period (Mathews 2008). The concept of 'cumulative harm' to children through prolonged neglect or repeat episodes of maltreatment has influenced some legislation, policy and practices.

Although Australia receives approximately nine times the number of notifications per thousand children as the United Kingdom, a similar proportion of children are removed from parental care. This suggests that many Australian families may be unnecessarily subjected to invasive forms of statutory assessment. Such interventions can also be expensive financially, drawing resources from supportive services for children and families (O'Donnell *et al.* 2008). Family support programmes aim to improve children's safety and wellbeing through the provision of direct support to parents and by assisting families to access other community services and resources (Wise 2003, p.188). Most early intervention efforts involve parenting education and counselling, monitoring and supervision of socially excluded families. Few early intervention or family support programmes improve families' economic circumstances (Walsh and Douglas 2009), despite the fact that many of the families referred to child protection have experienced economic disadvantage, often being sole-parent families reliant on government benefits. The rising number of children in out-of-home care indicates that many early intervention strategies have failed to provide the type of support families need to enable them to safely nurture children. These developments have occurred alongside widespread support for the use of intensive family preservation services as an alternative to removal of children from parental care, or to support the reunification process (Australia, Productivity Commission 2011). Yet, the alternative to removal of children – the provision of long-term support to those most at need – is rarely available to families, including those already involved with child protection services (Lonne *et al.* 2008). Once removed from parental care, children can experience multiple placements. There is mounting evidence that outcomes among many children are no better, and possibly worse, than if they had remained with their parents (O'Donnell *et al.* 2008). Kinship care, almost synonymous with care by grandparents, is the preferred policy option, as placements tend to be more stable (Horner *et al.* 2007).

Statutory interventions and the state as parent

When a child is removed from a parent, it is incumbent on the state to provide the conditions of care that might be expected of a caring parent. While this ideal is not always achieved, it is inherent in the principles of the 1989 *United Nations Convention on the Rights of the Child* (UNCRC) (UNICEF 2012). Australia contributed to the development of the UNCRC and was amongst the first countries to ratify it. Despite legislative, policy and practice differences, all Australian child protection systems reflect Australia's status as signatory and incorporate several key principles: the 'child's best interests'; early intervention to prevent children entering, or re-entering, the child protection system; children's participation in decisions that affect them; the provision of out-of-home care; and culturally sensitive services for indigenous children. Permanency planning, a relatively recent development, is not reflected in legislation in all jurisdictions, although it is usually referred to in policies and procedures. Each State and Territory provides a level of aftercare support for young people exiting the out-of-home care system. Some jurisdictions do not state a minimum age to which support is to be provided; others stipulate anywhere from 21 to 25 years of age (Holzer and Lamont 2009).

Article 3(1) of the UNCRC – the 'child's best interests' principle – has, in particular, influenced the drafting of child protection legislation and policy across Australian jurisdictions. Where Australia is deemed not to have implemented the UNCRC it may reflect a lack of uniform principles, or benchmarks, for child protection practice or the failure to develop and monitor laws and policies affecting children (Fogarty 2008). Philosophical commitment to the principle nevertheless influences practice. All courts with jurisdiction over child and family matters operate under the 'child's best interests' principle; however, the division between the family court, a federal jurisdiction, and child protection courts, linked to the legislative framework of individual States and Territories, has resulted in a degree of fragmentation, gaps and sometimes overlap between systems, particularly in response to family violence issues where children's safety and wellbeing can be seriously compromised (Peel and Croucher 2011, p.23). Similarly, there are gaps in coordination between child protection and juvenile justice systems. The close correlation between child maltreatment and adolescent offending, particularly amongst young people transitioning from out-of-home care when multiple placements have been experienced, means that many children are involved with both systems, each of which has its own philosophical underpinning and judicial requirements. Some progress in this area has been made. For example, there have been new initiatives that have introduced therapeutic or problem-solving courts, including some reserved for indigenous young people, and for those with serious substance use problems (Cashmore 2011, p.37).

The 'child's best interests' principle is variously interpreted and results in tensions between the rights of the child to protection from harm and parental rights to care for the child, a tension which must be resolved in the child's best interests through the least intrusive intervention in family life. It has been argued that, when confronted with risk to children, child protection services are more likely to resort to the removal of children from parental care rather than supporting families to safely care for their children (Walsh and Douglas 2009). There are concerns that children in different family constellations – those living in poverty, or those whose parents have a mental illness or intellectual disability – receive differential treatment from child protection authorities (Mathews 2008). Dominant cultural perspectives can also influence child protection practice. A racially defined understanding of 'best interests' principles led to the large-scale removal of children from families and communities across Australia (Bamblett and Lewis 2007, p.44). Historically, large numbers of indigenous children were removed from parents in a policy response now referred to as 'The Stolen Generations'. Systematic removal of children damaged the fabric of indigenous communities, severed kinship ties and destroyed the ability of parents to transmit cultural and childrearing practices (Cunneen and White 2002 as cited in Hunter 2008). At least 38 per cent of indigenous people have either been removed, or have a relative who was removed, from familial care (Gray 2006). For many of these communities 'the state as parent' has had a devastating legacy.

More recently, media attention to the plight of indigenous children in the Northern Territory, and in particular reports of high levels of violence and under-reporting of child sexual abuse, has resulted in the Northern Territory National Emergency Response (NTER), an unprecedented action by the Commonwealth Government in child protection matters. Introduced in 2007, the ensuing policy framework was aimed at restricting the availability of alcohol and quarantining income-support payments to ensure the basic needs of indigenous children for food, clothing and housing were met. Audits of computers to detect prohibited child pornography were conducted. Additional measures targeted land leases and tenure, the appointment of administrators to implement emergency measures, repeal of customary laws allowing for mitigating factors in sentencing, and changes of management to community stores to improve the quality of food. Whilst the reaction to the intervention has been divided, there has been significant criticism of the state's lack of consultation with indigenous communities, and a lack of recognition of the structural and cultural problems, such as social exclusion (sometimes as a direct result of earlier government interventions) that the communities face. In a dramatic breach of usual practice, the NTER was conducted by the Australian Defence Force, the Federal Police and other government representatives, rather than by the Territory's statutory child protection authority (Arney, McGuinness and Robinson 2009). As various policy initiatives have largely failed to improve social, economic or health measures among indigenous children and families (Gray 2006), writers have argued for the need of an approach that gives indigenous people more control over matters that concern them, as well as the ability to transmit culture (Bamblett and Lewis 2007).

Across other cultural domains, Australian child protection services are increasingly involved with refugee families, particularly from African and Middle Eastern countries. Many of these families share histories of trauma, dislocation and loss. These experiences, and the difficulty of settling in a new country, pose significant challenges to parenting practices. The maltreatment types recorded by child protection services among refugee families indicate the extent to which differences in cultural practices and social isolation contribute to notifications: physical abuse, often related to physical discipline; neglect when children are left alone without adult supervision, often occurring in large, single-mother-headed households; and exposure to domestic violence (Lewig *et al.* 2010). Australia's extensive migration, both historic and current, means that as many as one-third of children aged up to 17 years live in immigrant families. There is no national data on the involvement of children from immigrant families in child welfare, juvenile justice or out-of-home care systems. The limited available data suggests that some children face economic and social disadvantage, for example lower educational attainment, the effects of trauma and dislocation, racism and challenges in adjustment to a new culture, and have less access to formal and informal support. Difficulties are most pronounced among children from non-English-speaking backgrounds and those whose families arrive with less skills and resources. Overall, however, outcomes for children in immigrant families are comparable with their peers (Katz and Redmond 2010, p.439).

The UNCRC stipulates that children should be able to contribute to decisions that concern them, an expectation that has important ramifications for statutory services, and the state as a parent. Participation by Australian children involved with child protection, and their families, is limited. Unlike New Zealand, which has enshrined children's participation in legally mandated Family Group Conferences, the less formalized Australian context means that a child's contribution is more likely to occur at the discretion of child protection workers. Australia has avoided much contention around the language of child rights by referring to children's needs, an approach which perpetuates a welfare model in the delivery of services, rather than being necessarily embedded in a child-rights perspective. The distinction is nevertheless important. Families that come to the attention of child protection services tend to be socially and economically disadvantaged. From a children's rights perspective, children, and those that care for them, are entitled to economic and social programmes that the state is obligated to provide. International law acknowledges that social and economic development is an incremental process influenced by the availability of resources. With a thriving economy, Australian governments frequently operate with budgetary surpluses. Yet, under current practice, services working with families largely function within a welfare paradigm, most evident when fund-raising for children and families in need (Tobin 2008). In common with most OECD countries, Australian government spending is largely committed to social protection programmes, for example pensions, employment insurance and child welfare initiatives, but the greater proportion of funding is directed to health and education (OECD 2011). A child-rights-based approach would demand greater reallocation of resources to children in need and their families (Tobin 2008).

Most Australian parents believe they should convey their values and life philosophy to their children and are committed to caring for them when they are ill, and providing them with advice on a range of matters, from childrearing to finances, until well into their mid-twenties. Although most do not believe it is their role to provide adult children with food and clothing, or to assist them with their everyday needs, the majority are prepared to provide some form of financial assistance and emotional support. The decline of low-skilled, well-paying jobs for school leavers, higher rates of participation in tertiary education, financial stressors and the attraction of remaining in the familial home has resulted in more adults in their mid-twenties living with parents than in previous generations (Vassallo, Smart and Price-Robertson 2009). By contrast, young people transitioning from out-of-home care move towards independent living at an earlier age, and receive considerably less assistance with housing, education, training or employment than their peers. The legacy of trauma and abuse, and, for many, disrupted placements, renders this group of young people amongst the most highly vulnerable and disadvantaged in Australian society (Mendes, Johnson and Moslehuddin 2011). Government is therefore increasingly being lobbied to extend the in *loco parentis* role to provide at least some of the types of support typically provided by parents to adult children (Higgins 2011).

Conclusion

Child welfare legislation, policy and practice raise normative and practical questions for any country to consider about the nature of state intervention in family life. In many ways, the Australian child protection system has developed along similar lines to the UK and other English-speaking jurisdictions. There are, nevertheless, historical and cultural distinctions that have influenced the ways in which services have responded to children and their families over time. The child protection system in Australia grew out of concern for physically and sexually abused children, and for those subjected to serious or criminal neglect. The regulatory approach served its original purpose, but changes in community standards, and expectations that the child protection system attends to a broader definition of child maltreatment, resulted in a system inundated with notifications, few of which are substantiated (Higgins and Katz 2008). There are signals now that Australia is seeking to move away from a narrowly focused response to children's wellbeing based on investigation and short-term intervention towards a stronger public health approach (O'Donnell *et al.* 2008).

There is growing recognition that protection of children is everybody's business; but shared responsibility for children's wellbeing will not be easy to achieve. Much will depend on cultural, structural, organizational and systemic change (Higgins and Katz 2008). Addressing child safety and wellbeing by targeting the antecedents of child maltreatment – parental substance use, mental health problems, family violence, poverty and other forms of marginalization – will require sound policy initiatives, greater collaboration between adult services and child protection, and improved referral pathways to ensure families receive the full range of supports required without delays or duplication (Babington 2011; Higgins 2011; McCallum 2008). However, assessment of child protection matters by services other than child protection is contentious. There are significant barriers to adult services attending to children's needs, including, but not limited to, funding arrangements that only recognize the adult as the service user. Successful implementation of a public health approach will, therefore, require building the capacity of all services involved with families to be parent–child centred (O'Donnell *et al.* 2008). It will also require a cultural shift within the child protection workforce to embrace the whole family as the unit of attention (Scott 2009).

The National Framework for Protecting Australia's Children 2009–2020 provides policy direction on child protection, out-of-home care and support to young people transitioning from out-of-home care to independent living. But, the outcomes are yet to be evaluated. It is, therefore, early days, and time will tell whether it meets its future objectives (Babington 2011). Measuring progress in child protection and wellbeing is in fact a key challenge for Australian child protection services (Babington 2011). It is also necessary to know how many children are clients of the child protection and the juvenile justice systems (Cashmore 2011), as well as the number of families involved with both the family court and child protection. This will require the development of quality, nationally consistent data, comparable across jurisdictions and service sectors.

Developments in economic and social policy will be needed to create a more inclusive society, with integrated services to attend to children's needs across the service continuum. Sound child protection practice will also depend on strengthening the child protection workforce through education and greater professionalization, increased recruitment and improved retention of frontline child protection workers (Scott 2009). Realization of policy in Australia will demand resourcing of early intervention and prevention strategies (O'Donnell *et al.* 2008). Greater investment in family support and the adequate resourcing of parents should reduce child maltreatment, should reduce the need for state intervention in family life and should lower the number of children entering the already overburdened out-of-home care system. As Svevo-Cianci *et al.* (2010, p.51) note, 'the financial wealth of a country does not ensure protection for its most vulnerable children'. It will require considerable political will to overcome structural disadvantage and to create a more equitable society in which children not only survive, but also thrive, in parental care.

References

Ainsworth, F. and Hansen, P. (2006) 'Five tumultuous years in Australian child protection: Little progress.' *Child and Family Social Work 11*, 33–41.

Arney, F., McGuinness, K. and Robinson, G. (2009) 'In the best interests of the child? Determining the effects of the emergency intervention on child safety and wellbeing.' *Law in Context 17*, 2, 42–57.

Australia, Australian Bureau of Statistics (2011) *Australian Demographic Statistics* (March). Available at: www.abs.gov.au/ausstats/abs@.nsf/mf/3101.0.

Australia, Council of Australian Governments (2009) *Protecting Children is Everyone's Business: National Framework for Protecting Australia's Children 2009–2020*. Canberra, AU: Commonwealth of Australia.

Australia, Department of Foreign Affairs and Trade (2008) *About Australia: Religious Freedom*. Available at: www.dfat.gov.au/facts/democratic_rights_freedoms.html.

Australia, Productivity Commission (2011) *Report on Government Services* (Report of the Steering Committee for the Review of Government Service Provision). Melbourne, AU: Productivity Commission. Available at: www.pc.gov.au/gsp/reports/rogs/2011.

Australia, Productivity Commission (2012) *Report on Government Services* (Report of the Steering Committee for the Review of Government Service Provision). Melbourne, AU: Productivity Commission. Available at: www.pc.gov.au/gsp/rogs/2012.

Australian Government (2013) *The Economic Costs of Child Abuse*. Available at: www.aifs. gov.au/cfca/pubs/factsheets/a142118/index.html.

Babington, B. (2011) 'National framework for protecting Australia's children: Perspectives on progress and challenges.' *Family Matters 89*, 11–20.

Bamblett, M. and Lewis, P. (2007) 'Detoxifying the child and family welfare system for Australian Indigenous Peoples: Self-determination, rights and culture as the critical tools.' *First Peoples Child and Family Review 3*, 3, 43–56.

Black, A. (2010) 'Legal recognition of Sharia Law: Is this the right direction for Australian family matters?' *Family Matters 84*, 64–67.

Bromfield, L., Holzer, P. and Lamont, A. (2011) *The Economic Costs of Child Abuse and Neglect* (Resource Sheet). Melbourne, AU: Australian Institute of Family Studies, National Child Protection Clearinghouse.

Cashmore, J. (2011) 'The link between child maltreatment and adolescent offending.' *Family Matters 89*, 31–41.

Fogarty, J.F. (2008) 'Some aspects of the early history of child protection in Australia.' *Family Matters 78*, 52–59.

Gilbert, R., Fluke, J., O'Donnell, M., Gonzalez-Izquierdo, A. *et al.* (2011) 'Child maltreatment: Variation and trends in policies in six developed countries.' *The Lancet*, online, 9 December 2011.

Gordon, S. (2006) 'Family issues for indigenous children.' *Family Matters 75*, 77–79.

Gray, M. (2006) 'Indigenous families and communities.' *Family Matters 75*, 4–9.

Hayes, A. and Gray, M. (2008) 'Social inclusion: A policy platform for those who live particularly challenged lives.' *Family Matters 78*, 4–7.

Higgins, D. (2011) 'Protecting children: Evolving systems.' *Family Matters 89*, 5–10.

Higgins, D. and Katz, I. (2008) 'Enhancing systems for protecting children: Promoting child wellbeing and child protection reform in Australia.' *Family Matters 80*, 43–50.

Holzer, P. and Lamont, A. (2009) *Australian Child Protection Legislation* (Resource Sheet). Melbourne, AU: Australian Institute of Family Studies, National Child Protection Clearinghouse.

Holzer, P.J., Higgins, J., Bromfield, L.M., Richardson, N. and Higgins, D. (2006) *The Effectiveness of Parent Education and Home Visiting* (Resource Sheet). Melbourne, AU: Australian Institute of Family Studies, National Child Protection Clearinghouse.

Horner, B., Downie, J., Hay, D. and Wichmann, H. (2007) 'Grandparent headed families in Australia.' *Family Matters 76,* 76–84.

Humphreys, C., Harries, M., Healy, K., Lonne, B. *et al.* (2009) 'Commentary: Shifting the child protection juggernaut to earlier intervention.' *Children Australia 34,* 3, 5–8.

Hunter, B. (2009) 'Indigenous social exclusion: Insights and challenges for the concept of social inclusion.' *Family Matters 82,* 52–61.

Hunter, S.V. (2008) 'Child maltreatment in remote Aboriginal communities and the Northern Territory emergency response: A complex issue.' *Australian Social Work 61,* 4, 372–388.

Huston, A.C. (2011) 'Children in poverty: Can public policy alleviate the consequences?' *Family Matters 87,* 13–26.

Kalb, G. and Thoresen, T.O. (2010) 'A comparison of family policy designs of Australia and Norway using microsimulation models.' *Review of Economics of the Household 8,* 2, 255–287.

Katz, I. and Redmond, G. (2010) 'Review of the circumstances among children in immigrant families in Australia.' *Child Indicators Research 3,* 4, 439–458.

Lamont, A. and Bromfield, L. (2010) *History of Child Protection Service* (Resource Sheet). Melbourne, AU: Australian Institute of Family Studies, National Child Protection Clearinghouse.

Lewig, K., Arney, F. and Salveron, M. (2010) 'Challenges to parenting in a new culture: Implications for child and family welfare.' *Evaluation and Program Planning 33,* 324–332.

Lonne, B., Parton, N., Thomson, J. and Harries, M. (2008) *Reforming Child Protection.* London: Routledge.

Mathews, B. (2008) 'Protecting Children from Abuse and Neglect.' In G. Monahan and L. Young (eds) *Children and the Law in Australia.* Chatswood, AU: Lexis Nexis Butterworths.

McArthur, M. and Thomson, L. (2011) 'Families' views on a coordinated family support service.' *Family Matters 89,* 71–81.

McCallum, D. (2008) 'Punishing welfare: Genealogies of child abuse.' *Griffith Law Review 18,* 1, 114–128.

Mendes, P., Johnson, G. and Moslehuddin, B. (2011) 'Effectively preparing young people to transition from out-of-home care: An examination of three recent Australian studies.' *Family Matters 89,* 61–70.

Morphy, F. (2006) 'Lost in translation? Remote indigenous households and definitions of the family.' *Family Matters 73,* 23–31.

O'Donnell, M., Scott, D. and Stanley, F. (2008) 'Child abuse and neglect – is it time for a public health approach?' *Australian and New Zealand Journal of Public Health 32,* 4, 325–330.

OECD (2010) *Policy Brief: Australia – Moving to a Seamless National Economy.* Available at: www.oecd.org/dataoecd/44/16/44388793.pdf.

OECD (2011) *Government at a Glance* (released 24 June 2011). Available at: www.oecd.org/dataoecd/59/61/47875778.pdf.

Peel, S. and Croucher, R. (2011) 'Mind(ing) the gap: Law reform recommendations responding to child protection in a federal system.' *Family Matters 89,* 21–30.

Price-Robertson, R., Bromfield, L. and Vassallo, S. (2010) 'Prevalence matters: Estimating the extent of child maltreatment in Australia.' *Developing Practice 26*, 13–20.

Qu, L. (2011) 'Supporting families in challenging times.' *Family Matters 87*, 6–8.

Saunders, P. (2008) 'Measuring wellbeing using non-monetary indicators.' *Family Matters 78*, 8–17.

Scott, D. (2009) '"Think child, think family": How adult specialist services can support children-at-risk of abuse and neglect.' *Family Matters 81*, 37–42.

Simpson, B. (2008) 'Child Poverty, Homelessness and the Exploitation of Children.' In G. Monahan and L. Young (eds) *Children and the Law in Australia*. Chatswood, AU: Lexis Nexis Butterworths.

Spratt, T. (2008) 'Possible futures for social work with children and families in Australia, the United Kingdom and the United States.' *Child Care in Practice 14*, 4, 413–427.

Svevo-Cianci, K.A., Hart, S.N. and Rubinson, C. (2010) 'Protecting children from violence and maltreatment: A qualitative comparative analysis assessing the implementation of U.N. CRC Article 19.' *Child Abuse and Neglect 34*, 45–56.

Tobin, J. (2008) 'The Development of Children's Rights.' In G. Monahan and L. Young (eds) *Children and the Law in Australia*. Chatswood, AU: Lexis Nexis Butterworths.

UNICEF (2012) *United Nations Convention on the Rights of the Child*. Available at: www.unicef.org/crc/index_30229.html.

Vassallo, S., Smart, D. and Price-Robertson, R. (2009) 'The roles that parents play in the lives of their young adult children.' *Family Matters 82*, 8–14.

Walsh, T. and Douglas, H. (2009) 'Legal responses to child protection, poverty and homelessness.' *Journal of Social Welfare and Family Law 31*, 2, 133–146.

Wise, S. (2003) 'The child in family services: Expanding child abuse prevention.' *Australian Social Work 56*, 3, 183–196.

The Contributors

Alean Al-Krenawi PhD is President of Achva Academic College and Ben-Gurion University of the Nregev, Israel. He has been Dean of the School of Social Work at the Memorial University of Newfoundland, Canada. His research interests include multicultural mental health, political violence and social work with indigenous populations. He has conducted studies in Israel, Canada, Palestine and other Arab countries. He has written three books: on ethno-psychiatry; on helping professions and indigenous people; and on political violence. He also co-edited a book called *Multicultural Social Work in Canada: Working with Diverse Ethno-Racial Communities* (Oxford University Press, 1991). He is currently working on two books, *Social Work with Muslim Communities* and *The Psychosocial Impact of Polygamy in the Middle East*. He has authored numerous book chapters and articles. Recently published works appear, or are about to appear, in the *American Journal of Orthopsychiatry, British Journal of Psychiatry* and *British Journal of Social Work*.

Nazgul Assylbekova is the Principal Academic in the Faculty of Tourism and Social Work at Kokshetau State University named after Sh. Ualikhanov, Kazakhstan. She comes from the Kostanai region of Arkalyk, Kazakhstan. She studied at the Arkalyk Pedagogical Institute named after Y. Altynsarin, graduating in law and economics. She has also gained a Master's degree in Management, undertaking research on 'Competition, recovery and social and leisure services in the Akmola region of Kazakhstan'. She has pursued research, having studied in Kazakhstan, Russia and Bulgaria, and has published 21 works. She is Principal Academic member of staff for Social Work at Kokshetau State University, and is Pedagogic Coordinator for an international educational project (Tempus IV), working to introduce the principles of the Bologna Process for Higher Education in Kazakhstan. She has particular interests in ethics and values, and theory that relates to the regulation of the relationships between people and between people and society.

Teresa Bertotti PhD is an Adjunct Professor in Social Work at the University of Milano Bicocca, Italy. Based on her experience of direct work with families over the years, she is now a supervisor and trainer of professionals. She has also worked with national government commissions, and has been the President and Director of the CBM (Centre for Abused Children) in Milan. She is the founder of the National Network of Centres Against Child Mistreatment. Her research interests include: evaluation on social work practice, children and families' social policies, and professional ethics.

Annamaria Campanini PhD is Professor of Social Work at the University of Milano Bicocca, Italy. Her research interests mainly link to theoretical and methodological aspects of social work. In the 1980s, she was the first in Italy to experiment with systemic approaches in social work, publishing research and developing training courses on this new model. European education is another area of her research. She was coordinator of the EUSW Thematic Network (2002–2008), member of the EASSW Executive Committee (2003–2007) and EASSW President (2007–2011). She is co-founder of the 'China–Europa Forum', responsible for the permanent workshop on 'Social work education in China and Europe'. She was awarded an honorary degree in Human Sciences by Loyola University, Chicago, in 2009 in recognition of her distinguished contribution to social work education. She is the author of many books and articles on social work in Italian and English, and a board member of many international social work journals.

Clare Colton BA, MA (Social Work) is a Lecturer in Social Work at the University of Plymouth, England. She is a graduate of the University of Exeter. She has been teaching on the Masters Programme in Social Work at the University of Plymouth for five years. She is Joint Programme Lead for the Health and Social Care Undergraduate Programme, and Coordinator for Practice Learning for the Masters Programme in Social Work. She is the lead academic teaching Professional Practice and Integrated Practice. Prior to this she was a Senior Practitioner (Social Worker), and then Locality Manager, in an Independent Fostering Agency specializing in supporting adolescents with complex needs. She has studied as an international student at the University of California, Santa Barbara, where she specialized in slave literature. Clare has a specific interest in attachment disorders. Prior to becoming a social worker, Clare held a variety of jobs, travelling and working in many countries throughout Europe and the Middle East, including living in Greece and Israel. She now lives on Dartmoor in Devon with her three daughters.

Marie Connolly BA, Dip Soc Wk, MA, PhD is Professor of Social Work and Chair of the Department of Social Work at the University of Melbourne, Australia. She was formerly Chief Social Worker for the New Zealand government. Prior to this she was Associate Professor at the University of Canterbury. She was the founder and founding Director of the Te Awatea Violence Research Centre. Her professional practice background is in child protection social work. Her recent books include *Social Work: From Theory to Practice* (Cambridge University Press, 2012) and *Understanding Child and Family Welfare: Statutory Responses to Children at Risk* (Palgrave Macmillan, 2012) as well as numerous refereed journal articles, research reports and other research and theoretical publications.

John Dixon BEcon, MEcon, PhD (Public Administration and Management), AcSS is the Distinguished Professor of Public Policy and Social Work at KIMEP University in Almaty, Kazakhstan, where he has also been Dean of the College of Social Sciences. He has held senior academic appointments in Hong Kong (1993–

1997) and Australia (1981–1992). He is a Visiting Professor at the University of Northampton (UK, 2009–) and has been a Visiting Professorial Fellow at the Graduate School of Business at the University of Wollongong (Australia, 2007–2010). He has published extensively (including 13 authored books, 18 edited books, 11 journal symposia and 80 refereed articles, and 47 book chapters). His major works include: *The Chinese Welfare System: 1949–1979* (Praeger, 1981); *Social Security in Global Perspective* (Praeger, 1999); *Responses to Governance: The Governing of Corporations, Societies and the World* (Praeger, 2003); *The Privatization of Mandatory Retirement Income Protection: International Perspectives* (with M. Hyde and G. Drover) (Edwin Mellon Press, 2006); and *The Situational Logic of Social Actions* (with R. Dogan and A. Sanderson) (Nova Science, 2009). He is a fellow of the British Academy of the Social Sciences (nominated by the British Social Policy Association), and honorary life member of the American Phi Beta Delta Honor Society for International Scholars (nominated by the American Political Science Association and the Public Policy Organization).

Kathryn Goldfarb PhD (Cultural Anthropology) is an Advanced Research Fellow at the Program on US–Japan Relations, Weatherhead Center for International Affairs, at Harvard University, the United States. She is a graduate of the University of Chicago. She has conducted extensive ethnographic research in Japan, including fieldwork at a children's home and a support group for youth who were raised in child welfare institutions, and interviews with Japanese foster families, child guidance centre staff, children's home and baby home directors, and members of the Japanese Ministry of Health, Labour and Welfare. She is preparing a book manuscript on social inequalities, wellbeing and family in Japan, through an exploration of the legal and institutional frameworks that shape caregiving practices within Japan's child welfare system. Her research broadly focuses on the ways concepts of Japanese national and cultural identity articulate with understandings of 'normality', an investigation she situates within the international circulation of knowledge regarding medicine and child development, and humanitarian logics of public and private responsibility for population welfare.

Sven Hessle PhD is Professor of Social Work at Stockholm University, Sweden. His research concerns the study of poverty and children and their families from an international perspective, as well as international social work in general. He has published alone, co-edited or contributed to 37 books – most in Swedish, but some translated into a total of nine other languages. He is founder and Editor-in-Chief of the *International Journal of Social Welfare*. He was awarded the Katherine Kendall Award from IASSW in August 2006 for his distinguished contributions to international social work education. He is Honorary Professor at Beijing Normal University and Guizhou University for Ethnic Minorities in China. He is senior advisor for a number of organizations (including UNICEF, SIDA and NORAD). He gave the Friedlander Lecture at UC Berkeley in March 2008 and was invited to give the Terry Hokenstad Lecture at the 2011 Council of Social Work Education's 57th Annual Meeting in Atlanta.

Anuarbek Kakabayev PhD is Head of the Department of European Programmes (Eurasia), and a part-time Associate Professor of Geography and Ecology, at Kokshetau State University named after Sh. Ualikhanov, Kazakhstan. He graduated from Petropavlovsk Pedagogical Institute as a teacher of geography and biology. His doctoral studies specialized in Genetics in the Kazakh National State University named after Al-Farabi (Almaty). He was the holder of a scholarship for talented young scientists of Kazakhstan for 2004–2006. He is the main coordinator of four TEMPUS projects, and coordinator of other projects at the University, such as Erasmus Mundus 'e-Astana', 'Marco XXI' and 'CANEM'. He has published more than 50 scientific articles and abstracts. He speaks Russian, Kazakh, German and English. He has taken part in training in educational programme management at several European universities, including the University of Alicante, the Catholic University of Milan, Academy of Grenoble, Oldenburg University, Warsaw University of Technology and the University of L'Aquila.

Dennis Kimberley BA, MSW, PhD, RSW is Professor of Social Work at the Memorial University of Newfoundland, Canada. He is the Director of the Inuit BSW programme. He has been involved with social work education and human services in addictions, mental health, and children's protection for over 40 years. He has acted as a policy, programme and clinical consultant and trainer nationally and internationally. He has been on international governing bodies and consultation committees with the IASSW, the International Federation of Social Workers, the International Council on Social Welfare and WHO. He teaches advanced clinical practice in a range of fields, and has a special interest in addictions and parenting compromised by mental health problems, sibling incest, sex abuse and exploitation, Internet exploitation of children and youth and the sexual trafficking of children and youth. He also teaches and consults in the area of child protection with a special interest in aboriginal concerns and cross-cultural child welfare issues.

Otrude Nontobeko Moyo PhD is Associate Professor at the University of Wisconsin–Eau Claire, the United States. She is the author of *Trampled No More: Voices from Bulawayo's Townships* (University Press of America, 2007), which is about families, life, survival and social change in Zimbabwe. She has written about social development issues in southern Africa. Her current scholarship examines African immigrants' and African Americans' experiences with social welfare systems and public policies in the United States. She is part of the editorial collective of the *Journal of Progressive Human Services* and a guest editor for the Africa Issue.

Contiu Şoitu PhD is a Senior Lecturer at the Department of Sociology and Social Work of the Faculty of Philosophy and Social-Political Sciences, Alexandru Ioan Cuza University, Iaşi, Romania. He is also Vice-Dean of the Faculty of Philosophy and Social-Political Sciences and the Director of Research of the same faculty. He studied Psychology and Pedagogy of People with Special Needs, doing postgraduate studies in 'Social Intervention Programs' at Alexandru Ioan Cuza University. His PhD is in the psycho-social effects of residential care (2002) from the Faculty of Psychology and Educational Sciences of the same university. He has also studied at universities in the UK, France and Greece. He is involved, as a coordinator or member, with over 25 national and European Life Long Learning projects (Grundtvig 1 and 2; Tempus IV, Leonardo da Vinci, Erasmus Mundus). He has carried out funded national research studies and international studies, and his main interests are in persons with special needs; children and adolescents in residential care; victims of violence; offenders; adult education; and the social educational needs of various categories of population.

Daniela-Tatiana Șoitu PhD is a Senior Lecturer at the Department of Sociology and Social Work of the Faculty of Philosophy and Social-Political Sciences, Alexandru Ioan Cuza University, Iași, Romania. Her postgraduate studies include 'Social Resources Management' and 'Social Intervention Programs'. Her PhD, in the sociology of ageing and vulnerable groups, was undertaken at the same university. She has also studied at universities in the UK, France and Italy. She has been a coordinator or member of 20 national and European Life Long Learning programmes and has carried out national and transnational studies as a national coordinator. Her main teaching and research areas are in social work, counselling and communication competencies, and social work and better ageing. Her research includes topics such as education across the lifespan; adult education; the social and educational needs of various categories of population; cross-border cooperation; and social policies for vulnerable populations. She is the chief editor of *Analele Științifice ale Universității Alexandru Ioan Cuza at Iași, serie nouă: Sociologie și asistență socială* (*Scientific Annals of Alexandru Ioan Cuza University, Iași. New Series: Sociology and Social Work*) and of *Revista de Economie Sociala* (*Journal of Social Economy*).

Marie-Antoinette Sossou PhD is Associate Professor of Social Work in the College of Social Work at the University of Kentucky, the United States. She is a graduate of the University of Denver. She teaches social work practice, social policy and global poverty. Her research focus and interests are international social work, feminist and gender issues, child welfare and abuse of children, refugee issues and social development.

Selwyn Stanley MA (Social Work), PhD (Social Work) is a Lecturer in Social Work at the University of Plymouth, England. He is an alumnus of the Madras School of Social Work and the Bharathidasan University in India. He was Assistant Professor at the 'five star' (NAAC) Bishop Heber College, India, and later became Reader and Head of the Social Work Department. He has been intimately associated with the Childline project in India and establishing the social work department of the college as the nodal organization for Childline in Tiruchirappalli. He moved to the University of Plymouth in 2007. His research interests include mental health and family wellbeing, especially in terms of understanding parenting, domestic violence, conflict resolution and marital adjustment. Understanding quality-of-life issues in different populations constitutes another strand of his research interests. He has published widely on these issues, including a book entitled *Social Work Education in Countries of the East – Issues and Challenges* (Nova Science Publishers, 2010).

Menka Tsantefski PhD is a Lecturer in Social Work at the University of Melbourne, Australia. She specializes in child and family-related subjects. Her field of research is in child protection, substance dependency and children's rights, especially in the perinatal period. She is also interested in issues of work–life balance and its relevance for parenting. She has been a project worker on children's programmes prior to being an academic. Menka has provided services to children and families and family support, child protection and families first workers. Menka is affiliated with the Alfred Felton Research Program, a joint appointment between the University of Melbourne School of Social Work and the Centre for Excellence in Child and Family Welfare, headed by Professor Cathy Humphreys.

Penelope Welbourne BSc (Psychology), MA (Child and Family Law), MA (Social Policy and Social Work) is an Associate Professor in Social Work at the University of Plymouth, England. She gained her social work qualification from the London School of Economics. Before joining the University of Plymouth, she was a residential social worker, social worker and senior supervising social worker in a number of different local authority areas, mostly in East and North London. Her research interests reflect her practice experience, which was almost all childcare, and largely child protection practice, and range across areas of law, policy and practice. Her most recent publications are *Social Work as a Profession: A Comparative Cross-National Perspective* (with I. Weiss) (Venture Press, 2007) and *Social Work with Children and Families: Developing Advanced Practice* (Routledge, 2012).

Subject Index

Author Index